DISCOVERING SIERRA BIRDS
Western Slope

by
Edward C. Beedy
and
Stephen L. Granholm

with Foreword by
Les Line
Editor, Audubon Magazine

Illustrated by
Keith Hansen
John Petersen
Tad Theimer

To Susan and Holly

Published by
Yosemite Natural History Association
and
Sequoia Natural History Association

In cooperation with the
National Park Service
U.S. Department of the Interior

ISBN #0-939666-42-1
Printed in the United States of America

Cover illustration: Steller's Jay, Western Tanager, and Mountain Chickadee

Title Page illustration: Male Pileated Woodpecker

Table of Contents

Foreword

"The humming-bird of blooming waters, loving rocky ripple-slopes and sheets of foam as a bee loves flowers, as a lark loves sunshine and meadows." Ninety years ago, in his first book *The Mountains of California*, John Muir used these words to describe what is perhaps the most celebrated bird of the Sierra Nevada, the American Dipper, or as Muir called it, the Water Ouzel. Since the pioneering work of Muir, and later explorations of men like Joseph Grinnell and Tracy Irwin Storer, the list of western Sierra birds has grown to nearly 300 species. Of these, about 190 are sufficiently numerous or regular that a hard-working birdwatcher can expect to find them during the course of a year.

There are now several excellent field guides to the birds of the western United States, so that identification of Sierra birds presents few problems. But more and more these days, birdwatchers are going into the field with something more than mere identification in mind. They want to know about the ecology of the birds they see—how they interact with other birds, what their exact food and habitat requirements are, and the hows and whys of their seasonal movements. For this new breed of birdwatcher, Edward C. Beedy and Stephen L. Granholm, both men who know the Sierra Nevada intimately, have provided the perfect guidebook in *Discovering Sierra Birds*.

The Sierra Nevada, a spectacular mountain range that extends for more than 350 miles along the backbone of California, rises gradually on the west, and then plunges abruptly into the Great Basin on the east. The western slope receives more rainfall and has a greater diversity of habitats than the drier eastern slope. Beedy and Granholm have thus focused their attention on the richer birdlife of the western Sierra.

In easily understandable language they describe the general features of the Sierra Nevada and the annual cycle of its birds, and then discuss each of the Sierra habitats, from the foothill grasslands, where the mountains meet the floor of California's Central Valley, to the alpine zone, where rocky outcrops and wildflower meadows intermingle. For each habitat, they list the major plants, enabling the reader to learn the necessary botany quickly, and name some of the characteristic birds. Shorter chapters deal with the impact of human activity in the Sierra, the special birds of the eastern slope, and techniques of finding and identifying birds. Armed with this information, even a birdwatcher who has never set foot in the Sierra Nevada can "catch up" quickly, and know before he enters a habitat what birds he can expect to find there. All of these introductory chapters are full of insightful comments on ecology; the reader learns which habitat characteristics are best for flycatchers and other birds that sally out from perches

5

in pursuit of flying insects, how forest fires actually improve certain habitats for birds, and how some species withdraw from the Sierra entirely during the winter, while others merely move downslope.

The species accounts, which form the major part of the book, give information on the status and yearly cycle of each bird, describe the behavior a birdwatcher is likely to see, and give brief descriptions as an aid in identification. Here the reader learns about how the availability of food governs the winter distribution of birds like Townsend's Solitaire and the Western Bluebird, about the impact Brown-headed Cowbirds have had on the populations of some of their host species, about the complex social structure of the Acorn Woodpecker, and about how fiercely the Northern Goshawk defends the area around its nest, even from humans.

In the midst of all this solid information, gathered during the decades since John Muir wrote of the Water Ouzel, one finds that there is still much that we do not know. Do Vesper Sparrows nest in the western Sierra? What becomes of the Sierra's Pine Grosbeaks during the winter? When did the Brown-headed Cowbird invade the Sierra? By pointing out these gaps in our knowledge, Beedy and Granholm offer clues to how any of us can contribute new facts about the birds of the Sierra Nevada.

Although *Discovering Sierra Birds* is, as its title suggests, a book about the birdlife of this most famous of America's mountain ranges, it is also an introduction to the ecology of the Sierra Nevada. In the course of telling us about the life history and status of Sierra birds, Ted Beedy and Steve Granholm give us a broader insight into the interrelationships between all forms of life in the land that John Muir fought so hard to protect from human disturbance. In doing this they make us all more aware of the importance of the struggle begun by Muir so many decades ago. For this reason, as well as for the wealth of information they provide, I recommend this book to all who care for America's wild places. Take it with you when you visit the Sierra Nevada; you will soon come to see these mountains with the eyes of a seasoned ecologist.

Les Line
Editor, *Audubon Magazine*

The Authors and Artists

Ted Beedy and Steve Granholm share an enthusiasm for birds and natural history of the Sierra Nevada that dates from well before they met in graduate school in 1974. Since then they have birded and hiked together in many parts of the range and have contributed regularly to each other's research projects there. Both conducted their doctoral research on forest bird communities in Yosemite National Park and received Ph.D. degrees from the Zoology Department at the University of California, Davis. In addition to writing and presenting scientific papers on Sierran birds, they have authored many environmental reports and co-authored a wildlife-habitat relationships document on Sierran birds for the U.S. Forest Service. Ted has taught ornithology and ecology at U.C. Davis and ecology at California State University, Sacramento. He has conducted long-term research on birds near the headwaters of the American River and has recently studied the birds and vegetation of the lower Tuolumne River. He presently lives in Davis and works as a consulting biologist. Steve has taught animal ecology at U.C. Davis and is currently employed as a consulting biologist by Holton Associates in Berkeley, California. He has made studies of the birds and other wildlife inhabiting the lower Tuolumne and upper San Joaquin watersheds.

Keith Hansen, along with Tad Theimer and John Petersen, provided the original paintings from which the color plates in this book were made. Hansen, of Fresno, California, grew up among artists, and seven members of his family were represented in a local show. Much of his art training was from his mother and brothers, active artists and illustrators. A lifelong birder, Keith has spotted 826 species in the U.S., Canada, Guatemala and Mexico. Hansen spends some fall months banding migratory birds on the Farallon Islands off the central California coast. Among the publications to which he has contributed are *American Birds, Western Birds* and *Wings,* and he has illustrated *Birds of the Sierra,* a coloring book for young and old, and *A Distributional Checklist of North American Birds; Landbirds of California* is underway.

Tad Theimer currently is serving as a Naturalist/Artist at Fullersburg Woods Forest Preserve in Oakbrook, Illinois. He earned a B.S. degree in Biology from the University of Pacific in Stockton, California, and a Master's in Zoology from Colorado State University. Theimer's work has been published in *American Birds,* and he has exhibited at U.O.P. and at Indiana University. Possessed of a life-long interest in birds and birding, Theimer has participated in ornithological research at Point Reyes Bird Observatory, at Colorado State University and at Indiana University.

John Petersen's childhood visits to Yosemite with his parents kindled his interests in both nature and art. More formal exposure occurred during his undergraduate days at Chico State College. Upon moving to Sonoma County, where he is working on his M.A., he became more seriously interested in birds, birding and painting what he saw in the field. After completing his paintings for *Discovering Sierra Birds,* Petersen did a series of paintings of birds of Costa Rica, commissioned by the Costa Rica National Park Foundation. Currently, he is Resident Biologist at the Bouverie Audubon Preserve, a branch of the Audubon Canyon Ranch.

Acknowledgements

We wish to thank our many friends who have shared their knowledge and enthusiasm for birds during many years of hiking, birdwatching and research in the Sierra. We are particularly indebted to David S. Wilson for constructively editing the text and helping to shape it with his original ideas and prose. We gratefully acknowledge David DeSante, David Gaines, Keith Hansen, Steve Laymon, David Shuford and Rich Stallcup, who reviewed the entire manuscript for accuracy and in the process offered extensive information and invaluable suggestions. Special thanks also to David Graber, John Harris and Larry Norris for critiquing the introductory chapters and selected species accounts. Other portions of the manuscript were reviewed by Tim Kittel (climate and vegetation), Gary Page (water birds), Robert Holland and Rex Palmer (vegetation) and David Winkler (gulls).

We are grateful to Larry Norris for compiling most of the bird records from Sequoia and Kings Canyon National Parks included here, and to David Brennan for contributing his records from this region. Thanks also to Tim Manolis and Steve Laymon for northern Sierra Bird records and to Steve Morey for his observations from the foothills west of Yosemite. We appreciate the additional Sierran bird records or information provided by Tom Andrews, Bob Barnes, Jim Bergman, Steve Brougher, Gary Fugle, Mark Gatewood, Helen Green, Mike Green, Paul Green, Tina Hargis, Sallie Hejl, Craig Himmelwright, Tom Love, Jim Maddox, Marie Mans, Lyman Ritter, Randy Smith, Jared Verner, Mike Webb and Jon Winter.

Constructive comments by Shirley Beedy, Mary and Dennis Fox, Karl Olson, George Salt, Betty Sanders, Dr. and Mrs. Eugene Stern, Ed Vine and Martha Wilbur have improved the text substantially.

Susan Sanders' constant support, original ideas and creative energy deserve special thanks. She edited the book several times and gave hours and hours to all phases of its preparation. Special thanks also to Holly

McCulloch for her advice and support throughout the project and her useful suggestions on every draft.

We are indebted to Len McKenzie and Henry Berrey of the Yosemite Natural History Association and John Palmer of the Sequoia Natural History Association, who directed and supported the preparation of this book. We thank Holton Associates and Rex Palmer for use of office space and computer facilities. Finally, with great appreciation, we acknowledge the David and Lucille Packard Foundation and the William and Flora Hewlett Foundation for their financial assistance.

Preface

The idea for this book evolved while we were studying forest birds in Yosemite National Park for our doctoral dissertations. Through discussions with Chief Park Interpreter Len McKenzie and Henry Berrey of the Yosemite Natural History Association, we realized the need for a new park bird book, one that would appeal to anyone who appreciated birds. We welcomed the opportunity to write non-technically about the birds we had come to know during our years of scientific studies and birdwatching. Eventually the project grew to include Sequoia and Kings Canyon National Parks, and finally the entire western Sierra.

Along with Len McKenzie, Henry Berrey, and John Palmer, Sequoia-Kings Canyon's Chief Park Interpreter, we chose three artists to illustrate Sierran birds in their native habitats. The exquisite color plates by Keith Hansen, Tad Theimer and John Petersen form a central and essential feature of this book. With few exceptions, each plate portrays a grouping of birds that might naturally co-occur. Keith Hansen's masterful sketches depict other species and illustrate fine points of identification and anatomy.

Early on, we decided to limit the book's coverage to the western slope of the Sierra (see "Birds of the Eastern Sierra," p. 30). The boundaries covered by any regional guide are arbitrary to some degree, but this choice made sense for several reasons. Most of our own experience was on the west slope, and the three national parks, the destinations of many Sierra visitors, all lie west of the crest. Finally, the grand traverse from the Central Valley to the high Sierra makes for a complete elevational gradient and a well-defined geographical unit. To be more precise, our coverage starts just east of the Central Valley where noticeable rolling hills first appear.

The book is not meant to replace existing field guides, which already cover identification of most species adequately, nor to provide a detailed summary of distributional records, of limited interest to the general reader. Rather, it is intended to convey a feeling for birds' lives, specifically in the Sierra—to describe their behavior, habitats and normal distribution within this range.

There is no "first author" of this book; it was a mutual effort from start to finish and has benefited from our exhaustive editing and rewriting of each other's prose. To augment our own observations, we have drawn on countless publications about Sierran birds, of which only the more general works are listed in the Bibliography. Add to this the information we obtained from numerous unpublished reports, lists of bird observations, informal discussions, and reviews by other Sierran ornithologists (see Acknowledgements), and it becomes clear that the book truly represents the work of many. Nevertheless, we take full responsibility for the final synthesis and any errors it may contain. To avoid interrupting the flow of the text, we have not cited references, but will provide sources of specific information on request. (Write YNHA, P.O. Box 545, Yosemite National Park, CA 95389.) We would appreciate receiving readers' comments, including notes on errors or important omissions.

If this book stimulates greater interest in the birds and natural habitats of the Sierra Nevada and inspires some readers to urge broader protection of its remaining wild areas, then we will feel that our undertaking has been worthwhile.

Ted Beedy
Steve Granholm

Birds and the Sierra Nevada

From the rolling foothill grasslands, through oak-studded savannahs and giant conifer forests, up to alpine meadows and chilly, windswept peaks, the Sierra Nevada offers birds an extraordinary variety of habitats. The western slope boasts an elevation gradient unequalled in the 48 contiguous states, spanning over 14,000 feet from the lower foothills to the top of Mt. Whitney. No wonder Sierran bird life is so varied.

In addition, the Sierra's accessibility makes birdwatching there especially easy and rewarding. Public lands are plentiful, with huge pristine areas preserved in Yosemite, Sequoia and Kings Canyon National Parks and numerous national forest wilderness areas. Major all-weather highways such as Interstate 80 and U.S. 50 transect the range, as do many state routes, while other highways such as Highway 49 run north and south through the foothills. In a morning's drive, one can traverse the west slope from California's Central Valley up nearly to tree line at Sonora Pass on Highway 108 or Tioga Pass in Yosemite National Park.

Because birds can fly, they come and go as they please, moving to different habitats and elevations or migrating to distant regions where climate or food supplies are more inviting. Such movements are especially pronounced in a tall range like the Sierra, where seasonal changes vary tremendously with elevation and birds can switch from wintry snow-covered forests to warm foothill woodlands simply by descending a few thousand feet.

The Sierra rewards birdwatchers who take seasonal and elevational differences into account when planning trips, for those same lush foothills, full of singing birds in April, turn dry, brown, quiet and relatively lifeless by June. The cold, snowy subalpine forests, strangely still in April with only a few year-round residents in evidence, come alive by early June with an influx of migrants, energetically singing, nesting and defending territories. These seasonal changes at different elevations are more fully described below in "Highlights of the Sierran Bird Calendar." The following chapter, "Natural Environments of the Western Sierra," describes the features most important to birds, focusing on seven broad vegetation zones that correspond roughly to elevation on the west slope.

The 191 species accounts, which form the heart of this book, describe the ecology, distribution, and behavior of each bird species found regularly in the western Sierra. With two exceptions, these birds occur every year, either as year-round residents, breeding species, winter visitors or migrants. (Barrow's Goldeneyes and Bell's Vireos no longer nest regularly in the Sierra but deserve mention because of their disappearance.) Omitted are several species that occur irregularly or occupy only a limited, periph-

11

eral portion of the range. Ladder-backed Woodpeckers and Cactus Wrens, for example, live only near Walker Pass at the southern end of the Sierra; similarly, Summer Tanagers and Yellow-billed Cuckoos occur only in the nearby South Fork Kern River Valley. Several water birds and shorebirds that show up more or less regularly, but only in small numbers at scattered aquatic habitats in the foothills, have been left out as well. Appendix I lists all of these marginal and occasional species, along with extremely rare species reported only a few times in the western Sierra.

Highlights of the Sierran Bird Calendar

The lives of birds are tied intimately and inextricably to the passage of seasons, and radical changes take place in Sierran bird life as the year progresses. Birds migrate, stake out territories, court, nest, molt and change habitats in response to seasonal cues such as changing day length and weather patterns. Climate varies dramatically from the foothills, with their mild winters and hot, dry summers, through the wetter, cooler middle elevations, up to vast subalpine and alpine areas with harsh, long winters and short summers. Birds living at different altitudes thus follow radically different yearly schedules, as do birds of different species.

Some species' habits are less predictable than others. Great Gray and Spotted Owls apparently breed only in years when their small mammal prey are abundant. Red Crossbills are notorious for their unpredictable comings and goings; they may nest at almost any time of year, but only when they find a good supply of ripe conifer cones to feed on. Taking such variability into account, the following pages point out the highlights in each season of the Sierran bird calendar.

Spring (March, April, May)

As temperatures warm, snow melts and new leaves unfurl, spring migrants begin streaming through the western Sierra. At this season migrants generally keep to low and middle elevations where conditions are more hospitable than higher up. Many long-distance migrants like Western Tanagers, Nashville Warblers, and Dusky Flycatchers appear at elevations well below their Sierran breeding grounds. Some of these travel farther north to breed, while others simply linger at low elevations until conditions improve upslope.

Spring is the time when most birds begin courting, building nests and raising their young. This season brings abundant food in the form of swelling buds and emerging insects; and prey for raptors becomes plentiful as migratory birds arrive and small mammals venture from their winter hideaways. Because birds generally nest when food is abundant and climate favorable, breeding begins earlier in the foothills than in the mountains. By the end of May, many birds at higher elevations have still not begun nest-building, and some, such as White-crowned Sparrows, may not even have arrived.

Although birds call at all times of year, spring brings a resurgence of song. "Singing" refers to the complex, often melodic vocalizations that birds use to attract mates or advertise territories, which they defend against others of their kind. Males generally do most or all of the singing, but recent studies have discovered that females of many species sing too. Some birds, such as White-crowned Sparrows and Townsend's Solitaires, sing on sunny days throughout fall and winter, and many migrants sing in spring before reaching their breeding grounds. Golden-crowned Sparrows sing frequently in the Sierra but never breed there. Thus the fact that birds are singing in a given habitat or elevation does not guarantee they will stay to nest.

Many nonsingers, including owls, grouse and quail, make distinctive calls that serve the same function as song. Some birds employ dance-like rituals and other nonvocal displays for courtship and territorial defense. Woodpeckers, for example, drum on trees with their bills instead of singing, and hummingbirds, nighthawks, snipes and many hawks make spectacular aerial dives and maneuvers.

Summer (June, July, August)

For most species at middle and high elevations, breeding activities continue well into summer. Rosy Finches, Water Pipits and other high-elevation birds may not even start building nests until June. Most foothill birds raise their families by late May or June, and many, like Mourning Doves, start over again with a new clutch of eggs. At middle elevations Dark-eyed Juncos and some other species raise second broods, but double-brooding is probably rare at higher elevations.

Jays, warblers, sparrows and other small Sierran birds have "altricial" young, which hatch out blind, helpless and naked or skimpily clad in down. Until their insulating feather coats develop, their parents must "brood" them—sitting on the nest to shield them from excessive heat, cold or rain, just as they previously incubated the eggs. Parents must also feed these altricial young, which typically remain in the nest until they can fly.

"Precocial" young, including those of ducks, geese, grouse and quail, hatch out with thick coats of down, eyes open and legs capable of walking almost immediately. They leave the nest within a day and follow one or both parents, who brood and protect them for several weeks and in some cases feed them, too. Some newly-hatched birds, including herons, hawks and owls, cannot be classified as altricial or precocial, but rather fall somewhere in between.

Altricial young often cheep loudly when their parents bring food, making it easy for the alert hiker to spot their nest. They leave the nest when fully feathered, able to fly and nearly as large as adults, but usually need tending by their parents for two or three weeks longer. Called "nestlings" while in the nest, they are known as "fledglings" after leaving, until they can fend for themselves.

Family groups become a common sight as early as May in the Sierra foothills, but not until July in the higher forests. Ducks, quail and grouse, with their still-flightless young, may be easy to spot at this time as adults anxiously guard and call to their unwary offspring. No longer confined to the vicinity of the nest, families with fledged altricial young range widely beyond their nesting territories. Fledglings call noisily and beg for food, with wings fluttering and mouths gaping skyward. At first the parents make frantic efforts to satisfy their youngsters' appetites, but in time they begin to ignore the begging and the young must find their own way. Although adults and young frequently make simple calls to each other during this period, the parents rarely sing full songs, if at all. For many species, singing frequency drops off well before the young leave the nest, or even during incubation.

Following the fledgling period, by late June in the foothills and early August in the higher mountains, birds generally become less particular in their choice of habitats. Several species often flock together, ranging over broad areas to feed. One can walk through a forest for half an hour without encountering more than a few birds and suddenly be surrounded by 20 or 30 chickadees, kinglets and warblers. In addition to these flocks of insect-eaters, there are mixed flocks of seed-eaters such as sparrows, juncos and finches.

After nesting, many birds appear at higher elevations, well above their breeding range. Orange-crowned Warblers, for example, nest in foothill chaparral, but commonly occur up to tree line in August and September. It would appear that such birds have deserted the hot dry foothills and lower pine forests and moved up to cooler, moister elevations where food is more plentiful; this phenomenon has been termed "upslope drift." It is likely, however, that many of these high-elevation wanderers have migrated from northern breeding grounds rather than from the Sierra foothills below.

"Fall" migration actually begins in summer for many species, particularly long-distance migrants. Rufous Hummingbirds wing southward through the Sierra in large numbers beginning in June, and by late August many warblers, vireos, tanagers and flycatchers have departed. For many species the roving flocks of August may contain birds from the north as well as from Sierran breeding grounds.

Fall (September, October, November)

By early September, nesting activities have ceased, even at high elevations. Most fledglings have learned to find their own food and have molted into new plumage, usually resembling the adult females'. These young birds, now called "immatures," often flock with their parents for several more weeks or months, perhaps migrating or even wintering with them. Not surprisingly, most young birds starve, fall to predators or otherwise fail to survive the rigors of their first year.

In fall, great changes occur daily as migratory flocks pass through, and birds frequently appear in unexpected places. Many southward migrants avoid the hot, dry foothills, where insects have become scarce, and concentrate at middle and high elevations, where food and water are still plentiful. During August and September dozens or even hundreds of warblers may forage together at the edges of mountain meadows or riparian thickets. Large flocks of ground-feeding finches, sparrows and juncos gather on broad, grassy ridgetops. Hawks moving upslope or migrating south sometimes congregate in favorable updrafts above ridges or mountain peaks.

By the the end of September, most winter visitors have arrived in the Sierra, but many occupy habitats well above their winter range. Adult insects become much scarcer in fall, especially above the foothills, and many insectivorous birds depart. Those that stay often switch to alternate foods such as acorns, seeds, fruits, or larvae of insects and spiders. When the first big storms hit, many birds move downslope for the winter. Ground-feeding birds such as flickers, juncos and Hermit Thrushes remain below the heavy snow level; some may stay at middle elevations if sufficient ground is snow-free. By November many species have settled into winter "home ranges," relatively well-defined areas where they feed and rest until spring. Some, like Townsend's Solitaires, may even defend feeding territories in fall and winter. Many other species, particularly fruiteaters such as robins, bluebirds and waxwings, wander nomadically from one good food source to another.

Winter (December, January, February)

The higher, snowbound elevations become rather quiet in winter. Many birds have migrated southward or downslope where temperatures are less severe and food easier to find. Most insect-eating birds have departed, but some, including Mountain Chickadees, Golden-crowned Kinglets, Redbreasted Nuthatches and several woodpeckers, remain to search for overwintering larvae and pupae hidden in clusters of needles, furrows of bark or the wood beneath. Only a few seed-eaters brave the winter—like Red

Crossbills, which feed on pine nuts. Those alpine specialists, the Rosy Finches, may remain on high peaks through winter except in heavy storms. Other winter mountaineers include Steller's Jays, Townsend's Solitaires and Blue Grouse.

Much remains to be learned about how these hardy souls find sufficient food in winter and how and where they roost to avoid freezing to death. Woodpeckers, nuthatches, and chickadees, which nest in cavities, apparently also roost in them at night and during storms. How the tiny, cup-nesting Golden-crowned Kinglet survives is hard to imagine.

The winter range of many Sierran birds is still a mystery. Pine Grosbeaks have rarely been recorded in winter, and it is unclear whether they normally remain on their breeding grounds or move downslope. Williamson's Sapsuckers have been noted mostly below their breeding haunts, but the scarcity of sightings suggests that many of them migrate south.

Below the heavy snow belt, winter conditions are less severe and birds more numerous. Many foothill birds remain year-round, though large numbers even there migrate south for winter. Northern migrants swell the ranks of many Sierran breeding species such as American Robins and Fox Sparrows, while Golden Eagles and Lewis' Woodpeckers move in from east of the range. Only a few land birds that do not breed in the Sierra spend winter there; examples are Golden-crowned Sparrows, Varied Thrushes, and Cedar Waxwings. Wintering waterfowl and shorebirds, abundant in the Central Valley, occur much more sparsely in the Sierra, keeping mainly to low elevations. The stream-loving Dipper stays as high as the water remains unfrozen.

A few Sierran birds begin nesting in winter, particularly in the foothills. Great Horned Owls, Anna's Hummingbirds and California Thrashers may lay eggs as early as January, and Golden Eagles by late February or early March. Most surprising is the Clark's Nutcracker, which nests at high elevations, mostly east of the crest, and lays eggs as early as the first week of March.

Natural Environments of the Western Sierra

Forming an immense ecological barrier, the Sierra Nevada divides the productive lowlands of California's Central Valley from the high deserts of the Great Basin. It stretches more than 360 miles from near Lake Almanor, just south of Lassen Peak, south to Walker Pass east of Bakersfield (see Fig. 1).

Rising gently on its western slope to a lofty, jagged crest, this great range drops abruptly along its sheer eastern escarpment. The Sierra Nevada is only 60 to 80 miles wide, but because of its great elevational gradient supports the richest and most diverse assortment of terrestrial habitats, birds and scenic wonders in California. The Sierra serves as both a barrier to birds moving east and west and a vast bridge traversed by migrants between their northern breeding grounds and southern winter homes.

Travellers climbing the west slope pass from foothill grasslands and woodlands to vast coniferous forests that give way to alpine landscapes at the Sierra crest. As the vegetation changes with altitude so does the bird life. Most birds are tied to certain habitats and restricted elevation ranges, at least while breeding. Some, like American Robins, Western Wood-Pewees and Northern Flickers, range widely throughout the Sierra, while a few are restricted to one habitat — such as the Rosy Finch, which rarely strays from alpine rockfields, snow and turf. Most birds fall somewhere in between, occurring across an optimal range of a few thousand feet and sometimes a bit higher or lower where local conditions permit. A species' optimal zone frequently varies with the season. Hermit Warblers, for example, breed at middle elevations, but in August they wander through-out the high country.

Sierra Nevada means "snowy range" a name well-deserved, for the range has been blanketed by some of the heaviest snows ever recorded. Snowfall varies radically and unpredictably from year to year. For example, at the Central Sierra Snow Laboratory near Norden (6936 feet) in Nevada County, the greatest yearly snowfall was 812 inches during the winter of 1951-1952, while the lowest total was 182 inches in 1976-77. Similarly, temperatures measured at this station have ranged from -20 °F in winter to above 95 °F in summer. Such extremes of climate pose a great challenge to birds, especially those residing in the Sierra year-round. During winter most birds live below the lower limit of the snowpack — about 5000 feet in the central Sierra. A few hardy species, however, such as Red-breasted Nuthatches, Brown Creepers, Golden-crowned Kinglets and many wood-peckers survive severe storms high in the conifer forests, and Rosy Finches may winter amidst wind-swept alpine crags.

Vegetation of the Sierra reflects a gradual climatic change from the relatively warm, dry foothills to the cooler, moister middle elevations to the even colder mountaintops that receive somewhat less precipitation. As one traverses this gradient, dramatic changes in vegetation are evident. Grasslands give way to oak woodlands, then to pine forests and so on. Vegetation types usually overlap, forming broad transitional areas, and the boundaries are seldom abrupt or obvious. Nevertheless, it is conven-ient to classify Sierran vegetation into general elevation zones. The seven altitudinal zones defined below were adapted from those defined by Verner and Boss (see Bibliography).

Although these Sierran vegetation zones generally conform to elevation, other factors such as slope, exposure and soils can dramatically alter local conditions. North-facing slopes receive less direct sunlight and are cooler and damper than southern exposures. North-facing slopes thus may have lush forest and dense shrubs, while hillsides across a canyon are dry and open. A drive up the Merced River canyon along Highway 140 offers a particularly dramatic contrast between north and south slopes.

Latitude also has an effect; vegetation zones occur at higher elevations in the warmer climates of the southern Sierra than they do in the north. Ponderosa pine forests, for example, commonly extend down to 1500 feet in the north, but seldom below 4000 feet in the south (see Fig. 2). Birds stick to their preferred habitats and can usually be found higher up in the south. Most birds described in this book occupy the entire length of the range. A few species, however, occur only in limited areas; Chestnut-backed Chickadees have not been recorded south of Mariposa County, while Say's Phoebes breed exclusively in the southern foothills.

There are no bird species unique to the Sierra. Some, such as Great Gray Owls and Pine Grosbeaks, seldom occur elsewhere in California, but most species live in nearby mountains with similar habitats and topography. The key to the exceptional bird diversity of the western Sierra is the extreme elevation gradient and the great number of different habitats compressed together in a short distance. The most important of these habitats to birds are described below.

Vegetation Zones

Foothill Grassland Zone   **Plate 42**

Most travellers pass through foothill grasslands without registering them as "habitat." The fields east of Roseville (Interstate 80), Planada (Highway 140) and Centerville (Highway 180) exemplify this open, gently rolling terrain, vivid green in winter and early spring, but parched to a golden-brown in summer. Many areas have valley or blue oaks[1] scattered over open savannahs. Wintering Horned Larks and Water Pipits flock together in grazed pastures and plowed furrows, and Savannah Sparrows forage in the deeper grasses. In spring Western Kingbirds and Loggerhead Shrikes stake out territories on fencelines or lonely oaks. "Tombstones" of

[1]*Common and scientific names of all plants mentioned in this book are listed in Appendix II.*

ancient metamorphic rock rise abruptly here and there (easily seen along Highway 120 east of Oakdale), offering perches for American Kestrels and Red-tailed Hawks. On hot afternoons Turkey Vultures float lazily above low ridges and hillsides.

Perennial grasses once dominated the lowlands of California, but now introduced grasses brought by European settlers have almost wholly replaced the indigenous species. Sheep and cattle, by their trampling and grazing, prevent the re-establishment of native grasses. In spring wildflowers still flourish in the foothills, and specialized blooms form rings around the receding waters of vernal pools. Killdeer nest near these ephemeral habitats and ducks occasionally dabble in their shallows.

Foothill Woodland and Chaparral Zone   Plate 42

Above the grasslands and oak savannah, denser groves of blue and interior live oaks crowd Sierran hillsides. In spring these oaks come alive with the trilling songs of Orange-crowned Warblers and the whistled notes of Ash-throated Flycatchers. Gray pines[1], with their wispy, gray-green needles, grow along with the oaks in the northern and central Sierra and in the extreme south. White-breasted Nuthatches search the deeply furrowed bark of these pines and sound their horn-like calls. In steep ravines canyon live oaks cling to rocky slopes, while toyon, laurel and redbud grow in cooler glades below. Northern Pygmy-Owls hide in these canyons by day and emerge at dusk to hunt for songbirds.

In the Mother Lode country, Highway 49 cuts through broad expanses of foothill woodland. On nearly any turnout the strident calls of a Scrub Jay or Plain Titmouse can be heard. California Quail work through tangles of poison oak, and Acorn Woodpeckers flash back and forth between trees, flycatching, chattering and tending their acorn caches.

Impenetrable seas of brush cover hot, dry slopes the length of the Sierra. Interspersed with foothill woodlands, this chaparral vegetation generally occupies the steeper, more arid exposures, and the most extensive stands occur south of the San Joaquin River. Turnouts along the new Priest Grade (Highway 120) and the slopes near Ash Mountain in Sequoia National Park are easy places to view this habitat.

The pungent odors of chamise, whiteleaf manzanita, buckbrush, coffeeberry and shrubby oaks fill the air. These shrubs grow together in thickets forbidding to people, but offering shade and shelter to birds. Chaparral birds usually sing, defend territories and forage in the cool early-morning

[1]*This species is called the "digger pine" by most authors after the "Digger Indians," a name given to the native people of the Sierra foothills. Their descendants consider the term demeaning, and in the 1930's had a ceremonial burning of the word "digger."*

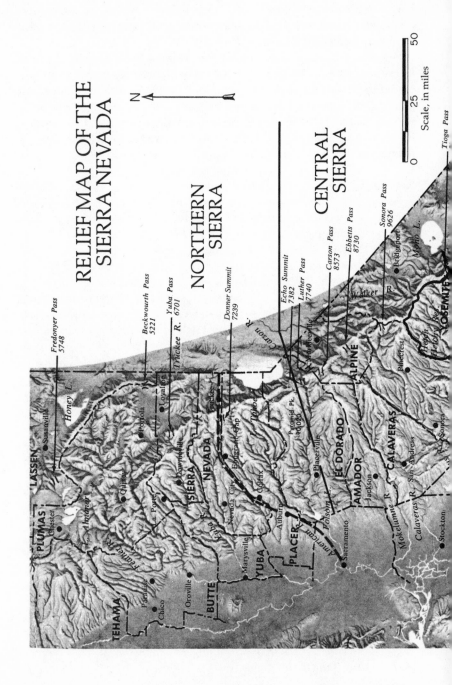

RELIEF MAP OF THE
SIERRA NEVADA

NORTHERN
SIERRA

CENTRAL
SIERRA

N

0   25   50

Scale, in miles

Fredonyer Pass
5748

Beckwourth Pass
5221

Yuba Pass
6701

Trickee R.

Donner Summit
7239

Echo Summit
7382

Luther Pass
7740

Carson Pass
8573

Ebbetts Pass
8730

Sonora Pass
9626

Tioga Pass

Carson R.

Walker R.

Honey L.

Mono L.

LASSEN

PLUMAS

SIERRA

NEVADA

PLACER

EL DORADO

AMADOR

ALPINE

CALAVERAS

YUBA

BUTTE

TEHAMA

Susanville

Chester

Almanor

Quincy

La Porte

Downieville

Portola

Loyalton

Truckee

Emigrant Gap

Nevada City

Colfax

Auburn

Pyramid Pk.
10,000

Placerville

Folsom

Sacramento

Jackson

San Andreas

Sonora

Stockton

Marysville

Oroville

Chico

Paradise

Tahoe

Markleeville

Pinecrest

Bridgeport

Feather R.

Yuba R.

American R.

Mokelumne R.

Calaveras R.

YOSEMITE

Hetch Hetchy Res.

Tuolumne R.

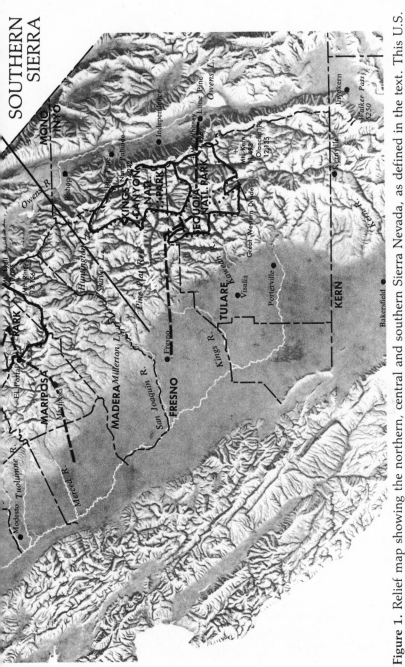

Figure 1. Relief map showing the northern, central and southern Sierra Nevada, as defined in the text. This U.S. Geological Survey photo was reproduced with slight modification from Storer and Usinger (see Bibliography), with permission from University of California Press. Dashed lines (━━━) indicate the locations of the cross-sections depicted in Figure 2.

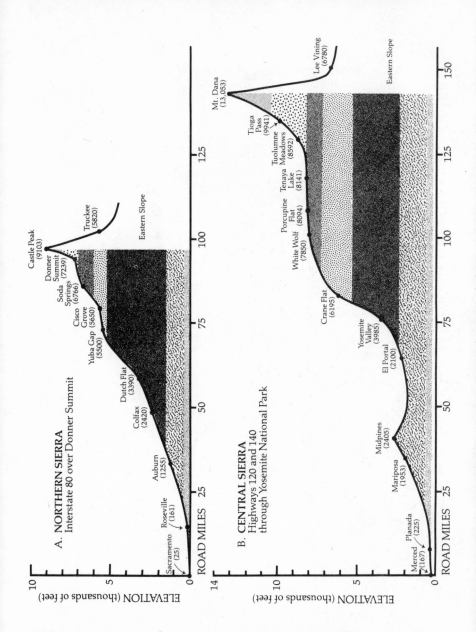

Figure 2. Approximate cross-sections of the northern, central, and southern Sierra, showing the seven vegetation zones and representative localities, with elevations in parentheses. This figure was modified extensively from Storer and Usinger (see Bibliography) with permission from University of California Press.

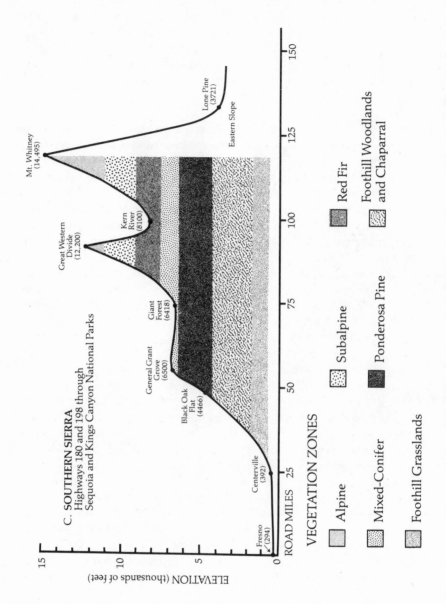

C. **SOUTHERN SIERRA**
Highways 180 and 198 through
Sequoia and Kings Canyon National Parks

Mt. Whitney
(14,495)

Great Western
Divide
(12,200)

Kern
River
(8100)

Lone Pine
(3721)

Eastern Slope

Giant
Forest
(6418)

General Grant
Grove
(6500)

Black Oak
Flat
(4466)

Centerville
(392)

Fresno
(294)

ELEVATION (thousands of feet)

15
10
5
0

ROAD MILES   25   50   75   100   125   150

VEGETATION ZONES

Red Fir

Foothill Woodlands
and Chaparral

Subalpine

Ponderosa Pine

Alpine

Mixed-Conifer

Foothill Grasslands

hours. Pre-sunrise visits to these arid shrublands are often rewarded by a chorus of Common Poorwills, Wrentits, California Thrashers and Rufous-sided Towhees. As early as January, Anna's Hummingbirds defend patches of shrubs with squeaky calls, and in spring Blue-gray Gnatcatchers and Sage Sparrows raise their families within this protective cover.

Conifer Forests

At their upper limits the foothill woodlands give way to groves of magnificent conifers. A wide variety of trees may dominate these forests or grow together in mixed stands, depending on elevation and local conditions. Most forests are broken by meadows, rock outcrops or streams. Yellow-rumped Warblers, Western Wood-Pewees, Olive-sided Flycatchers and many other birds prefer to forage in open airspace near forest edges, which harbor abundant flying insects. Some "edge" species such as Mountain Quail and White-crowned Sparrows use trees and shrubs for cover but feed in open areas nearby. Open forests with understories of shrubs, wildflowers and grasses draw Dark-eyed Juncos, Chipping Sparrows and Purple Finches, which search the ground for insects and seeds. In many forests where fires have not occurred for decades, thickets of young conifers crowd together and prevent the establishment of other understory plants. In closed-canopy forests, especially in mature stands, dead trees or "snags" provide nest sites for hole-nesting birds like woodpeckers, nuthatches and many owls.

Brushfields of huckleberry oak, greenleaf manzanita, snowbrush or chinquapin occupy steep, rocky slopes or forest clearings created by treefalls, logging or fire. Especially prevalent on south-facing exposures, this "montane chaparral" may grow in impenetrable thickets but can be quite open on severe or recently established sites. Although usually dry, these shrubfields are cooler than their foothill counterparts. Here the whistled melodies of Fox Sparrows mingle confusingly with the similar songs of Green-tailed Towhees. Although they are often found in moist streamside habitats, Yellow Warblers and MacGillivray's Warblers also nest in montane chaparral. Mountain Quail sneak through the underbrush and nest under this protective cover. Widespread above the foothills, such shrubfields can be easily seen along Interstate 80 near Dutch Flat, Highway 120 west of Crane Flat in Yosemite and on the slopes below Giant Forest in Sequoia National Park.

Conifer forests of the western Sierra fall into four general vegetation zones that are described separately below.

Ponderosa Pine Zone   Plate 43

Rising above the heat and haze of the foothills, this zone is where many people first feel they have reached the mountains. Breezes rustle the trees, and though hot in summer, these forests are distinctly cooler than the lowlands. They also receive more rainfall and snow, enabling them to survive the summer drought. Ponderosa pines, the namesake of this zone, are often the first large conifers encountered above the foothills. They tolerate hotter and drier climates than most other west-slope conifers and are the most common and widespread trees in this lowest conifer belt. Incense cedars, white firs, Douglas-firs or sugar pines often join the ponderosas in mixed stands.[1] Hairy Woodpeckers, Brown Creepers and Red-breasted Nuthatches forage on tree trunks and branches, and Warbling Vireos and Black-headed Grosbeaks make music from the foliage above. Black oaks, with dark trunks and bright green leaves, grow in patches mixed in with conifers — especially on open, rocky ridges and in forest clearings. These deciduous oaks turn gold in fall like the aspens, willows and cottonwoods. Black oaks harbor hordes of caterpillars and flying insects that attract Nashville Warblers, Black-throated Gray Warblers and Solitary Vireos to forage and sing. In many ponderosa pine forests kit-kit-dizze (a member of the rose family) covers the forest floor. Its pungent odor permeates the forest and clings to boots and clothing, earning it another name: "mountain misery."

Near campgrounds and other developed areas, Steller's Jays squawk and patrol their picnic tables and Brewer's Blackbirds strut across the pavement. In areas where fire has been prevented for many years, shade-tolerant white firs and incense cedars often outnumber the pines and oaks. Yosemite Valley offers a vivid example of the effects of fire control — formerly open vistas of walls, domes and waterfalls have been lost to dense groves of young trees. Most birds avoid such forests, but even in the deepest stands one might find a watchful Great Horned Owl or a Red-tailed Hawk perched in a snag above.

Mixed-Conifer Zone   Plate 43

The ponderosa pine zone at its upper margin blends into the cooler, moister mixed-conifer forest. At places such as Crane Flat in Yosemite and near the Giant Forest in Sequoia National Park, huge conifers echo the songs of Western Tanagers, Hermit Warblers and Warbling Vireos. Hammond's Flycatchers sound their buzzy notes from the deeper, shaded woods while Pileated Woodpeckers call loudly from ancient snags. Golden-crowned Kinglets thrive in these forests, whispering high-pitched

[1]Sometimes such stands are called mixed-conifer forests. In this book, however, the mixed-conifer zone is defined as the elevation belt above the normal range of ponderosa pines. The ponderosa pine zone, by the definition used here, includes forest stands with a variety of conifers, usually but not always dominated by ponderosa pines.

notes throughout the day. In the mixed-conifer zone, ponderosa pines give way to Jeffrey pines, with larger cones and an aroma like vanilla rising from their bark. White firs often outnumber all other trees, but usually incense cedars, Douglas-firs, sugar pines and even a few red firs grow there, too. Mixtures of four or five species of conifers are typical in this zone, as its name suggests. Black oaks reach this high, but are fewer than farther down. Where the soil is rocky or wet, especially near meadows, lodgepole pines may grow in scattered stands. Typically, tangles of fallen branches and decomposing logs clutter the ground in mature forests where fires have not occurred for years. If forest canopies are open, growths of bracken fern, huckleberry oak, snowbrush, manzanita or chinquapin may flourish. Deep within these shrubs, Fox Sparrows scratch in litter and MacGillivray's Warblers deliver their penetrating songs.

Giant sequoias, the world's largest known living things, occur naturally only in the western Sierra, primarily in the mixed-conifer zone. A few grow north as far as Placer County, but most of the 75 groves are south of the Kings River and the largest, most majestic stands are in Sequoia and Kings Canyon National Parks. These groves contain essentially the same birds as surrounding forests; White-headed and Pileated Woodpeckers thrive there and the tiny Winter Wrens like to nest among their gnarled roots.

Red Fir Zone   Plate 43
Red fir forests receive the heaviest Sierra snows. In these shady groves deep drifts often last long into summer, gradually releasing moisture into the soil. Small numbers of red firs grow on north slopes in the mixed-conifer zone, but higher up, their silent columns reign supreme. Entire forests consist of only these trees, with rings of chartreuse lichen circling their trunks above the snow line. Often lodgepole and western white pines are mixed in, as are white firs at the lower edge of this zone. Particularly common in the northern and central Sierra, red firs grow only in limited areas farther south. At Porcupine Flat and Badger Pass in Yosemite and near Soda Springs on Interstate 80, impressive stands of red firs and lodgepole pines grow together. Lodgepole pines may form extensive stands in this zone, particularly in cold sites, around meadows and on dry, rocky slopes. Heavy snows and deep forest litter prevent much growth of shrubs, grasses or flowers; most birds in the red fir zone search bark surfaces and sprays of conifer needles for food, often avoiding the ground. Red fir forests often seem lacking in birds, but if one looks and listens, Mountain Chickadees, Yellow-rumped Warblers and Golden-crowned Kinglets can be found in the treetops and flocks of Pine Siskins or Evening Grosbeaks may fly overhead. The rhythmic tapping of Williamson's Sapsuckers resounds through these forests, and Blue Grouse occasionally utter their deep, ventriloquial calls.

Subalpine Zone   Plate 44

Backpackers head for these high forests where serrated ridges, perpendicular cliffs and massive granite domes form spectacular vistas. Mountain lakes and springs spawn tiny streams that meander through meadow grasses and open stands of lodgepole pine. These pines dominate the subalpine zone, especially in the northern and central Sierra, where they are sometimes joined by mountain hemlocks. Wind-sculptured whitebark pines grow with stunted lodgepoles on exposed ridges up to tree line. In the southern Sierra, erect stands of foxtail pine largely replace the gnarled whitebarks. Much of the high country in Sequoia and Kings Canyon National Parks is dominated by these trees.

Echo Summit (U.S. 50), Donner Summit (Interstate 80), Tuolumne Meadows in Yosemite and the higher slopes of the Great Western Divide in Sequoia-Kings Canyon have good examples of subalpine forest. Clark's Nutcrackers bound from tree to tree searching for pine nuts, and Golden-mantled Ground Squirrels dive for cover if the shadow of a Prairie Falcon skims by. Mountain Chickadees move along sprays of lodgepole needles and swing down to inspect them from below. Dusky Flycatchers sound their familiar calls from forest edges and open ridgetops while flocks of Red Crossbills rove the treetops.

Alpine Zone   Plate 44

Freezing temperatures are possible any day of the year in the alpine zone, the land above tree line, and even the intense high-elevation sun does little to warm the cool, clear air. Life in the alpine zone is severe and most plants are stunted by high winds, bitter cold and shallow soils. Rock faces, boulder fields and talus dominate much of the landscape, providing abundant habitat for Rock Wrens. In summer wildflowers bloom profusely in alpine meadows, and juncos and White-crowned Sparrows forage near shrubby willows. Rosy Finches feed on low turf or snow banks and American Kestrels hover above. Mountain Bluebirds perch on boulders and suddenly dart out to snatch flying insects, the stunning blue of their plumage rivaling the alpine sky.

In the northern Sierra few peaks exceed 9000 feet and alpine habitats are limited to the summits of a few mountains such as the Sierra Buttes in Sierra County and Castle Peak in Nevada County. Farther south, many peaks exceed 13,000 feet, including Mt. Whitney (14,495 feet), the highest mountain in the contiguous states. Alpine environments are particularly extensive in Sequoia and Kings Canyon National Parks. Most Sierran alpine areas occur above the reach of highways, but a short hike from Carson Pass (Highway 88), Sonora Pass (Highway 108) or Tioga Pass (Highway 120) puts one amidst the rugged cliffs, glacial cirques and rock gardens of this zone.

Special Habitats

The habitats described below are of limited extent in the western Sierra but provide key resources for birds. Because of their importance, and because each occurs across a wide range of vegetation zones, they are described separately here.

Lakes, Marshes and Rivers
Margins of lowland lakes, marshes and streams teem with bird life. Marshes are limited in the Sierra and most foothill "lakes" are artificial reservoirs. Where shorelines are clogged by tules, cattails or rushes, however, these aquatic habitats harbor Marsh Wrens, Common Yellowthroats and throngs of Red-winged Blackbirds. Ducks and coots swim in open water and Great Blue Herons stand like statues in the shallows. Trees adjacent to lakes and rivers support cavity nesters such as Wood Ducks and Common Mergansers. Grebes, diving ducks and gulls visit deep lakes, reservoirs and sewage ponds, and shorebirds flock to exposed mudflats. Because most Sierran rivers flow through steep-sided canyons, extensive mudflats are scarce, but they occur around reservoirs with gentle slopes.

Turbulent mountain streams are home to American Dippers and, rarely, Harlequin Ducks. Nearby sandbars may harbor nesting Spotted Sandpipers or pehaps a family of Killdeer. Although unequalled in beauty, clear alpine lakes offer little food to birds. Probably the most common visitors to alpine waters are California Gulls travelling to and from their Great Basin breeding grounds. Compared to the surrounding landscape, lakes take longer to warm in summer and cool more slowly in winter, making the climates around them slightly warmer in winter and cooler in summer. Mountain birds flock to their margins to feed, perhaps attracted by the milder climate as well as by abundant insects and other foods.

Riparian Forests   **Plate 44**
Only small fragments remain of the shady jungles of sycamores, cottonwoods and willows that once flourished along meandering streams of the Sierra foothills. Most were cleared long ago for lumber, firewood and agriculture. Lowland riparian forests are critical to birds, and good-sized stands support more breeding and migratory species than any other habitat. A few species such as Red-shouldered Hawks and Yellow-breasted Chats live only there. Narrow stands of moisture-loving deciduous trees still border some stretches of rivers, creeks and lakes. Draped in wild grapes, berry vines or poison oak, these lush groves offer moisture and shade during the hot summers. Yellow Warblers, Warbling Vireos, House Wrens and Lazuli Buntings sing above the constant din of humming

insects, while Downy and Nuttall's Woodpeckers drill on branches and flake off bark.

In the ponderosa pine and mixed-conifer zones, riparian forests mostly become narrow, discontinuous corridors of dogwood, black cottonwoods and aspens or, more typically, tall willows or alders. Conifers often replace deciduous trees along streams, especially in steep terrain. Yellow Warblers and Wilson's Warblers breed in broadleaved trees, and migrants flock to them in late summer and fall. In the red fir and subalpine zones shrubby willows and alders form a narrow and patchy border along most streams.

Meadows   Plate 44

Mountain meadows sometimes begin as lakes and many will someday become forests. Grasses, sedges and rushes share the moist central portions with wild onions, corn lilies, shooting stars and countless other wildflowers, while young trees gradually colonize the edges. Growths of shrubby willows harbor birds such as Willow Flycatchers, Lincoln's Sparrows and MacGillivray's Warblers. Abundant mosquitoes, dragonflies and butterflies dance in the air while Western Wood-Pewees and Olive-sided Flycatchers perched at meadow's edge scan for these and other insects. Wet meadows stay green all summer, while dry grassy sites atop domes and ridges usually turn brown and go to seed by the end of August. The margins of many Sierran meadows are ringed by aspens or cottonwoods that display a brilliant gold when framed against a blue October sky.

Whether rimmed with broadleaved trees or ranks of conifers, forest-meadow edges attract birds like Western Bluebirds, Yellow-rumped Warblers, Chipping Sparrows and Purple Finches, which forage among meadow plants for insects and seeds and take to the trees for cover. During the night cold air flows down into meadow depressions and by dawn these areas become significantly colder than nearby forests. Like humans, birds seek warmth at dawn and usually flock to the sunny sides of meadows.

Sierran meadows range in size from small forest clearings to wide expanses such as Tuolumne Meadows in Yosemite that encompass hundreds of acres. Wet meadows are most numerous and extensive in the glaciated terrain of the subalpine zone, but they are scattered throughout the coniferous forests.

Rocks and Cliffs

In the northern Sierra ancient volcanoes spewed molten lava across the landscape, but the central and southern Sierra display vast expanses of glacier-polished granitic cliffs, domes and scattered boulders. Some of the earth's finest rock work graces the canyons of the Merced and Tuolumne Rivers in Yosemite and the high country of Sequoia and Kings Canyon National Parks. Rock crevices and ledges high on steep canyon walls provide nesting sites for swifts, Golden Eagles and the rare Prairie and Peregrine Falcons. Rock Wrens and Rosy Finches scuttle confidently across alpine talus slopes and Canyon Wrens inhabit jumbles of boulders in river gorges.

Birds and Habitats of the Eastern Sierra

Although this book focuses on the western Sierra, much of the information also applies to the east slope. This section briefly compares the habitats and bird life of the two slopes for the benefit of those watching birds east of the crest.

The great bulk of the Sierra Nevada lies west of the divide, and the east side drops off sharply to the deserts of the Great Basin. On this steep escarpment, altitudinal vegetation zones overlap extensively, making them less apparent than on the west slope. Some of the larger basins, however, such as those surrounding Lake Tahoe and Mammoth Lakes, have extensive subalpine, red fir and mixed-conifer forests much like those to the west. North of Lake Tahoe the main crest is flanked on both sides by other high ridges, making the distinction between the western and eastern Sierra less obvious.

The east slope is relatively arid, as moisture-laden clouds from the Pacific drop most of their rain and snow on the west slope. Precipitation may be substantial at high elevations east of the crest, but declines rapidly with decreasing elevation. Thus the high country on the two slopes is similar down to the red fir zone, but the lower vegetation zones, and their birds, become increasingly different. Red fir forests occupy smaller areas in the eastern Sierra and are restricted to the moister locations. The mixed-conifer zone has great forests of Jeffrey pines (central and southern Sierra) or ponderosa pines (northern Sierra) that are relatively dry and open, with scattered shrubs typical of the Great Basin. White fir dominates some stands, particularly in the Tahoe Basin.

At lower elevations is an even drier habitat, pinyon pine woodland, which is almost nonexistent on the west slope except at the southern end, where extensive stands occur in the drainages of the South Fork Kings River, the Kern River and the South Fork Kern River. The shrubby single-leaf pinyons usually grow in open stands, sometimes mingling with western junipers and Jeffrey pines, with understories of scattered sagebrush, curl-leaf mountain mahogany, bitterbrush and rabbitbrush. In large areas east of the Sierra only the shrubs remain, forming the dominant habitat of the Great Basin. Sagebrush scrub also extends up to high elevations on dry hillsides of the east slope and locally west of the crest, as near Donner Summit. A denser shrub habitat, montane chaparral, carpets many slopes up to the red fir zone. It resembles its west-slope counterpart, but has sagebrush, bitterbrush and mountain mahogany mixed in.

Streams flowing down the east slope support narrow bands of riparian woodland, much like western watersheds. The most notable difference is that quaking aspen forms extensive stands along many eastern streams and moist slopes. These islands of productive riparian habitat serve as important stopovers for migratory birds moving north and south along the relatively dry east side.

Not surprisingly, the bird communities at higher elevations on the east slope, and the habits of each species, closely resemble their counterparts in the western Sierra, while those of pinyon pine woodlands and sagebrush scrub are quite different. A few east-side land birds rarely occur on the west slope, and vice versa (Tables 1 and 2).

The eastern and western Sierra show even greater differences in their aquatic bird life. The west has little marshland and few large lakes, except for relatively unproductive reservoirs. On the east slope, sizable marshes, as at Sierra Valley, and large lakes such as Tahoe and Almanor provide habitat for numerous water birds. Waterfowl, shorebirds and other aquatic species are also abundant just east of the Sierra, as at Mono Lake and Honey Lake. A discussion of these diverse and teeming bird communities is beyond the scope of this book.

TABLE 1. East-slope Sierran land birds that are absent or much less common on the west slope.

Species	Status on east slope of Sierra
Lewis' Woodpecker	Breeds and winters locally in open forests at low elevations. Numbers vary from year to year; generally uncommon.
Gray Flycatcher[1]	Uncommon, breeding in sagebrush scrub at low elevations.
Pinyon Jay[1]	Breeds and winters locally in pinyon, ponderosa and Jeffrey pine forests; also feeds in sagebrush scrub. Uncommon to fairly common.

Black-billed Magpie	Common year-round in open habitats east of the mountains, but uncommon on the east slope itself.
Pygmy Nuthatch[2]	Common year-round in Jeffrey and ponderosa pine forests; less common in pinyon pine woodlands.
Virginia's Warbler	Breeds in brushy habitats with scattered trees up to 8500 feet, in a few localities in Mono and Inyo Counties.
Green-tailed Towhee[2]	Common, breeding in open sagebrush scrub, usually with a mixture of shrub species.
Brewer's Sparrow[1]	Common, breeding in open sagebrush and other brushy habitats up to 9000 feet or above.
Yellow-headed Blackbird	Common summer resident locally, breeding in marshes as high as the Tahoe Basin.

[1]*Regularly breeds on the west slope, on the Kern Plateau.*
[2]*Widespread breeder on the west slope, but much more common on the east slope.*

TABLE 2.   Montane breeding birds[3] of the western Sierra that are absent or extremely localized on the east slope.

Great Gray Owl	Western Flycatcher
Black Swift	Black Phoebe
Acorn Woodpecker	Chestnut-backed Chickadee
Pileated Woodpecker	Winter Wren
Hammond's Flycatcher	Hutton's Vireo

[3]*Regular breeders in the ponderosa pine zone or above.*

Human Impacts

Much of the High Sierra is still pristine, but large portions of the foothills and middle elevations have been altered by human activities. Since the Forty-niners swarmed into the Sierra during the Gold Rush, these impacts have become increasingly evident. Early on, hunters decimated populations of quail, pigeons and other game, and many people slaughtered birds of prey they considered harmful to game or livestock. Hawks, eagles, herons and other large birds, intolerant of disturbance near their nests, were driven away from settled areas. Although such problems continue, wildlife protection laws have enabled previously overhunted populations to increase, and raptors such as Ospreys and Peregrine Falcons have returned to some former nesting sites.

By far the greatest historical changes in Sierran bird populations have resulted from human impacts on their environment. Mining, grazing, logging, housing developments and hydroelectric projects continue to degrade habitat quality. Long before European settlers arrived, native peoples regularly burned out forest understories to make travel easier and improve conditions for game. Such low-intensity ground fires, frequently started by lightning as well, occurred every 5 to 20 years in ponderosa pine and mixed-conifer forests, maintaining them in an open, park-like condition. Ironically, one of the settlers' most pervasive impacts resulted from preventing fires, a policy intended to protect their environment, especially housing, livestock and timber. Over the years, fire suppression has become more and more efficient. As a result many forests, especially at low and middle elevations, are now choked by nearly impenetrable growths of young trees and deep accumulations of decaying wood. These unnatural forests have a dangerous potential for massive, uncontrolled wildfires. Although some birds live in these dense understories, most species prefer a more open forest floor; such habitats are dwindling.

Recognizing these problems, the National Park Service and U.S. Forest Service have reintroduced fire to selected areas, to consume debris and undergrowth and restore forests to their formerly open condition. Visitors to the giant sequoia forests in Yosemite and Sequoia National Parks can observe the results of this restorative process.

Fire prevention in foothill and montane chaparral has had similar effects on birds, favoring species that prefer dense, tall brushfields over those that inhabit sparser, younger stands. Management burns could convert some old, senescent stands to vigorous, productive brushfields, creating a patchwork of old and young chaparral more representative of the days when fires burned unchecked. Unfortunately, management burns in chaparral have been less extensive than in forests, and more are sorely needed.

Logging and timber management activities have also altered bird habitats tremendously. Until 1975, nearly all Sierran logging was selective: the best and biggest trees were removed, leaving more open forests and smaller trees. In recent years more forests have been clear-cut. Large clear-cuts are detrimental to forest birds, but smaller harvests, especially in narrow strips, actually may be preferable to selective logging, as they create openings beneficial to wildlife.

Probably the greatest problem for birds is that logging has severely depleted tall, relatively dense "old growth" forests, and cutting continues at an alarming rate. These forests are important habitat for birds like Great Gray Owls, Spotted Owls, Northern Goshawks and Pileated Woodpeckers. Once cut, such forests may never return, due to short timber harvest schedules of 50 to 80 years. Second-growth forests often feature dense growths of brush and oaks that may harbor a wide variety of birds; the danger is not that all bird species will decline, but that birds preferring old-growth forests will have too little remaining habitat to maintain their populations.

Another problem is that foresters traditionally have tried to control the spread of harmful insects by removing dead trees, which provide important resources for many birds and other animals. Most woodpeckers and nuthatches prefer these "snags" for foraging and excavating nest holes, while other birds like chickadees, owls, bluebirds and Wood Ducks raise their families in cavities abandoned by woodpeckers or created by natural decay. Forest Service policy now recognizes the value of snags to wildlife and preserves some of them from cutting, but they are typically in short supply in logged forests.

Hydroelectric development has changed Sierran watersheds extensively. Reservoirs on most of the major rivers have inundated meadows and riparian deciduous forests, the most productive habitats for birds and other wildlife. Hetch Hetchy Reservoir on the Tuolumne River and New Melones Reservoir on the Stanislaus eliminated especially magnificent river canyons. Such developments have increased the available habitat for water birds and shorebirds, particularly in the foothills and lower elevations, but in general the habitat is of low quality. Most reservoirs provide less plant and animal food for water birds than do natural lakes and ponds. Their shorelines are frequently too steep to serve as good shorebird habitat, and their fluctuating water levels inhibit the shoreline vegetation that many birds seek out.

Sheep, cattle and horses have altered meadows and stream channels dramatically by trampling, cropping grasses and wildflowers and favoring the spread of exotic plants. Birds such as Lincoln's Sparrows that thrive among tall meadow plants suffer if meadows are heavily grazed. Browsing by cattle has severely reduced the abundance of willows, required by the rare Willow Flycatcher and favored by the Lincoln's Sparrow, Song Sparrow and several warblers. Despite such important impacts on native plants and animals, livestock grazing is permitted still on most National Forest land, even within designated Wilderness Areas.

Mining has degraded wildlife habitats, particularly in the foothills. In the 1800's, water cannons scoured away entire hillsides in search of gold, causing severe silting of streams. Such hydraulic mining is no longer permitted, but now the prospect of large open pit mines raises the possibility of even more extensive disturbance. Fortunately, some of these impacts will be temporary, due to requirements that mined areas be revegetated.

Besides changing birds' habitats, people have increased the food supply around stables, picnic areas, campgrounds and settled areas, allowing Common Ravens, American Robins, Northern Mockingbirds and other species to expand their ranges in the Sierra. Unfortunately, Brown-headed Cowbirds and Steller's Jays also have benefited, reducing populations of songbirds in developed areas by parasitizing their nests and preying on eggs and young. The introduced European Starling and House Sparrow, which frequently evict native birds from their nests, have invaded developed areas at lower elevations, but have not yet penetrated the high country.

The lower elevations, which are settled most heavily, have suffered the greatest impacts from human developments. Although relatively undisturbed foothill habitats harbor a great diversity of birds and other wildlife, they have so far received little protection. The productive river bottoms that are rapidly being converted to farms and reservoirs particularly deserve preservation as dwindling and critical habitats.

Fortunately, large portions of the higher Sierra are now protected by National Parks and Wilderness Areas. Yosemite, Sequoia and Kings Canyon National Parks include some of the most magnificent examples of Sierran natural diversity, encompassing dramatic elevational gradients from the upper foothills to summits of the highest peaks. Along with large Wilderness Areas, they preserve entire natural communities for future generations.

How to Find and Identify Sierran Birds

In the Sierra, as elsewhere, it is often possible to use information on habitat needs to predict which birds will be found in a given forest or meadow at a particular time of year. While some species such as Steller's Jays and American Robins traverse a wide range of altitudes and habitats, others such as Flammulated Owls are highly localized. Many birds avoid developed areas, so it is best to walk at least a short distance from campgrounds and roads. The more habitats one visits, the more birds one is likely to see.

Birding is best in early mornings when birds feed and vocalize and in late afternoon when there is another burst of activity. Birds are inactive and call infrequently during midday, particularly on hot afternoons in exposed habitats.

Songs and calls often provide the first and sometimes the only clue to a bird's presence. Bird sounds may best be learned by searching patiently for the sources of any unfamiliar vocalizations, but commercial recordings of bird songs also can be helpful. Better yet is the experienced ear of a birder friend.

Some birds, such as male Western Tanagers and Clark's Nutcrackers, can be identified at a glance, while others like many flycatchers and finches demand close attention to "field marks," behavior and habitat. It is important to note whether a bird forages on bark as does a woodpecker, or in foliage like a warbler or vireo. Does it occur alone or in flocks? Does it walk or hop? Does it pump its tail up and down, or flick its wings? Another clue to its identity is its style of flight — some birds soar or continually beat their wings, some follow a direct path, while others undulate. Physical features to note include posture, body size, bill shape, color patterns on the tails and wings, and facial markings like eye rings and eye stripes.

The species accounts in this book describe field marks and characteristic behaviors, and the plates illustrate most Sierran species. Field guides such as those listed in the Bibliography are also useful. Unfamiliar birds often can be identified later if observations are recorded in the field. Dates, approximate locations and habitats are important to note, and sketches can be helpful for comparisons with field guides. Identification is only the first step in birdwatching. Many people also enjoy making detailed observations of nesting and feeding behavior, habitats and geographical distribution.

Visitors to the Sierra should know that many species such as raptors are sensitive to human disturbance, especially while nesting; and accordingly, they should respect the retreats of such wildlife. A pair of Great Gray Owls, listed as endangered in California, abandoned their nest in Yosemite National Park after groups of overzealous birders approached too closely. Tape recordings of songs to attract birds can also disrupt nesting efforts and should not be overused. Eager birders in large numbers can easily trample a fragile mountain meadow. If visitors are cautious, however, birdwatching becomes a nondestructive and immensely rewarding hobby that will enhance their appreciation of the Sierra and its rich natural history.

Naming and Classifying Birds

Many people enjoy birds, along with flowers, trees, and mountain scenery, simply as wondrous and beautiful elements of nature and feel no need to name them. But to learn more about birds by reading and comparing observations with others, one must know names.

Bird names can be confusing. The birds that some people in the Sierra foothills call Angel Hawks are called White-tailed Kites by many birdwatchers and Black-shouldered Kites by up-to-date birders. Scientific names, however, cross cultural and regional barriers; ornithologists in Paris, Beijing and California all call this species by its scientific name, *Elanus caeruleus*. They further classify it by family (Accipitridae) and order (Falconiformes) to indicate its kinship to other hawks, vultures and falcons.

In this book Sierran birds are called by their common names first— Black-shouldered Kite, White-crowned Sparrow, American Robin. These English-language names (as well as the scientific names) have been standardized across the country by the American Ornithologists' Union (AOU, 6th ed.; see Bibliography). Because the AOU changes bird names occasionally, the species accounts below mention recently revised names in footnotes, for the benefit of readers who may not know the current nomenclature. Some names are in dispute; a few scientists still call the Black-shouldered Kite in North and South America by its former common and scientific names (White-tailed Kite, *Elanus leucurus*) because they consider it a separate species from Black-shouldered Kites on other continents.

Birdwatchers often are intrigued by the origins of bird names. Some such as the falcon, kite and harlequin date back to the Middle Ages. Others memorialize early naturalists: Wilson's Warbler, named for the early ornithologist and poet, Alexander Wilson; Bewick's Wren, for the famous eighteenth-century English artist and naturalist Thomas Bewick, Lewis' Woodpecker and Clark's Nutcracker for those two early explorers of the great Louisiana territory. For stimulating reading on this subject see Robert Gruson's *Words for Birds* (Quadrangle, 1972) and Joseph Kastner's *A Species of Eternity* (Knopf, 1977).

Subspecies (or races), species, genera, subfamilies, families, orders— with these categories ornithologists sort birds in ways that reflect our best understanding of how they evolved and how they are related. Evolutionary relatedness, as currently understood, also determines the official AOU sequence of bird species, which was followed in arranging the species accounts in this book.

Species Accounts

The following species accounts describe the life histories of 191 species of Sierran birds[1], arranged in the American Ornithologists' Union checklist order (6th edition; see Bibliography). At the bottom of each account, a **"Where Found"** section lists representative locations where the species has been observed in Yosemite, Sequoia and Kings Canyon National Parks. For many low-elevation and rare species, localities outside (but near) the parks are also given. Generally the listed sites have good habitat where future searches might be successful.

Most families of birds, such as tyrant flycatchers or vireos, are prefaced by a brief description of the features shared by their member species.

Approximate abundance of each species is described using the following subjective categories, which indicate the frequency that an experienced birder might expect to find a given species in the proper habitat and season during peak birding hours.

Abundant - Many individuals observed during every outing.
Common - Observed on most outings, sometimes many individuals.
Fairly Common - One or a few individuals observed on most outings.
Uncommon - Observed on relatively few outings.
Rare - Seldom encountered, often highly localized.

GREBES *(Family Podicipedidae)*

At a distance, grebes look something like small ducks, but sit higher in the water and have pointed bills. Rather than webbed feet, they have lobed toes that fan out when pushed through water. They dive deep with great strength and agility, propelled by legs set so far to the rear that they cannot walk upright but must use both wings to flap along on their bellies. Grebes are rarely seen in flight as most migrate at night and flee from predators by diving. They are suspected to be strong fliers, however, as a few species such as Eared Grebes travel thousands of miles between their breeding and wintering grounds.

Pied-billed Grebe *(Podilymbus podiceps)*   Plate 2, Figure 7

Swimming along the margins of cattail- or tule-bordered ponds, Pied-billed Grebes may go unnoticed. These solitary birds prefer to feed in the

---

[1]*Marginal, occasional and very rare bird species in the Sierra Nevada are listed in Appendix I.*

shallows, diving for small fish, crustaceans or aquatic invertebrates. After feeding, they may move out into open water with the larger coots or diving ducks. Most water birds take flight when predators approach, but Pied-billed Grebes sink quietly beneath the surface. When they reappear they may lurk in the grasses and reeds at pond's edge with only their heads out of water. Their bills are noticeably broader and thicker than those of most grebes, and adults have black bands circling them during the breeding season. These bands, as well as the black throat patches, disappear in winter.

Although they are common residents of the Central Valley, Pied-billed Grebes are uncommon in the Sierra Nevada. They breed and winter at scattered quiet lakes and ponds bordered by dense reeds or tules. A few nest up to the mixed-conifer zone, but most montane sightings have been after breeding in late summer and fall. In the foothills they breed from March through August. Both parents gather dead plant materials to build a thick mat nest that occasionally floats free, but is more often anchored to plants growing from the bottom ooze. Each pair defends a small territory around the nest, where the young are fed and reared. Often, newly-hatched chicks will ride on the adults' backs or hide beneath their wings during dives.

Where Found:
Yosemite: Recorded on the lower portion of the Merced River below Yosemite Valley; also west of the park at Don Pedro Reservoir, Hardin Flat and foothill ponds near Highway 120, west of Yosemite Junction.
Sequoia-Kings Canyon: Observed at Clover Creek below the Generals Highway and on the Middle Fork Kaweah River below Pumpkin Hollow Bridge. Nests west of the parks at Allen Gap. Also common below Terminus Dam (Lake Kaweah).

Eared Grebe *(Podiceps nigricollis)* Plate 2

These small, thin-billed grebes with bright scarlet eyes are uncommon visitors to ponds, lakes and reservoirs of the western Sierra. Most sightings have been in the foothills during fall, winter and early spring, but migrants may turn up rarely at high elevations in late summer and autumn. They nest locally in freshwater lakes east of the Sierra crest, but have not done so recently on the west slope.

During the nonbreeding season, Eared Grebes congregate in brackish or salty water along coastal California, and enormous numbers gather at Mono Lake directly east of Yosemite. Hundreds of thousands concentrate there in late summer and fall to feed on the abundant brine shrimp that thrive in the salty, alkaline water. Diversions of Mono's feeder streams have caused the lake's level to drop precipitously in recent years, and the water has increased in salinity to the point that even the brine shrimp are threatened. If the shrimp disappear, it will be a disaster for Eared Grebes and other long-distance migrants that depend on Mono for food during their journeys north and south across the inhospitable Great Basin.

In the nonbreeding season, Eared Grebes lose their golden ear tufts and molt into subdued plumage of brown and gray. When swimming, they sit high on the water and have a noticeably high-rumped appearance.

Where Found:
Yosemite: Recorded in Yosemite Valley, Harden Lake, Tuolumne Meadows and Lyell Canyon.
Sequoia-Kings Canyon: Recorded at Hume Lake, Moose Lake, Heather Lake, Moraine Lake, Lake South America (Kern Basin), Wolverton and the Ash Mountain sewage ponds.

CORMORANTS *(Family Phalacrocoracidae)*

Double-crested Cormorant *(Phalacrocorax auritus)*
Though confined mainly to the lower foothills, these large, black fish-eaters regularly winter in the western Sierra now that construction of numerous reservoirs has expanded their preferred habitat. They frequent large bodies of water that provide ample room for their labored takeoffs and plentiful small fish, their favored prey. These they take by diving from the water's surface. Because their feathers are not fully waterproofed like ducks', cormorants must leave the water periodically to dry in the sun. With wet wings spread, they perch like awkward gargoyles on snags or branches along the shore.

Double-crested Cormorants occur regularly in the foothills as far south as Lake Isabella (Kern County) and occasionally show up at higher elevations. Uncommon in winter and rare in summer, they breed at Butt Valley Reservoir in Plumas County and probably at other foothill lakes and reservoirs. At such inland areas they build nests of sticks and debris in large trees, dead or alive.

Where Found:
Yosemite: Recorded at Yosemite Valley, Hetch Hetchy Reservoir and Tenaya Lake; regular in foothills west of park at Don Pedro Reservoir, Dawson Lake (near La Grange), Turlock Reservoir and the Tuolumne River below La Grange.
Sequoia-Kings Canyon: Occurs west of parks at Lake Kaweah and Lake Success.

HERONS *(Family Ardeidae)*

These birds have long legs for wading in shallow water, long necks to extend their reach and pointed bills for grasping or spearing aquatic prey. In the western Sierra, herons are rather uncommon except in the foothills. Greater numbers, and more species, occur in the lowlands west of the range.

Great Blue Heron *(Ardea herodias)* Plate 2

Few Sierran birds are more majestic than this largest of North American herons. Standing fully four feet tall, with a wingspread of seven feet, it dwarfs other herons and shorebirds of the region.

A solitary feeder, the Great Blue Heron forages night and day but is most active around dusk and dawn. Great Blue Herons stalk fish, frogs, crayfish and aquatic insects in the shallows of lakes, ponds and quiet streams. Less often, they venture into grasslands and agricultural fields to hunt for mice and other small animals. Recent studies have shown that they do not have a significant impact on game fish, which constitute only a small fraction of their diet. When hunting, a Great Blue Heron shows great patience, standing motionless for several minutes or inching forward stealthily, with neck outstretched. Suddenly it strikes, grasping small prey in its bill, or spearing larger animals.

This successful and widespread species is the most common Sierran heron and the only one regularly seen above the foothills. Great Blues are fairly common at low elevations, and a few may remain all year as high as Yosemite Valley. Rarely they wander to higher elevations, even up to tree line, in late summer.

Great Blues nest colonially, usually building their platforms of sticks in the upper parts of tall trees. They also nest on cliffs or amidst marsh vegetation. Most of them breed in lowlands west of the Sierra, but a few rookeries exist along rivers and reservoirs in the foothills.

The only bird that could be confused with a Great Blue Heron is the Sandhill Crane, which is occasionally seen migrating over the western Sierra, but rarely if ever alights. The Crane, however, is heftier, flies with its neck outstretched, and almost always appears in flocks. The Great Blue is less social, except when breeding, and like all herons, flies with its neck curled into an S-shape. Although its plumage shows a tinge of blue in good light, it generally appears grayish. Usually silent, it sometimes utters deep, harsh croaks when startled or when interacting with others of its species.

Where Found:
Yosemite: Occasionally seen in Yosemite Valley and above, but more common west of park along foothill streams, ponds and reservoirs: as at the Moccasin Creek arm of Don Pedro Reservoir and at farm ponds east of Oakdale.

41

Sequoia-Kings Canyon: Frequently seen flying high above the Middle Fork Kaweah River near Ash Mountain and Three Rivers. Rookeries west of parks along the South Fork Kaweah River and Dry Creek.

Green-backed Heron[1] *(Butorides striatus)*

When flying or perching with its long neck hunched in, this chunky, crow-sized bird may be difficult to recognize as a heron. At a distance it appears black or bluish on its crown and back, but good lighting reveals a beautiful dark green. Its chestnut face and neck complete the striking and unmistakable color pattern.

Green-backed Herons stalk small fish and other aquatic animals by wading or standing in shallow water, much like Great Blues. Sometimes they hunt from logs or streambanks and may even dive headfirst at their prey. They are also known to "fish" with lures such as feathers or bread crusts. They often perch by the water's edge on logs or on dead branches of trees. Unlike other herons, pairs nest solitarily, rather than in colonies.

In the Central Valley, these small herons are fairly common year-round, and they also occur rarely in the lower Sierra foothills. Present from April to October, they are usually found along tree-bordered lakes, ponds, and quiet streams. They nest and roost in willows, oaks and other trees and prefer to forage in their shade. Because so many riparian woodlands have been destroyed or heavily disturbed, this species may be less numerous than in the past.

Where Found:
Yosemite: May still nest, as it did formerly, along slow-moving stretches of the Merced and Tuolumne Rivers in the lower foothills west of park.
Sequoia-Kings Canyon: Probably nests below Terminus Dam (Lake Kaweah).

DUCKS AND GEESE *(Family Anatidae)*

Millions of ducks, geese and swans crowd the wetlands of California's Central Valley in winter, forsaking the frozen marshes and tundra of their northern breeding grounds. Because of its proximity to these waterfowl concentrations, about 25 species in this family have been seen in the western Sierra Nevada. Most occur only sporadically (see Appendix I) and none is common.

In the Sierra, waterfowl frequent wetland habitats ranging from low-elevation reservoirs, lakes and rivers to turbulent streams of the high country. All species are excellent swimmers and are well adapted to aquatic

[1]*Formerly, Green Heron.*

living, with webbed feet, long necks for underwater feeding, a thick coat of down and a large oil gland beneath to keep the feathers dry. Only the most frequently observed migrants, and species that have nested in the region, are described here.

Canada Goose *(Branta canadensis)*

The honking of Canada Geese is often heard before their V-shaped flocks are seen flying overhead. A few nest in meadows above Paradise, Butte County, and possibly elsewhere in the northern Sierra. They primarily breed farther north in the Cascades and in the Great Basin. Rarely, a few land in wet meadows or lakes of the Sierra to feed on grasses and cereal grains while in transit between their wintering and breeding grounds. The identical males and females can be distinguished from all other waterfowl by their large, dark bodies and long black necks with white cheek and throat patches.

Canada Geese form pair bonds during their second or third winter, and like all geese and swans, mated birds stay together for life. Extremely clannish, they maintain family groups throughout the year. These strong social bonds have led to the isolation of small breeding populations and the rapid evolution of new races across North America. The twelve currently recognized races range in size from the rare Giant Canada Geese of the northern Great Plains to the Cackling Geese, only a little larger than Mallards. The race most likely to be seen in the western Sierra is the large Honker, which nests in the Great Basin.

Where Found:
Yosemite: Has been noted at Yosemite Valley, Lake Eleanor and Tuolumne Meadows.
Sequoia-Kings Canyon: A few flocks have been seen flying over Ash Mountain; once noted at Zumwalt Meadows.

Wood Duck *(Aix sponsa)* Plate 2

As their name suggests, Wood Ducks are partial to densely forested backwaters where oaks, willows or cottonwoods offer cover. They search for oaks with abundant acorns, an especially favored food. Wood Ducks usually hunt for acorns in leaf litter of the forest floor, but unlike most ducks may also land in trees and pluck them from the highest branches. They also forage in water for aquatic plants, insects and other foods.

Extensive clearing of riparian forests has greatly reduced Wood Duck habitat throughout their range. Where suitable lakes and rivers persist in the Sierra foothills, they still occur uncommonly. Although a few have nested up to the ponderosa pine zone, breeding is normally confined to the lower foothills and floor of the Central Valley. After breeding, Wood

43

Ducks may follow stream courses up to black oak woodlands of the ponderosa pine zone, but they never remain there for winter.

Pileated Woodpecker holes and natural tree cavities are the Wood Duck's preferred nesting sites. The down-lined nest holes provide safe places for the females to incubate their eggs. Females coax their young from the nest, usually within a day after hatching. Their light weight and downy bodies allow them to flutter uninjured to the ground from heights up to 50 feet and then tumble into the water and swim away. Artificial nest boxes have greatly benefited local populations in areas with few natural cavities. Sometimes starlings, flickers or owls compete for these homes.

The exquisite plumage of male Wood Ducks reflects metallic patterns of green and violet when bathed in sunlight. They are the only North American waterfowl with entirely iridescent wings and backs. Females are similar in shape, but wear subdued tones of grayish-brown. In flight Wood Ducks appear generally dark with long, squared-off tails; they may make loud, nasal shrieks.

Where Found:
Yosemite: Historical nesting in Yosemite Valley; recorded at farm ponds west of Yosemite Junction on Highway 120; probably occurs in bottomlands of the Merced and Tuolumne Rivers.
Sequoia-Kings Canyon: Regular west of parks, below Terminus Dam (Lake Kaweah) and to the west, at Dry Creek. Also regular in stock ponds on Globe Drive in Springville (Tulare Co.).

Mallard *(Anas platyrhynchos)* Plate 2, Figure 7

The Mallard is the most widely distributed and best-known duck in the Northern Hemisphere. Bred in captivity since ancient times, it is the ancestor of most domestic varieties. In nature, Mallards mate rarely with other species, but captive birds have produced fertile offspring with more than 40 different species of ducks and geese. Domestic flocks of ducks in urban parks and barnyards often feature the odd-looking progeny of such mixed matings.

In contrast to geese and swans, ducks select new partners each year. The brilliant plumages of the males are used in elaborate courtship displays to attract the more subtly patterned females. Male Common Mergansers are probably the only birds in the western Sierra for which male Mallards could be mistaken. Unlike diving ducks such as mergansers, Mallards feed at the surface. They and other "puddle ducks" tip up rather than dive when feeding, walk proficiently on land, and fly directly up from the water when flushed. Mallards in flight have large, broad bodies with slower wingbeats than most other ducks.

Small resident populations of Mallards breed in freshwater ponds, rivers and marshes, and large concentrations winter throughout the lowlands of the state. These hardy ducks will nest almost anywhere there is a supply of pondweeds or aquatic insects for the young. In the western Sierra, Mallards nest fairly commonly at low elevations and rarely up to the subalpine zone. They lay 10 or 12 bluish eggs in ground nests hidden by tall grasses or marsh vegetation. Like most ducks, male Mallards abandon their mates soon after the eggs are laid, leaving the female to incubate her clutch and care for the young. The precocial ducklings can walk, swim and feed shortly after hatching. In late summer and fall small groups of migrating Mallards and other surface-feeding ducks visit lakes, ponds and slow-moving streams of the western Sierra. Snowstorms and freezing temperatures drive most of them downslope for the winter.

Where Found:
Yosemite: Regular breeding along slow stretches of the Merced and Tuolumne Rivers and at Hardin Flat; uncommon breeding in Yosemite Valley, rarely up to Tuolumne Meadows and ponds near Tioga Pass; also recorded in Pate Valley, Little Yosemite Valley and at Harden Lake.
Sequoia-Kings Canyon: Regular breeding at Kern Lake and lower portions of the Kern River; nests also found at Hume Lake, Hockett Lake and Sawdust Meadow; also recorded at Evolution Meadow, Paradise Valley, Zumwalt Meadows and Sand Meadow; in foothills at Ash Mountain, below Terminus Dam (Lake Kaweah) and at Allen Gap and Dry Creek.

Ring-necked Duck *(Aythya collaris)*

Despite its name, the male Ring-necked Duck has a chestnut collar so faint it is difficult to see even at close range. From a distance the dark head and back, vertical white stripe before the wing, and white ring around the bill tip make much better field marks. The female can be told by her similar white bill markings, white eye ring and overall brown coloration. The Ring-necked Duck occurs on ponds and lakes, where it dives for pondweeds, other aquatic plants and occasionally insect larvae. Ring-necks and other diving species run across the water surface before taking flight.

In the Sierra, Ring-necks are uncommon winter visitors to low-elevation lakes, ponds, and reservoirs, where they often associate with other diving ducks. They have nested at Buck's Lake in Plumas County and possibly breed at other deep lakes of the northern Sierra.

Where Found:
Yosemite: Noted historically in Yosemite Valley; recent sightings at foothill ponds along Highway 120 west of Yosemite Junction and along the Wards Ferry Road south of Sonora.
Sequoia-Kings Canyon: Recorded at Allen Gap and at lakes below Terminus Dam (Lake Kaweah).

Harlequin Duck *(Histrionicus histrionicus)* Plate 1

Turbulent headwaters of Sierran streams from the Stanislaus River south to the upper San Joaquin formerly harbored nesting Harlequin Ducks. Unlike other North American waterfowl, they prosper amidst swirling torrents and rapids. Sadly, they have been nearly extirpated from the Sierra Nevada. The only recent recorded nestings occurred above Salt Springs Reservoir on the Mokelumne River in Amador and Calaveras Counties. The exact cause of their decline is unknown but is probably related to increased numbers of fishermen and backpackers and to damming of historic nesting streams. Harlequins from northerly, healthier breeding populations still occur sparingly along the coast in winter, where they dive for marine animals along exposed, rocky headlands. They occasionally show up in the western Sierra as well.

These hardy ducks nest on the ground under the shelter of driftwood or rocks, and always beside swift-flowing rivers. Harlequins are adept underwater swimmers, and prefer to dive in clear, cold rapids where they search rock crevices for larvae of caddisflies, mayflies and stoneflies.

Named after the brightly costumed clowns of the medieval stage, the slate-blue males have bright orange-brown sides and white facial and body markings, and indeed appear to be dressed for a performance. The less distinguished-looking females are mostly dark gray, with three circular white head markings.

Where Found:
Yosemite: Historical breeding on Tuolumne River from about 4,000 feet up to the headwaters, and on the Merced River in Yosemite Valley, the South Fork Merced River, Lake Ediza in the headwaters of the San Joaquin River (Madera Co.), and Cherry Creek (Tuolumne Co.); recent records of nonbreeding birds in Tenaya Canyon and the South Fork Merced River near Wawona.
Sequoia-Kings Canyon: Nonbreeding birds noted historically near the Clough Cave Ranger Station on the South Fork Kaweah River, and near Cedar Grove on the South Fork Kings River.

Common Goldeneye *(Bucephala clangula)* Figure 3

Unlike most ducks, Common Goldeneyes winter regularly above the foothills of the western Sierra. They prefer lakes and large ponds, where they dive for small fish and crustaceans. Though rare, they occur the length of the range, lingering regularly well into January up to the mixed-conifer zone. At higher lakes and rivers they mingle mainly with Common Mergansers, which look similar in coloration but have a sleeker profile and larger, narrower bills and wings. Male Goldeneyes on the water appear mostly white with dark backs and heads and circular white face patches.

Figure 3. The nearly identical female Barrow's (a) and Common (b) Goldeneyes can be distinguished by the shape of their heads and bills. The Common has an evenly rounded head sloping gently down to a large, black bill, which often has a yellow-orange tip. The Barrow's has a slight bump on the back of the head (at the nape), and its steep forecrown creates a sharp angle where it meets the mostly yellow-orange bill. Reproduced with permission of Point Reyes Bird Observatory.

The gray females have brown heads with white collars. Females and immatures are easily confused with the much rarer Barrow's Goldeneyes (see Fig. 3).

Where Found:
Yosemite: Recorded in winter at Mirror Lake (Yosemite Valley), and outside the park at Hardin Flat, White Pines Lake (near Arnold), Burgson Lake (near Donnell Lake), and regularly at Pinecrest Lake (Tuolumne Co.).
Sequoia-Kings Canyon: No records in or west of the parks. Observed to the south in the Kern River Valley and to the north at Bass Lake (Madera Co.).

Barrow's Goldeneye *(Bucephala islandica)* Figure 3

Barrow's Goldeneyes probably have always been rare in California. Most nest in secluded lakes of the Cascades, Rockies and mountainous portions of Alaska. Before the 1940's there were a few nesting records from the Lassen region and south in the Sierra to Fresno County. Most of them were from high-elevation lakes bordered by forests that provided tree cavities for nesting. Breeding has not been observed recently in the Sierra, and the few birds that regularly winter in California are doubtless migrants from the north. A few Barrow's Goldeneyes winter regularly on the Feather River at the De Sabla Reservoir and below the Oroville Fish Hatchery, and there are also winter records from the Lower American River.

Despite the scarcity of recent sightings, birdwatchers in the Sierra should be alert for these strikingly beautiful birds. The male has a purple-glossed head with a white crescent before its golden eye. From a distance it appears mostly white with a dark head and back, distinct white wing markings, and a dark bar extending downward from each shoulder (lacking in the Common Goldeneye). The gray female has a white collar and a large, brown head; typically at least half her bill is a bright yellow, while the similar Common Goldeneye's is all dark or barely tipped with yellow (see Fig. 3).

Where Found:
Yosemite: Historical nesting at Smedberg Lake and Table Lake; also at a small lake outside the park near the headwaters of Cherry Creek (Tuolumne Co.).
Sequoia-Kings Canyon: Recorded historically at a small lake in Grand Cirque (Fresno Co.).

Bufflehead *(Bucephala albeola)*

The rounded heads of these dapper little ducks reminded early ornithologists of a buffalo's profile, hence the name Bufflehead. They sit buoyantly high on the water and can fly up directly from the surface rather than having to skitter across the water to gain speed like most diving ducks. Buffleheads fly rapidly, flashing white patches on their whirring wings. Much like their close relatives, the goldeneyes, they dive for small fishes or search the bottom oozes for shellfish and other prey. Less commonly they feed at the surface.

Buffleheads visit deeper lakes and rivers of the Sierra foothills in winter and occasionally range up to the ponderosa pine zone. They breed in forested mountain lakes of the Cascades and farther north, but not in the Sierra. Before flying north, drakes get a headstart on breeding: they actively court females and threaten other males by swimming at them with wings flapping. At a distance males look black and white, but close views reveal a bright purple and green iridescence on their heads. Females have dark grayish bodies with white wing patches and white spots behind their eyes.

Where Found:
Yosemite: Has been observed a few times in Yosemite Valley.
Sequoia-Kings Canyon: A "flock" was once recorded near Ash Mountain in early spring; one fall observation at Bullfrog Lake (Fresno Co.).

Common Merganser *(Mergus merganser)*   Plate 1

These expert underwater hunters require fairly clear water to see their prey. Their long, thin bills have horny tooth-like projections, which prevent slippery fish from escaping their grasp. This feature has earned them the epithet "sawbill." Mergansers have been accused of depleting fisheries, but recent studies indicate they mostly take non-game species that are slower and more easily caught. In the western Sierra, Common Mergansers do eat some trout, but their total impact on the fisheries is negligible.

Mergansers breed in small numbers along forested lakes and streams of the western Sierra. Eggs are laid in tree cavities or rock crevices. They usually nest below 6,000 feet, but range to above 9,000 feet in late summer and fall. Flocks of 5 to 30 individuals occasionally remain on ice-free lakes and rivers through the winter.

Like other diving ducks, Common Mergansers are clumsy on land and must run across water to take flight. Once flying, their long, straight bodies knife through the air just above the water's surface, flashing white wing patches. They can be told from all other Sierran ducks by their sleeker profiles and long, narrow bills, which are bright orange in both sexes.

Where Found:
Yosemite: Has nested in Yosemite Valley and Hetch Hetchy, where several pairs have been observed in recent years during the breeding season; uncommon along the Merced and Tuolumne Rivers at other seasons.

Sequoia-Kings Canyon: Summer resident along the Upper Kern River (near Lower Funston Meadow); noted in small lake near Crabtree Meadow. Breeds regularly on Middle Fork Kaweah River near Three Rivers. Winters at Lake Kaweah (west of parks) and Kaweah River near Ash Mountain.

Ruddy Duck *(Oxyura jamaicensis)*

Stout, chunky birds with thick heads and necks, Ruddy Ducks sit low in the water and cock their stiff tail feathers upward. Males have conspicuous white cheeks and retain their grayish-brown winter plumages longer than most other ducks. In spring and early summer they molt into a bright chestnut or "ruddy" plumage, while their bills turn a startling blue. Females are brownish with a dark line crossing each cheek.

Although uncommon in the western Sierra, Ruddy Ducks may dot the surfaces of deep lakes, reservoirs and sewage ponds in fall and winter. They remain primarily in the foothills, but have ranged up to the mixed-conifer zone. They feed by diving for seeds, roots and shellfish. To become airborne they must run across water with their short wings beating furiously; usually they dive rather than fly to escape danger.

Where Found:
Yosemite: Has been recorded at Lake Eleanor and in Yosemite Valley.
Sequoia-Kings Canyon: Uncommon in open waters below Terminus Dam (Lake Kaweah), and at Allen Gap. No recent records in the parks.

VULTURES *(Family Cathartidae)*

Vultures are large scavengers that soar great distances in search of carcasses. These carrion-eaters have extraordinary vision and can spot dying or recently dead animals from high in the air. They often feed by thrusting their heads into the body cavities of rotting animals; baldness helps them avoid any problem with chronically soiled head feathers.

Turkey Vulture *(Cathartes aura)*   Plate 5, Figure 6

Spiraling almost effortlessly on warm updrafts, Turkey Vultures soar over open grasslands, chaparral and oak-lined canyons of the foothills. Their long wings, slightly smaller than those of the Golden Eagle, are held in a flattened "V" with the grayish flight feathers spread almost like fingers. They wobble unsteadily from side to side, only rarely flapping their wings. At close range the naked red heads of adults resemble those of turkeys, hence their name. Juveniles have black heads.

Turkey Vultures often search for carrion alone, but when one finds a choice carcass, others soon gather and descend to join the feast. Unlike most birds, Turkey Vultures have a keen sense of smell, which helps them locate decaying flesh. They often begin their meals with the soft parts, such as eyes and internal organs. Although their talons are strong, they are not adapted for seizing or killing prey.

A few Turkey Vultures reside year-round in the foothills of the Sierra, but their numbers increase dramatically in March and April when migrants return to breed. Mated pairs do not build nests, but lay their eggs in simple depressions on cliffs, ledges, in caves or in hollow stumps. Nest sites are usually inaccessibly situated to insure protection from predators that might otherwise be attracted to the odor of rotting meat. Parents feed regurgitated food to their young for 70 to 80 days before they leave the nest.

Turkey Vultures patrol the Sierra foothills throughout the summer, providing a useful clean-up service. They seldom wander up to the conifer forests, where the terrain is less open for foraging. In late summer and fall, a few may be seen wheeling over the higher mountains, and at least one bird reached an elevation of 10,000 feet on the slopes of Mt. Dana in Yosemite. With the arrival of cool, crisp days in September and October many gather into loose flocks and migrate to wintering grounds in southern California and Mexico. Those that remain in the Sierra foothills and Central Valley typically roost communally in tall trees or on rock outcrops at night, but disperse to forage during the day.

Where Found:
Yosemite: Commonly observed west of the park along Highways 120 and 140 and lower portions of the Merced and Tuolumne Rivers; a few records up to Yosemite Valley, Crane Flat and Wawona.
Sequoia-Kings Canyon: Commonly observed near Three Rivers and Ash Mountain; in summer and fall recorded up to Hume Lake, Grant Grove, Giant Forest and Cherry Gap.

California Condor *(Gymnogyps californianus)* Figure 4

During the Pleistocene, California Condors searched open expanses of western North America for decaying carcasses provided in abundance by vast herds of bison, elk, deer and pronghorn antelope. Mass exterminations of these herds during the Ice Ages decreased food supplies and probably started the Condor's long-term decline. Prior to European colonization they occurred from British Columbia to Baja California, but shooting, nest disturbance and other human intrusions caused further dramatic declines. By 1940 they numbered only about 100, and today there are fewer than 10.

California Condors, with their massive nine-foot wingspans, are the largest land birds in North America. These giants routinely make round trips of seventy miles or more between roosting and feeding sites. They always feed on the ground in open areas such as grasslands and roadsides where there is sufficient space for their labored landings and takeoffs. Decomposing carcasses of cattle, sheep, deer and ground squirrels are now the mainstays of their diet.

Most active Condor nests found in recent years have been in rugged coastal mountains of the Los Padres and Angeles National Forests in southern California. In 1984 a new site was discovered east of Porterville, Tulare County, in the southern Sierra. Reproductive rates are low and a successful pair will generally hatch only one egg every other year. They usually nest in simple depressions on cliff ledges or potholes in caves. Condors do not breed until at least their sixth year and mated pairs often remain together for long periods, re-using the same nesting sites. Non-breeding birds regularly travel north to the Coast Range and foothills of the southern Sierra. Reliable observations have been reported in Kern, Tulare, Fresno and Madera Counties from late May until October. Recent radio-tracking studies have revealed an important roost-site in the Sierra foot-

Keith Hansen 81

Figure 4. California Condor (adult). Reproduced with permission of Point Reyes Bird Observatory.

hills northeast of Bakersfield. Immature Condors occur there year-round, and adults during the nonbreeding season.

Shooting and poisoning are known to have contributed to the California Condor's decline, and pesticides, urbanization and loss of natural food supplies have probably also been responsible. One died recently from lead poisoning, acquired by eating an animal killed with lead shot. Their nesting sites are now protected, but they also need freedom from human disturbance when feeding and roosting. Key habitats must be identified and preserved. The small population, localized nesting areas and low reproductive rates increase the precariousness of their existence. Unquestionably human activities have brought California Condors to the threshold of extinction, and superhuman efforts will be required to avert this tragedy.

Where Found:
Yosemite: No records.
Sequoia-Kings Canyon: Historical records from Moro Rock, Castle Rocks, Salt Springs and Yokohl Valley. At least 20 sightings since 1960 from numerous points including Park Ridge Lookout, Wolverton, Colony Mill Road below Ash Peak Lookout, Milk Ranch Peak Lookout, Three Rivers, Hockett Meadow and Blue Ridge.

HAWKS AND EAGLES *(Family Accipitridae)*

All species in this large family are primarily daytime predators with keen eyesight, sharp talons and hooked beaks to capture and devour prey. Like owls, they often consume whole animals and digest them in their highly acidic stomachs. Fur, feathers and bones are then passed on to the gizzard, compressed into pellets and regurgitated. These pellets, or castings, provide useful information about diets that biologists could otherwise collect only by killing birds. Females are larger than males, but usually look the same. Immatures typically take two or more years to achieve adult plumage. Ornithologists recently lumped many birds of prey into this single, diverse family that includes ospreys, kites, eagles, forest-dwelling *Accipiters* and soaring *Buteos*.

Osprey *(Pandion haliaetus)*   Plate 3

Few birds are as widespread as Ospreys. Despite their worldwide distribution, they seldom concentrate in large numbers at any single place. Ospreys rarely stray far from large lakes, rivers, or coastal areas with clear water and ample fish. They search for fish from perches on rock outcrops and snags or by flying low above the water. They prey on many species but prefer fishes 6 to 12 inches long that school near the surface. Ospreys

53

attack by swooping down rapidly and striking the water with outstretched talons. Their long toes have tiny spikes that help grip and subdue slippery prey. They usually fly back to a favored perch to eat, holding fish tightly with heads pointing forward to reduce air resistance or to prevent theft by other birds. Also fish-loving, Bald Eagles sometimes bully Ospreys into dropping their prize rather than fishing for themselves. Ospreys occasionally feed on other aquatic animals such as turtles and frogs.

In the western Sierra, Ospreys nest at New Melones Reservoir in Tuolumne County, Bass Lake in Madera County and a few other localities in Tehama, Butte and Plumas Counties. Their nearest nesting strongholds are to the north and east at Shasta, Almanor, and Eagle Lakes. They arrive on their breeding grounds in March or April and build large stick nests on hollow stumps, flattened treetops or cliff faces, rarely far from water. Pairs nest alone or in small colonies if the fishery is especially productive. Most observations of Ospreys in the western Sierra have been made in the late summer and fall when migratory birds move south to their wintering grounds. During this period, they might be seen at lakesides or along rivers at almost any elevation, but mostly below the red fir zone.

Where Found:
Yosemite: Mostly observed in late summer and fall at Hetch Hetchy, Lake Eleanor and Cherry Lake; also noted in Yosemite Valley, Tuolumne Meadows.
Sequoia-Kings Canyon: Recorded at Three Rivers, along the Kaweah River and at Lake Kaweah, west of the parks. Nests south of the parks at Lake Isabella on the Kern River (Kern Co.).

Black-shouldered Kite[1] *(Elanus caeruleus)*
Black-shouldered Kites are still called "Angel Hawks" by many longtime residents of the Sierra foothills for their habit of hovering in one spot or "kiting," with light graceful flight. Prior to 1900, they were abundant in the Central Valley and adjacent lowlands, but were easy targets for hunters. Furthermore, plowing of open grasslands for unirrigated agricultural fields reduced the population of small mammals that kites eat. By the 1930's fewer than 50 pairs remained in California. In the late 1940's kites began a remarkable comeback due to strict prohibition of shooting and their adaptation to modern farming practices. Extensive irrigation of agricultural crops increased populations of meadow mice, the kites' preferred food. Today they reside commonly in the Central Valley, but uncommonly in the Sierra foothills. Kites concentrate in areas with especially high prey densities and attack by slow vertical descents using their long

[1]*Formerly, White-tailed Kite.*

pointed wings and flared, white tails to parachute downward. By hunting in this manner, they can achieve extremely high capture rates, sometimes approaching 80%.

Black-shouldered Kites are rare above the foothill grasslands of the Sierra but have been recorded in higher meadows up to the alpine zone. Nests are usually in lowland groves of oaks, willows or sycamores, often near small streams. Sticks and twigs are gathered into loose masses and hidden in dense foliage at the tops of trees. In winter, groups of birds roost together in stands of trees or in orchards. At dusk, they return with direct flights from surrounding farmlands to settle and spend the night. They sound their eerie whistles while whirling together in the sunset.

Where Found:
Yosemite: Probably in foothill grasslands east of Oakdale and Planada; recorded in Yosemite Valley.
Sequoia-Kings Canyon: Occasionally observed hovering over pasture-lands in Three Rivers.

Bald Eagle *(Haliaeetus leucocephalus)* Plate 3

Bald Eagles are familiar to most people as our national symbol. They are the largest land birds in North America, other than California Condors, with wingspreads exceeding seven feet. Like many large predatory animals, these great birds are now endangered. Shooting, human destruction of nesting and feeding areas, and contamination of their food supplies by pesticides and pollution all threaten their continued existence.

Historically, Bald Eagles probably nested throughout the Sierra Nevada, but now only a few pairs breed there and only in Butte and Plumas Counties. Fifteen or more pairs also nest north of the range in Shasta and Lassen Counties. From October to April, Bald Eagles still can be seen regularly though rarely in the central and southern Sierra. They travel great distances and might be observed over any type of habitat, but occur most often near large rivers, lakes and reservoirs such as Lake Oroville, Folsom Lake and New Melones Reservoir. Most birds winter in the foothills or the lower ponderosa pine zone.

For successful nesting, Bald Eagles usually require large bodies of water with dependably productive fisheries, suitable nest sites and little human disturbance. Peak nesting in the Sierra takes place from March to June, and pairs often use the same sites year after year. Massive stick structures, built high in conifers, cottonwoods, snags or occasionally on cliff ledges, the nests are usually well-shaded by foliage or rock overhangs and are seldom farther than one-half mile from water. Fish, living or dead, form the bulk of their diet. Eagles capture them by swooping down from perches or from flight. When possible, eagles steal from Ospreys, which as a rule are more

55

efficient hunters. In some parts of the Sierra, wintering eagles feed primarily on coots, injured waterfowl, muskrats, squirrels, rabbits and decaying animal carcasses.

Bald Eagles are only distantly related to the more common Golden Eagles, but immature birds of one species may be taken for the other. Young Bald Eagles have brown plumage irregularly mottled with white on the underwing linings and sides of the body, rather than the distinct white wing and tail patches of the immature Goldens. Bald Eagles also have noticeably larger heads and more massive beaks. They tend to soar with rather flat wing profiles. Both species of eagles require about five years to reach their adult plumage.

Where Found:
Yosemite: In winter rare but regular at Don Pedro Reservoir, Cherry Lake and Lake Eleanor.
Sequoia-Kings Canyon: Observed along the Middle Fork Kaweah River near Three Rivers and Ash Mountain and along the South Fork Kaweah River near Clough Cave. Occasionally seen at Lake Kaweah, west of the parks. South of the parks, recorded every winter at Lake Success (Tulare Co.).

Northern Harrier[1] *(Circus cyaneus)*

Scanning the grasslands and marshes of the Central Valley one can often see these low-flying hawks with long, swept-back wings and narrow tails. Northern Harriers almost always hunt near the ground and rarely soar. More like owls than hawks, they use their acute hearing to locate meadow mice and other prey concealed beneath grasses. Unlike most hawks, adult sexes differ in appearance, with females brownish and males gray, black and white. At a distance the males might be mistaken for Black-shouldered Kites, but the white rump patch is the surest identification mark for either male or female Northern Harriers. They might also be mistaken for Prairie Falcons, especially when flying into the wind.

Northern Harriers do not range above the foothill grasslands of the Sierra when nesting. Migrant or post-breeding birds, however, have been seen skimming over meadows or open ridges up as high as the alpine zone in late summer and fall.

Where Found:
Yosemite: Probably resident in lower foothills west of the park; late summer and fall records at Yosemite Valley, Wawona Meadow, Tuolumne Meadows and Mt. Hoffmann.
Sequoia-Kings Canyon: Recorded at Moro Rock and in the Giant Forest; in late summer observed at Rae Lakes.

[1]*Formerly, Marsh Hawk.*

Sharp-shinned Hawk *(Accipiter striatus)* Plate 4, Figure 5

Perched motionlessly on a stump beside a meadow or gliding swiftly over an open hillside, the Sharp-shinned Hawk is constantly on the alert for flocks of small songbirds, its primary prey. Finch-sized birds are captured in midair or plucked from the ground or from foliage. Rarely it takes other small vertebrates such as mice or lizards. This adept hunter attacks its prey from a low, chasing flight or by darting out suddenly from a concealed perch. The relatively short, rounded wings and long tail of the Sharp-shin make it exceedingly agile as it pursues elusive, darting birds into dense thickets. If successful, the hawk returns to a favorite perch to pluck the prey fastidiously before it is eaten or fed to hungry nestlings. Feathers scattered on the forest floor are often the first clue a Sharp-shin is near.

In the Sierra Nevada, Sharp-shinned Hawks primarily breed in the northern half of the range from the ponderosa pine to the red fir zone. Between these elevations, they nest in groves of oaks and conifers or in riparian woodlands. They hide their nests high on horizontal branches near the trunks of dense-foliaged trees. Pairs may reuse nests in successive years; those in current use are loosely constructed with twigs and sticks and lined with bark. They usually nest in moist portions of forests with water, open hunting terrain, plucking perches and an abundance of small birds nearby. During the late summer and fall, Sharp-shins range above their normal nesting elevations and follow flocks of songbirds to the Sierra crest. They retreat below the heavy snows for winter.

This smallest of North American *Accipiters*, or forest hawks, is easily confused with its close relative the Cooper's Hawk, even by experts. Adult plumages of the two species are nearly identical, but the Sharp-shin has a distinctly smaller head and shorter neck. It also appears to have a squared tail when the feathers are not fanned out. The brownish, immature birds have light colored breasts covered by irregular broad streaking. Possibly due to its relatively small wing surface area, this species tends to soar less than the Cooper's Hawk or Northern Goshawk.

Where Found:
Yosemite: Yosemite Valley, Hetch Hetchy, Big Meadow, Crane Flat; recorded up to Mt. Conness in fall.
Sequoia-Kings Canyon: Occasional at Grant Grove, Wolverton Meadow and Round Meadow in Giant Forest.

Cooper's Hawk *(Accipiter cooperii)* Plate 4, Figure 5

Stealthy hunters of riparian groves and oak woodlands, Cooper's Hawks always use the element of surprise when attacking prey. Often they wait patiently on hidden perches for birds or mammals to venture danger-

57

Keith Hansen 1984

c

b

a

Figure 5. Tails of the immature *Accipiters,* or forest hawks, provide useful clues for identification. Immature Northern Goshawks (a) have tails that show wavy, irregular banding when spread, unlike the more even banding on the spread tails of immature Cooper's and Sharp-shinned Hawks. Cooper's Hawk tails (b) are clearly longer, relative to their body size, than the other two species' and may appear rounded when closed. The Sharp-shinned Hawk's tail (c) usually appears squared or notched when closed.

ously far from cover. Small birds and those up to the size of Mountain Quail are their primary victims, but Cooper's Hawks also attack rabbits, squirrels, mice and reptiles. These powerful hawks avoid eating feathers or fur and prefer to pluck their prey at favored perches. Like the other *Accipiters*, they traverse open hillsides and ravines while hunting or pursue birds through dense thickets, maneuvering with ease. Occasionally these hawks land on the ground in search of prey hiding in cover; they resume the chase when their quarry takes flight.

The smaller size of the Cooper's Hawk renders it an only slightly less formidable and aggressive nest defender than the Northern Goshawk. Both deserve caution and respect. Near the North Fork American River in Placer County, a pair of Cooper's Hawks built their nest in a dense mixed-conifer forest near a well-traveled trail. Despite the frequency of human traffic, the stealthy adults were never seen flying from their nest to distant feeding grounds. Their stick platform was finally discovered high in a white fir tree lodged between the trunk and a large branch. Excrement or "whitewash" splattered the foliage and ground. The plucked remains of a chipmunk and a Steller's Jay dangled from nearby branches. Three juveniles peered from the nest, but the adults were gone. The parents returned suddenly and attacked the human intruders with frenzy—driving them about 100 yards through the forest.

Cooper's Hawks begin nest building or reconstruction of old nests as early as March, and most pairs have produced eggs by May or June. Scattered dense stands of live or blue oaks and lowland riparian forests are preferred breeding habitats, but a few pairs build their nests in the thick fir and pine forests up to the mixed-conifer zone. They may nest in more open woodlands than the Sharp-shin. Small streams are often nearby, but nests have also been found in arid forests and foothill canyons. In the late summer and fall, after nesting is completed, Cooper's Hawks occasionally pursue their prey in subalpine forests.

Intermediate in size between Sharp-shins and Goshawks, Cooper's Hawks are about as large as crows. Like their relatives, these long-tailed hawks have somewhat short, rounded wings. Sharp-shins and Cooper's have virtually identical plumage, but the latter have noticeably longer necks, larger heads and slightly rounded tails. Immatures have the same size and body proportions as the adults, but their plumage is brownish with distinct teardrop-shaped streaks on the whitish breasts.

Where Found:
Yosemite: Lower canyons of the Merced and Tuolumne Rivers up to Yosemite Valley and Hetch Hetchy. Recorded at Crane Flat and Tuolumne Meadows in fall.
Sequoia-Kings Canyon: Uncommon in the Ash Mountain area, at

Potwisha and from Hospital Rock up to Wolverton Meadow. Nests below Terminus Dam (Lake Kaweah).

Northern Goshawk[1] *(Accipiter gentilis)* Plate 4, Figure 5

Harsh, screaming "kak-kak-kak" issuing from the deepest conifer forests announces the presence of nesting Northern Goshawks. If approached too closely, these largest and most powerful of North American *Accipiters* will defend their nesting territories like demons. They peer down at intruders with defiant red eyes and fly boldly at their targets with talons spread. The best strategy when attacked is to protect head and eyes and quickly leave the nesting territory. They generally give up a chase 150 to 300 feet from the nest. The National Park Service has on several occasions temporarily closed the popular Four-Mile Trail in Yosemite to protect hikers from a nesting pair of Northern Goshawks.

In the western Sierra, Goshawks nest in mature forests from the ponderosa pine through the lodgepole pine zones, usually in dense stands near openings used for foraging. Because they require extensive forest stands, Goshawks are especially vulnerable to logging. Males and females may combine efforts to build their large, bulky stick nests in the middle or upper portions of conifers. Often concealed by foliage, nests may be two or three feet across and supported by horizontal limbs near the trunk. As early as March, Goshawks, which often mate for life, begin to build a new nest or reline an old one with bark and conifer needles. The larger females are clearly the dominant partners as they hunt, defend territories and incubate the young with only minimal help from the males. The streaky-brown immatures are capable of flight about 45 days after hatching.

On relatively short, rounded wings these cunning predators glide silently and swiftly beneath the forest canopy in search of prey. A chorus of alarm calls from chipmunks, chickarees or Steller's Jays is often the first clue to their presence. Even the silhouette of a Goshawk in its distinctive flap-glide flight is sufficient to trigger a flurry of nervous activity from small forest animals. Goshawks often hunt in clearings or along meadow edges. They attack from a perch or while in flight, pursuing birds in midair at tremendous speeds. Foliage of trees and shrubs are brushed aside as they crash through close behind a bird or rabbit. Goshawks also attack on the ground; one in the Sierra hopped around a small lake for more than an hour chasing Mallard ducklings and eventually caught three.

Northern Goshawks are uncommon residents of Sierran conifer forests. In late summer, some travel above tree line and soar over open ridgetops in search of Belding's Ground Squirrels and other alpine prey. In severe winters they may descend to the foothill woodlands where food is more

[1]*Formerly, Goshawk.*

abundant.

Adult Goshawks cannot be confused with other species of *Accipiters* when viewed at close range. Immatures are very similar to Cooper's Hawks, but they have larger bodies, relatively longer wings, and tail banding that is irregular and wavy even when the tail is spread (see Fig. 5).

Where Found:
Yosemite: Yosemite Valley, Merced Grove, Crane Flat, White Wolf, Tuolumne Meadows, Ostrander Rocks, Wawona.
Sequoia-Kings Canyon: Grizzly Creek, Little Baldy Trail, Giant Forest and the Hockett Plateau (primarily Hockett Meadow). Observed as far south in the Sierra as Redwood Meadow and the Greenhorn Mountains (Kern Co.).

Red-shouldered Hawk *(Buteo lineatus)*

The piercing screams and rapid wingbeats of a Red-shouldered Hawk adeptly maneuvering through dense forests suggest an *Accipiter* rather than a soaring *Buteo*. When landing on a perch or wheeling overhead, the striking black and white barring of the wings and tail flash boldly. Red-shoulders keep almost entirely to wooded river bottoms. In the Sierra Nevada, they reside year-round along the Kern River and nest up to about 3000 feet. They also breed in some foothill river drainages to the north such as the Lower American River and in extensive tracts of riparian forest throughout the Central Valley. Transients wander along low elevation streams the length of the Sierra, especially in fall.

The loss of most of California's streamside forest has reduced the available habitat for Red-shouldered Hawks and they have declined greatly. In addition their nests frequently fail, possibly due to high pesticide levels in their prey. Surprisingly, they tolerate humans and sometimes nest in densely settled farming country. In April or May, they weave sturdy stick platforms between forked branches of cottonwoods, oaks, eucalyptus or other trees and line them with grasses and moss. Once they find a suitable nesting site, they tend to re-use it in successive years. Although they reside in forests, Red-shoulders often hunt over grasslands and agricultural fields. Their prey, including small birds and mammals, reptiles, amphibians and large insects, usually are captured on the ground. Red-shoulders attack from perches or low flight and do not hunt while soaring.

Where Found:
Yosemite: Bottomlands of the Merced and Tuolumne Rivers; historically observed near Snelling; now occurs along the Tuolumne up to La Grange.
Sequoia-Kings Canyon: Uncommon nester in the riparian zone of the North, Middle and South Forks of the Kaweah River; Three Rivers and

Ash Mountain areas. Nests south of the parks on the South Fork Kern River (Kern Co.).

Swainson's Hawk *(Buteo swainsoni)*

Unlike most of their relatives, Swainson's Hawks migrate long distances to winter in the plains of South America. In the spring and summer they breed in bottomland forests and oak woodlands of the Central Valley, but probably do not nest in the Sierra Nevada. As early as June, a few Swainson's Hawks may venture up the west slope to forage over high meadows prior to their southward migration in fall. Most montane observations of these birds have been made in August and September, but rarely even during these months.

They prefer dense-foliaged trees for nesting but generally forage over open grasslands or agricultural fields. Small mammals and birds are their primary prey, but they may also gather into large flocks to pick grasshoppers and other large insects from recently plowed furrows. Throughout California the once-common Swainson's Hawks have declined alarmingly due to shooting, pesticides, habitat destruction and disturbances on their wintering grounds.

Swainson's resemble Red-tailed Hawks in shape, but have narrower, pointed wings held in a slightly uptilted "V." Swainson's occur in light, dark and intermediate plumages; these are color phases rather than sex or age differences. Unlike most soaring hawks, Swainson's have dark flight feathers that contrast with white wing linings on light-plumaged birds. Their tails are grayish and narrowly banded.

Where Found:
Yosemite: Records from Yosemite Valley, near Tuolumne Meadows, Mt. Conness and Tioga Pass.
Sequoia-Kings Canyon: A few fall observations at Rae Lakes, Sequoia Lake View and Crescent Meadow.

Red-tailed Hawk *(Buteo jamaicensis)*   Plate 5, Figure 6

More often than not, a large raptor seen wheeling above the western Sierra is a Red-tailed Hawk. Red-tails frequent a greater range of habitats than any other Sierran raptor, but prefer open terrain such as river canyons, mountain meadows, granite outcrops, chaparral, broken forests and even alpine fell fields where their ground-dwelling prey can be more easily spotted. With broad, outstretched wings and fanned tails they often soar high in the air in transit from one place to another, but not while hunting. Red-tails search for prey from exposed perches, from low, quartering flight and rarely while hovering. Unlike the agile *Accipiters* that chase songbirds through woodland thickets, Red-tails search open habitats, using their extraordinary eyesight to detect ground squirrels, gophers, mice, snakes or lizards that stray from cover. Rarely they attack larger birds such as American Kestrels and Western Meadowlarks. They kill with a direct dive, stunning their unsuspecting victims with powerful legs and sharp talons.

Courting pairs may fly high above their nesting territories, shrieking and diving at each other with legs dangling. The sexes can sometimes be distinguished by size when seen flying together; females, like most raptors, are slightly larger than males. Pairs build their sturdy nests between forked limbs of tall trees or, less often, on cliff faces well above the reach of ground predators such as coyotes or raccoons. Nests may be re-used year after year unless they are first appropriated by Great Horned Owls, aggressive birds that never build their own. Red-tails reside in the foothills all year and breeding activities may extend from January to September. In the summer months they also nest very rarely at meadow edges and other suitable spots throughout the conifer forests. In fall, Red-tails might be seen soaring anywhere in the Sierra, even up to tree line. They remain in the high mountains until driven downslope by heavy snows.

Red-tailed Hawks are relatively large and bulky. Individuals vary in color from light streaky to chocolate brown, but their heads are almost always dark. Immatures have gray-brown tails with obscure barring, rather than the rusty adult coloration. Red-tails sometimes utter shrill, melancholy cries. Steller's Jays are masters at imitating these calls, though the point of this mimicry, or how it came to be, are unknown.

Where Found:
Yosemite: Fairly common in the foothills along Highways 120 and 140; widespread in late summer and fall at Yosemite Valley, Hetch Hetchy, Hodgdon Meadow, Foresta, Crane Flat, Tuolumne Meadows, Bridalveil Meadow and Wawona.
Sequoia-Kings Canyon: Uncommon at Cedar Grove, Grant Grove, Giant Forest, Ash Mountain and Mineral King.

Golden Eagle *(Aquila chrysaetos)* Plate 5, Figure 6

Silently gliding among granite cliffs, domes and canyons, the keen-eyed Golden Eagle betrays little of the awesome power of its great bulk and talons. It inhabits the entire length of the Sierra Nevada wherever undisturbed nesting sites, open terrain for foraging and dependable food supplies are to be found. This majestic bird has a wingspan exceeding seven feet; only the rarely seen California Condor is significantly larger.

Golden Eagles build huge stick nests on steep cliff ledges or in tall trees with commanding views of open country. These bulky structures are often five or six feet across and may weigh a ton or more. They are re-used by mated pairs in successive years but may be abandoned if disturbed. One pair in Yosemite Valley recently deserted a nest with eggs because too many people climbed up for closer views. Golden Eagles have a prolonged nesting period extending from January through September. Early in the season adults mount high in the air and make as many as twenty successive courtship dives. They nest most frequently in the foothills, but breeding has been observed to the crest of the mountains. Thus, Golden Eagles might be seen at any elevation, particularly over open habitats preferred for foraging and in terrain that provides updrafts to ease their flight. Winter storms drive most eagles below the snow belt where hunting is more productive. Eagles from the Great Basin invade the Sierra foothills in winter, noticeably swelling the population.

Whether gliding above lowland grasslands or over alpine meadows, Golden Eagles search for unwary squirrels, rabbits, marmots, pikas, carrion, and rarely large birds. They occasionally scan for prey while perched but more often hunt from low, quartering flight. Despite their protected status, they have been trapped, shot and poisoned by ranchers who accuse them of attacking sheep and other livestock. When game is scarce, they readily feed on carcasses of domestic animals but rarely feed on livestock in the Sierra.

Somewhat like the smaller Turkey Vultures, Golden Eagles often soar with their wings slightly uptilted. Adults appear uniformly dark, but have light barring on their tails and wings, visible at close range. Adults and immatures have a golden hue to the tops of their heads and necks, and noticeably dark-tipped bills. Immatures have distinctive white patches on their wings and white tails with broad, dark terminal bands. These white markings gradually fade as the birds grow older; adult coloration is reached in about five years.

Where Found:
Yosemite: Lower gorges of the Merced and Tuolumne Rivers—especially in remote areas west of Hetch Hetchy where they nest; recent nests have also been found in Yosemite Valley and near the Arch Rock Entrance Station. In summer, birds soar above Tenaya Canyon, Little Yosemite Valley, White Wolf, Mt. Hoffmann and Tuolumne Meadows.
Sequoia-Kings Canyon: Observed at Cedar Grove, Kearsarge Pinnacles, Tokopah Valley (nested 1979), Marble Fork Canyon below Giant Forest, Ash Mountain, Sky Parlor Meadow, Siberian Pass, Franklin Pass, Farewell Gap and Mineral King. In winter recorded soaring above Pear Lake, Wales Lake, the Great Western Divide and west of the parks at Lake Kaweah; often observed south of the parks at Lake Success (Tulare Co.).

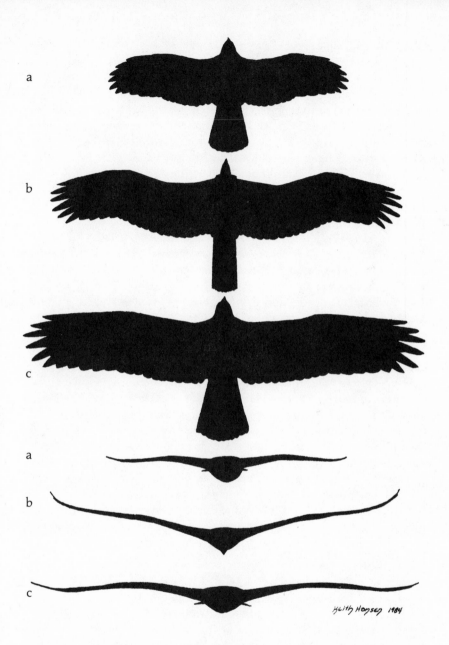

a

b

c

a

b

c

Keith Hansen 1984

Figure 6. Silhouettes of the Red-tailed Hawk (a), Turkey Vulture (b), and Golden Eagle (c) in flight. The vulture holds its wings in a slightly uptilted "V"; it has a relatively long tail and small head, compared to the other two raptors. The eagle's wings may also tilt up. It is much larger than the Redtail and has longer wings relative to its body size.

FALCONS *(Family Falconidae)*

Compared to other birds of prey, Falcons are streamlined and compact. They have small heads, short necks, stiff feathers, long, pointed wings and narrow tails, all adaptations for rapid flight. When pursuing prey, they rocket through the air at enormous velocities and kill with powerful blows from outstretched talons. Their hooked beaks are sharply notched about halfway between the tip and base, useful for tearing flesh or breaking the necks of their victims. Like many other predatory birds, falcons dissolve food in their highly acidic stomachs and then regurgitate indigestible feathers or fur as compressed pellets.

American Kestrel[1] *(Falco sparverius)* Plate 6

Along virtually any country road in the Central Valley and Sierra foothills American Kestrels can be seen perched on telephone lines, poles or fenceposts. These small, colorful falcons are California's most abundant raptors, particularly in open terrain such as grasslands, woodland edges and chaparral. Active hunters by day, Kestrels circle with quick, graceful flight or stop to hover with rapid wingbeats. Often they alight on nearby perches with their tails bobbing. Kestrels hawk grasshoppers and other large insects in midair or capture small birds, mammals and reptiles on the ground.

From April to August, Kestrels breed fairly commonly in the lowlands of the Sierra and rarely up to the mixed-conifer zone. They nest in abandoned woodpecker holes, magpie nests, cavities in cliffs, earthen banks and old buildings. After breeding, they sometimes travel upslope to forage over open hillsides, mountain meadows and talus slopes near the Sierra crest. A few remain in the alpine zone until storms force their return to more productive lowland hunting grounds. In winter, their numbers in the Central Valley and Sierra foothills increase dramatically.

Unlike the larger falcons, male and female kestrels have very different plumage. The bright reddish backs and slate-blue wings of the males are replaced in the females by rusty upperparts with black crossbarring.

Where Found:
Yosemite: Yosemite Valley, El Portal, lower canyons of Merced and Tuolumne Rivers; post-breeding birds wander up to Peregoy Meadow, Crane Flat, White Wolf and Tuolumne Meadows.
Sequoia-Kings Canyon: Common at Three Rivers, Ash Mountain and Potwisha; occasional at Wolverton Meadow and Sugarloaf Valley.

[1]*Formerly, Sparrow Hawk.*

Merlin *(Falco columbarius)*

Perhaps the wizardry of its flight earned this small northern falcon the title of Merlin, the magician. Rather than diving from above, it pursues small birds—sandpipers, swallows and swifts—snatching them in midair. Like the slightly smaller kestrel, it also captures dragonflies in flight.

Merlins breed to the north of California, but small numbers invade the state during fall and winter. Though rarer than along the coast or in the Central Valley, they apparently winter regularly in the Sierra foothills, as far south as the Kern River Valley. They typically linger in open habitats with abundant prey, as along lakeshores or in grasslands or meadows, often with scattered oaks. Trees, fenceposts or rock outcrops serve as launching sites for their aerial pursuits.

Merlins lack the rufous coloring of American Kestrels, and never stop to hover like these smaller falcons. In flight Merlins can be told from *Accipiter* hawks by their pointed wings. When perched, the immatures could be mistaken for immature Sharp-shinned Hawks, which also have brown backs, banded tails and streaked underparts, but Merlins have much longer wings, extending well over half the length of their tails.

Where Found:
Yosemite: Recorded above the Tuolumne River near Groveland, east of Coulterville and exceptionally as high as 10,000 feet near Vogelsang Peak.
Sequoia-Kings Canyon: Recorded at Little Five Lakes in late summer, below Terminus Dam (Lake Kaweah) in fall and at Paradise Creek in the Kaweah River drainage in winter.

Peregrine Falcon *(Falco peregrinus)*   Plate 6

Peregrine Falcons, among the world's fastest fliers, attain speeds up to 175 miles per hour when diving with rapidly beating and partially folded wings. From lofty, exposed perches or from searching flights, these powerful predators survey the landscape for flying birds such as jays, woodpeckers, gulls, pigeons and even the darting swifts. When they spot likely victims, they hurtle down and kill in midair with a single blow of their talons. They usually pluck and eat prey on the ground or on cliff ledges, but sometimes consume it in flight.

Eyries, or nesting sites, usually are simple recesses on inaccessible cliffs that offer expansive views of the surrounding landscape, often near lakes or rivers. Peregrines typically mate for life, reusing the same eyries year after year. Although mates are faithful to each other during their lives, if one bird dies the other may return to the same site with a new mate. If both die, the eyrie is often reoccupied by a new pair.

Never common, Peregrines have declined in California from about 100 pairs in 1940 to fewer than 40 pairs in the 1980's. Historically, nesting sites were scattered throughout the Sierra from the foothills to the highest peaks. Low and mid-elevation sites, however, were more common. Now, most of the historically known eyries have been abandoned. After many years of absence, Peregrines returned to breed in Yosemite Valley in the late 1970's, and there have been other recent nesting records in Yosemite and elsewhere in the Sierra, indicating at least a partial recovery. Probably most leave the Sierra or move down to the foothills in winter, although those in Yosemite Valley apparently remain, except during harsh weather.

These magnificent falcons reached their present endangered status primarily because of eggshell-thinning (due to DDT and other pesticides) and nest robbers who sold nestlings illegally to unscrupulous falconers. In recent years their prospects have improved. DDT and other chlorinated hydrocarbons have been banned in the U. S. and Canada. Wild populations have begun to increase on their own and a captive breeding program has been successful in reintroducing falcons to areas of former occurrence. Eggshell-thinning is still a major problem, however, particularly with older females that have accumulated illegally applied DDT and long-lived residues remaining in the environment. Falcon biologists have placed young peregrines in eyries in Yosemite and elsewhere, taking the fragile eggs to incubate in the lab. These young they then place in other pairs' nests. Peregrines may never again attain their historical abundance, but perhaps a stable population level can be achieved and reverse a 30-year decline.

Where Found:
Yosemite: Recent nesting in Yosemite Valley; observed in Tenaya Canyon and gorges of the Merced and Tuolumne Rivers.
Sequoia-Kings Canyon: Recorded near Moro Rock, Amphitheater Point, Ash Mountain and Cirque Rock.

Prairie Falcon *(Falco mexicanus)*   Plate 6

Like Peregrines, Prairie Falcons are large, powerful hunters that dive on prey from above. Occasionally they mount high in the air and overtake small and medium-sized birds, but more often they attack from perches or when in low, rapid flight, striking ground squirrels and other rodents on the ground.

These falcons, partial to open, arid country, are uncommon throughout the Sierra. Breeding extends from May through August, and nesting sites, or eyries, are situated on steep rock walls. Instead of building nests, they lay eggs in slight depressions in dirt or gravel, on sheltered ledges or potholes in cliffs. They often use abandoned raven nests. Sites range in height from low rock outcrops to the highest cliffs, but most offer wide views of the surrounding landscape. Historically, Prairie Falcons nested fairly commonly in the Sierra foothills, but only a minority of these eyries are still active. Small numbers continue to nest on foothill cliffs throughout the length of the western Sierra and possibly at a few high elevation localities in the southern Sierra. They usually nest near level or gently rolling open terrain with a good supply of rodents. The most commonly cited reasons for the Prairie Falcon's decline are pesticides, vertebrate control programs that reduce potential prey, and nest robbing by falconers.

In late summer and fall, Prairie Falcons wander fairly commonly amid the open landscapes of the high Sierra. Even during this period, they have been recorded only a few times in the mid-elevation coniferous forest zones. Some birds remain in the high mountains until the first heavy snows drive them to the foothills. In the winter they frequent lowland grasslands on the west slope and sagebrush plateaus of the Great Basin.

In addition to their paler coloration, dark feathering along the bases of the underwings is the surest field mark for distinguishing Prairie Falcons from Peregrines, which they resemble in shape and size.

Where Found:
Yosemite: Post-nesting birds observed at Mt. Conness, Mono Pass, Mt. Dana, Mt. Hoffmann, Vogelsang Lake, Ten Lakes.
Sequoia-Kings Canyon: Records from Mt. Gould, Upper Kern River Canyon and Tamarack Lake (historical breeding). Winter records from Ash Mountain and Ash Peaks Ridge.

FOWL-LIKE BIRDS *(Family Phasianidae)*

These stout-bodied birds with their strong feet and legs are well suited for dwelling on the ground. Though capable of short, swift flights, they often run to escape danger. The turkeys, ptarmigans, and chukars of the Sierra were introduced for hunting; the native grouse and quail also are game birds. All Sierran species nest on the ground, making them vulnerable to predators, but the drab, mottled females are difficult to spot. Their precocious young are well-developed upon hatching, with strong legs, open eyes and thick coats of down. Within hours the young leave the nest and begin feeding while one or both parents lead them to food and provide protection.

Chukar *(Alectoris chukar)*

Introduced from Eurasia, these quail-like birds have bright red legs, strikingly barred sides and black "necklaces." They thrive only on steep, rocky hillsides, in open areas with less than 20 inches of precipitation per year. To escape danger, they fly and run up slopes, and at night they roost among the rocks or shrubs. Green leaves, small seeds and a few insects make up their diet. More widespread east of the Sierran divide, breeding populations have become established on the west slope only along the crest in Fresno County, from the foothills up to 12,000 feet in Tulare and Kern Counties, and possibly in the foothills below Yosemite. During the dry summer months, coveys of up to 40 or more birds concentrate near sources of water. Like Mountain Quail, they descend below the heavy snow line for the winter.

Where Found:
Yosemite: Introduced in the 1960's, and possibly still present, at two locations west of the park: the Red Hills south of Chinese Camp and Horseshoe Bend Mountain near Lake McLure.
Sequoia-Kings Canyon: Observed several times near New Army Creek, west of New Army Pass, and recorded south of the parks near Spanish Needles, on the Kern Plateau.

Blue Grouse *(Dendragapus obscurus)*   Plate 7

From late April to early July, male Blue Grouse proclaim their territories with a series of resonant, booming hoots. These calls are lower in pitch than those of any other Sierran bird, so low that some people cannot hear them. Two yellow air sacs on the neck, usually hidden, are inflated to produce these unmistakable notes. Finding a hooting male is seldom easy, because he makes ventriloquial calls from a hidden perch, typically high overhead in the foliage of conifers.

Most Blue Grouse breed in the mixed-conifer and red fir zones. They prefer open or partly brushy slopes, with nearby stands of dense-foliaged conifers for roosting and hooting. Throughout the nesting season, males remain on their territories and attempt to court and mate with receptive females attracted by their calls. Once mated, a female prepares a nest by lining a shallow depression under a shrub, tree, or log with leaves and grasses. Although a female usually nests near her mate's territory, she cares for the eggs and young alone.

The young eat mostly insects, a source of protein, for ten days after hatching. By late summer, mothers with young disperse both up- and down-slope from their nesting grounds, feeding in meadows and on brushy hillsides. During spring, summer, and fall, Blue Grouse forage mostly on the ground, eating seeds, berries, green shoots and insects. Adults also fly up into conifers to browse on needles and buds.

These hardy birds survive fearsome high-elevation winters by taking shelter in dense firs, pines and hemlocks and eating needles, buds and pollen cones. In British Columbia, Washington and Montana, Blue Grouse actually migrate upslope for the winter, and they apparently undertake this "backward" migration in Sequoia National Park and possibly other parts of the Sierra. East-slope Blue Grouse studied at Sagehen Creek (Nevada County), however, remained at their breeding elevations through the winter.

Where Found:
Yosemite: Olmsted Point, Mt. Hoffmann, slopes below Harden Lake, Mt. Watkins, Porcupine Flat, Glacier Point and vicinity.
Sequoia-Kings Canyon: Grant Grove, Moraine Ridge, Cloud Canyon, Little Baldy Trail, Tokopah Valley, Giant Forest, Mineral King Valley.

White-tailed Ptarmigan *(Lagopus leucurus)*

Brown and white in summer, these arctic grouse molt into pure white plumage in winter to match their snowy surroundings. White-tailed Ptarmigans feed and nest in alpine meadows strewn with rocks and boulders. Heavily dependent on alpine willows throughout the year, they feed on buds, twigs, leaves, flowers and seeds of these and other plants. Their chicks mainly eat insects and spiders. These ptarmigans have been seen in spring at an elevation of about 8000 feet in Lundy Canyon (on the east slope in Mono County), suggesting they had moved downslope for the winter.

Ptarmigans are not native to the Sierra, and there is good reason to believe that their recent introduction will have serious impacts on the fragile alpine ecosystem. Ecologists have long known that non-native animals can have unpredictable and disastrous effects on native plants and animals, which have coevolved over thousands of years. Nevertheless, the California Department of Fish and Game, as recently as 1971 and 1972, released White-tailed Ptarmigans on the Sierran crest simply because the alpine zone had no game birds for hunters. Conflicting reports make it unclear whether these birds were released at Mono Pass, just east of Yosemite National Park, or around Eagle Peak, 10 miles northwest of Bridgeport. In any case, the population prospered and by 1976 had spread at least to Matterhorn Peak, 20 miles north of Mono Pass, and at least one bird travelled to Mt. Williamson, almost 100 miles to the south.

Where Found:
Yosemite: Matterhorn Peak, Granite Lakes, Gaylor Lakes, Dana Plateau, Mono Pass.
Sequoia-Kings Canyon: Recorded at Mt. Williamson, in John Muir Wilderness, east of Sequoia N.P.

Wild Turkey *(Meleagris gallopavo)*

With their dazzling, iridescent bronze plumage, Wild Turkeys are streamlined versions of the barnyard bird, a breed domesticated during pre-Columbian times in Mexico. They are not native to California, but were introduced for hunting beginning in 1908. Most of the successful introductions have been wild-trapped birds from Texas. Established populations now live near Kernville, Groveland, and Nevada City, as well as the Mt. Lassen area and parts of the east slope.

Turkeys roost in trees but nest on the ground and feed in forest openings, eating insects, green plants, seeds, acorns and fruit. Typically they summer in the ponderosa pine zone, but some wander up to 10,000 feet in the Kern River drainage of the southern Sierra. In winter they move as much as 50 miles to downslope locations with plentiful food and little snow, often in foothill woodlands and chaparral.

Throughout the year Wild Turkeys associate in groups, which consist during the breeding season of a "gobbler" male and his harem of four to six hens. Winter flocks are larger, as the young remain with their parents until the next breeding season.

Where Found:
Yosemite: Near Groveland: just west of Pine Mountain Lake Airport, and east to Smith Station Road (south of Highway 120). Also at Horseshoe Bend Mountain near Lake McClure.
Sequoia-Kings Canyon: Rare along Colony Mill Road and at Badger, southwest of Grant Grove. Occurs locally south of the parks in Lloyd Meadows Basin, east of Quaking Aspen.

California Quail *(Callipepla californica)*   Plate 7

These exquisitely plumaged quail were a favorite game bird of native Sierran tribes who snared them along their runways and shot them from blinds with bows and arrows. Enormous numbers were killed by professional market hunters during the nineteenth century. Probably less numerous now than before that era, these gentle birds are common once again in suitable habitat. Back-road travelers in the Sierra foothills often startle large coveys, sending them running for cover or erupting into whirring flight in all directions.

Rarely found above the foothill woodlands, California Quail take shelter in chaparral and streamside thickets, but feed in grassy openings. They do not migrate and may spend their entire lives in areas only two miles across. During the long, dry summers, they seldom venture far from streams or seeps that supply their daily water. At night, quail prefer to roost in heavily foliaged trees, but will use dense shrubbery if necessary.

In fall and winter California Quail feed and roost in large coveys numbering 25 to 60 birds. They make a variety of clucks and calls for courtship, aggression, alarm and maintaining contact. When separated visually, covey members utter a three-note assembly call, "chi-ca-go," with

72

the second note higher than the others. This call is given frequently in spring by pairs that are separated and by single birds seeking mates.

Males and females form monogamous pairs in late winter, gradually leaving the covey in early spring to find nesting sites. At this time, the older unmated males establish small "crowing territories" to attract females. Their "cow" calls, similar to the last note of the assembly call, are repeated several times per minute, usually from exposed perches in shrubs or trees.

Each mated male defends his mate from other suitors but does not hold a nesting territory. The female lays a huge clutch, averaging 14 eggs, in a small, well-hidden depression in the ground. The young stay with both parents through their first winter. In late summer, two or more of these family groups band together, along with nonbreeding individuals, to form a covey once again.

The staple foods of California Quail are seeds and leaves of herbaceous plants, especially legumes, but fruits and insects are also important. They usually forage on the ground, picking food from plants or scratching like chickens. Sometimes they move up into shrubs or even leap off the ground to snatch insects or seeds from plants.

Where Found:
Yosemite: Widespread in foothills west of the park, as at El Portal, Mariposa, Big Oak Flat, Groveland.
Sequoia-Kings Canyon: Widespread in the Kaweah River drainage, at Hospital Rock, Potwisha and Ash Mountain.

Mountain Quail *(Oreortyx pictus)* Plate 7

These large, handsome quail are easy to miss but may be located in April, May and June by the loud, mellow "wook" calls of unmated males. At a distance these calls could be mistaken for the single whistled notes of Northern Pygmy-Owls. These secretive birds seldom fly, but instead run under dense brush when disturbed. The young are less cautious, however, and may sometimes be seen at close range as their parents call anxiously or even feign injury to distract the human "predators." Like California Quail, Mountain Quail live in chaparral, but they breed at higher elevations, from the lower ponderosa pine zone up nearly to tree line. They prefer slopes with dense thickets of manzanita, ceanothus and other shrubs, interspersed with grassy openings. They do not perch in trees like California Quail, although scattered trees are usually present in their habitat.

Mountain Quail hide their nests in well-concealed hollows on the ground, and both parents care for the young, which hatch in late June or July. Family groups remain together through the winter, often joined by nonbreeding adults, but unlike California Quail, they do not typically band together with other families. In the Sierra these winter coveys average only seven individuals. A striking feature of the annual cycle is the altitudinal migration in spring and fall, sometimes covering over 20 miles each way, nearly all of it on foot. During migration, coveys may traverse atypical habitats such as dense coniferous forests. They winter below the heavy snow line down to the foothill chaparral, where some coveys live side by side with California Quail. In spring they move upslope again. Their feeding habits are much like those of California Quail, suggesting that competition between these two species may have contributed to their apparent altitudinal segregation while breeding.

Where Found:
Yosemite: Yosemite Valley, Chinquapin, Peregoy Meadow, Ostrander Rocks, Mariposa Grove, Gin Flat, ridge east of Smoky Jack.
Sequoia-Kings Canyon: Paradise Valley, High Sierra Trail, Giant Forest, Colony Mill Road, Mineral King Valley. In winter and spring — Ash Mountain and Elk Creek.

RAILS AND COOTS *(Family Rallidae)*

Virginia Rail *(Rallus limicola)*

Few visitors to the Sierra actually see these chunky, long-billed "marsh hens," for they rarely emerge from dense marsh cover. Like owls, however, rails can be recognized by their distinctive calls, most often uttered at night or at dawn and dusk. Virginia Rails make a loud, harsh descending "rak, rak, ... rak" and several shorter calls. None is likely to be confused with the high-pitched "whinny" of the Sora, a shorter-billed rail which occupies similar habitats.

More common east of the crest, these secretive birds apparently breed in small numbers in the western foothills and ponderosa pine zone. Only a small patch of cattails, tules, or tall sedges is necessary to harbor a nesting pair and provide sufficient quantities of insects, worms, snails, seeds, or marsh plants to eat. Virginia Rails are fairly common year-round in Butte County, uncommon in the South Fork Kern River Valley and regular winter visitors up to 3500 feet in Tehama and Shasta Counties. Systematic surveys for these elusive birds would probably reveal larger populations in the central and southern Sierra than the few records suggest.

Where Found:
Yosemite: Not known to occur regularly in the park; has been recorded at Yosemite Valley (one nest record) and Hodgdon Meadow.
Sequoia-Kings Canyon: Found in summer at Big Meadows on the Kern Plateau, south of the parks; in winter, below Terminus Dam (Lake Kaweah), west of the parks.

Sora *(Porzana carolina)*

Like other rails, this seldom-seen marsh bird reveals its presence by distinctive calls, but rarely emerges from dense cattails or reeds. The Sora makes an unmistakable whinny—a rapidly descending series of clear-toned notes—as well as a harsh "keek" and a clear, whistled "er-weeeee" that rises in pitch. A patient observer may be rewarded with a clear view of this small rail's black mask, short yellow bill and stubby cocked tail as it steps gingerly along a muddy marsh edge or swims across a small stretch of open water.

Like Virginia Rails, Soras require only a small patch of marsh plants along a pond or stream, and the two species often occur together. In the western Sierra, Soras reside uncommonly all year in the South Fork Kern River Valley and winter regularly at foothill marshes up to 3500 feet in Tehama and Shasta Counties. They rarely have been reported in between (see below). Soras have nested as high as Lake Tahoe on the east slope and occur fairly commonly in the Central Valley, suggesting that careful searching on the west slope could reveal more populations, particularly in the lower foothills.

Where Found:
Yosemite: Recorded once in Yosemite Valley; common, possibly breeding, at foothill dredge ponds along Tuolumne River up to La Grange, in foothills west of park.
Sequoia-Kings Canyon: Recorded at Bullfrog Lake (10,634 feet).

American Coot *(Fulica americana)*   Plate 8, Figure 7

Often mistaken for ducks, American Coots are actually members of the rail family. Coots and ducks provide a good example of convergent evolution; over the millenia they have come to resemble each other superficially in adapting to similar aquatic lifestyles. Both are excellent swimmers and divers, due largely to their specialized feet. While ducks have webs connecting their toes, coots have "lobed" feet, with separate webbing around each toe (see Fig. 7). This adaptation, lacking in other members of the rail family, allows coots to swim and feed efficiently in deeper water. They dive as much as 25 feet below the surface or tip up like Mallards. Coots jerk their heads backward and forward while swimming and have fleshy structures called frontal shields on their foreheads. They are game birds, but are spurned by many hunters who call them "mudhens" and consider their flesh distasteful. Although this reputation has been disputed, it has allowed coots to prosper.

Coots occur rarely in the higher Sierra, almost always during spring and fall migration. They are fairly common year-round in the foothills and breed locally along the edges of ponds, lakes and slow-moving streams.

Augmented by migrants from the north, foothill populations increase during fall and winter. These highly adaptable birds feed on a great variety of aquatic plants and occasionally on small fish, tadpoles and invertebrates. Often they come ashore to graze on grasses and tender shoots.

Coots prefer water bordered by large patches of cattails, rushes or tules, used as building materials and for concealing nests. They first construct a large floating platform and attach it to standing plants, and then build a mound-shaped nest on top. Separate rafts are built for courtship and for brooding the young. The downy young are surprisingly gaudy, with black bodies and bright reddish-orange heads. Fiercely territorial, the parents defend a small area around their nest throughout the year, and a larger one during the breeding season.

Where Found:
Yosemite: Widespread in foothills west of the park during winter and migration; probably breeds locally. Recorded occasionally at higher elevations, as at Hardin Flat (west of the park) and Lake Eleanor.
Sequoia-Kings Canyon: Possibly nests at Hume Lake and Sequoia Lake (both outside the parks near Grant Grove); also recorded at Rae Lakes and Big Kern Lake.

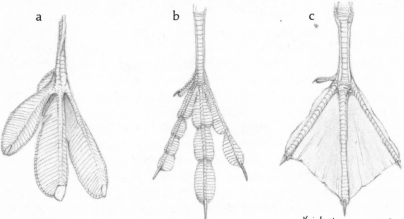

Figure 7. Feet of the Pied-billed Grebe (a), American Coot (b), and Mallard (c) illustrate convergent evolution. These water-loving birds belong to three separate families that have evolved different methods of paddling. The lobed toes of coots and grebes fan out when pushed through water, but collapse together on the recovery stroke. Ducks have entirely webbed feet.

SHOREBIRDS AND GULLS *(Order Charadriiformes)*

Members of this diverse order share an attraction to water and at inland areas may be found at marshes, wet fields and meadows, lakes, rivers and even on dry land. Hundreds of thousands of phalaropes and other Charadriiformes migrate north and south along the eastern base of the Sierra, relying on aquatic habitats such as Mono Lake for feeding and, in some cases, nesting. Another major migratory flyway follows California's Central Valley, bringing migrating shorebirds, gulls and terns into the Sierra foothills on occasion (see Appendix I). Only the few species that breed in the western Sierra or occur regularly above the lower foothills are discussed below.

PLOVERS *(Family Charadriidae)*

Killdeer *(Charadrius vociferus)* Plate 8

Named for its loud, high-pitched "kill-deer'" cries, this ring-necked shorebird can be heard at any hour, night or day. The Killdeer commonly lives along the edges of lakes and streams, but unlike many shorebirds does not require a substantial body of water. It will settle for a small seep, wet meadow, irrigated field, or even a golf course, as long as the terrain is flat and free of tall plants that would obstruct the view or impede its movements. There must also be an ample supply of ground-dwelling insects, spiders, snails and worms. Like robins, Killdeers run quickly along the ground and stop short, scanning motionlessly, before suddenly pecking at their prey.

For nesting, Killdeers scrape small depressions in gravel, turf or bare earth in areas with little or no vegetation — often on river bars. The downy young, which leave the nest soon after hatching, depend on their parents for protection but must find food by themselves. Because their eggs and young are in the open and vulnerable to predators, Killdeers have become particularly adept at luring enemies away from their nests. Before a predator approaches too closely, the incubating parent sneaks quietly away and makes a great racket from a different direction. Another tactic is to feign a broken wing and flap awkwardly along the ground to entice predators farther and farther from the nest or young. Many ground-nesting birds have evolved such distraction displays, but the Killdeer's are among the most skillful and convincing.

Killdeers reside fairly commonly all year in the Sierra foothills, but their abundance apparently drops off toward the southern Sierra. Small numbers nest in the higher mountains up to the subalpine zone and descend to winter below the snows. Although Killdeers may gather by the dozens or even hundreds in favorable feeding areas, they seldom travel in flocks.

77

Where Found:
Yosemite: Breeds at Yosemite Valley, Tuolumne Meadows and west of the park at Groveland and Hardin Flat; more common in the foothills.
Sequoia-Kings Canyon: Recorded in spring or summer at Hume Lake, Wolverton Meadow, and Slick Rock; winters in irrigated pastures near Three Rivers. Nests west of the parks below Terminus Dam (Lake Kaweah).

SANDPIPERS, SNIPES AND RELATIVES *(Family Scolopacidae)*

Spotted Sandpiper *(Actitis macularia)* Plate 8

Between late summer and winter, the Spotted Sandpiper loses its dark polka dots but retains its characteristic mannerisms, making identification easy. Over short distances it flies with stiff, shallow wingbeats, interrupted by frequent, brief glides on downcurved wings. On land it "teeters," holding its head low while bobbing its tail end vigorously up and down.

Except while breeding, Spotted Sandpipers usually lead a solitary existence. In the Sierra they feed on insects and other invertebrates along sandy or pebbly shores of lakes and streams. They also venture into quiet waters and may even dive down and walk on the bottom like Dippers, though much less frequently.

They nest in a simple depression along the shore, often hidden among low plants, rocks or logs. The parents display an interesting reversal of roles. Males incubate the eggs and care for the young with little help from their mates, while females often mate with two or more males and defend large territories where the males raise their broods. Soon after hatching, the young leave the nest; although they must find their own food, the parents brood and protect them.

Less common in the southern Sierra than farther north, Spotted Sandpipers are the only shorebirds that nest fairly commonly above the foothills. They breed at all elevations in appropriate habitat, but mostly from the ponderosa pine zone up to tree line. Some remain in the foothills through the winter, but they desert the higher mountains.

This species could be mistaken for the Solitary Sandpiper, which occurs rarely but fairly regularly along mountain streams on the west slope in late summer. The Spotted is somewhat smaller, with a shorter bill, a white wing-stripe (absent in the Solitary) and an eye line instead of an eye ring.

Where Found:
Yosemite: Breeds in Yosemite Valley and Tuolumne Meadows and west of the park at Hardin Flat.
Sequoia-Kings Canyon: Along Kern River in Sequoia N.P.; also Center Basin, Upper Kern Basin, Hume Lake, and Hockett Meadow. Winters west

of the parks below Terminus Dam (Lake Kaweah).

Common Snipe *(Gallinago gallinago)*

This chunky, long-billed shorebird feeds and nests in wet grasslands, meadows, and short marsh vegetation, and is difficult to spot until flushed. Then it bursts forth in rapid zigzag flight, suddenly settling into another hiding place. It is conspicuous only during the breeding season when either sex may perform an impressive "winnowing" display. After circling high above its nesting territory, the snipe dives steeply, forcing air through outspread tail feathers and producing a rapid series of hollow, owl-like notes.

With their extremely long, slender bills, Common Snipe probe in mud for worms and insect larvae and pick adult insects from the ground. In their marshy habitat, they build cup-nests in dry spots such as hummocks of grass. Snipe are rare and localized on the west slope, breeding, for example, in the South Fork Kern River Valley and at Meadow Valley, Plumas County. While breeding they are confined to the mixed-conifer zone and below. In fall and winter, they occur sparsely throughout the western foothills, and fall migrants occasionally reach higher elevations.

Where Found:
Yosemite: Recorded occasionally in Yosemite Valley and at higher elevations, as at Peregoy Meadow and Lyell Canyon. Common locally in foothills west of the park, as at the inlet to Turlock Reservoir.
Sequoia-Kings Canyon: Recorded near Slick Rock (Kaweah River). Winters west of Three Rivers below Terminus Dam (Lake Kaweah), and to the south in Yokohl Valley.

GULLS AND TERNS *(Family Laridae)*

Ring-billed Gull *(Larus delawarensis)*

Because it resembles the more common California Gull in appearance and habits, the Ring-billed may often go unnoticed in the Sierra. Like the California, it breeds in the Great Basin and migrates across the mountains to winter in the Central Valley or coastal California. The Ring-billed, however, does not nest south of Honey Lake (Lassen County) in California. It is most often seen in the northern Sierra, usually during June or July, and only very rarely visits mountain lakes in the central and southern parts of the range. In fall and winter, a few visit reservoirs and city dumps throughout the foothills.

At close range, adult Ring-bills can easily be distinguished from adult California Gulls, which usually have a black spot on the bill but never a complete ring. Better clues at a distance are the smaller bill and paler gray back and wings of the Ring-bill. Second-year California Gulls, which also have ringed bills, may be mistaken for adult Ring-bills, but the former can be told by the brown on their wings. Distinguishing one immature gull from another is among the more difficult challenges for birdwatchers. For more information on identification of adult and immature gulls, see guides by Cogswell, National Geographic Society, and Farrand (in Bibliography).

Where Found:
Yosemite: A few records from Yosemite Valley.
Sequoia-Kings Canyon: Occasional fall migrant in Kings Canyon at high mountain lakes. Occurs in winter and spring around Lake Kaweah (west of Three Rivers) and Lake Success (east of Porterville).

California Gull *(Larus californicus)* Plate 8

Many people are surprised to find "sea gulls" in the Sierra, far from the ocean. In fact, several species of gulls spend significant parts of the year inland, and some even nest there. In the United States, California Gulls breed primarily in the lakes and marshes of the Great Basin, south in California to Mono Lake. Most gulls seen in the Sierra are California Gulls in transit between their breeding grounds east of the Sierra and wintering grounds along the coast and in the Central Valley. They often linger at mountain lakes (usually above 7,000 feet) in the central Sierra for long periods during July and August. From August to April, moderate numbers can be found at reservoirs, city dumps and wet fields in the foothills, where they feed on insects, earthworms, fish, garbage, carrion and even mice.

Sadly, fewer California Gulls may be seen in the Sierra in the future, due to the decline of the Mono Lake nesting population. The nesting colony that until recently occupied Negit Island was the second largest in the world, with about 50,000 birds. Since 1940, however, diversion of Mono's feeder streams into the Los Angeles Department of Water and Power aqueduct has stopped the natural replenishing of Mono's waters. More than half the lake's volume has been lost to evaporation, lowering its level until a landbridge to Negit Island emerged in 1979, allowing coyotes and other mainland predators to reach the island and destroy all the nests. Recent wet winters have increased Mono's level temporarily, but if diversions continue the lake's level will fall once again. Increased salinity of the remaining water threatens to kill off the brine shrimp, the staple food of Mono's gulls and other water birds. Unless diversions are curtailed, Mono may become a dead sea like Owens Lake to the south, a sterile sump, useless to the nesting gulls and the millions of migrating Eared Grebes, Northern and Wilson's Phalaropes and other water birds that depend on it.

Where Found:
Yosemite: Regular in summer at Olmsted Point, Tenaya Lake, Roosevelt Lake and just east of the crest at Saddlebag Lake and Tioga Lake.
Sequoia-Kings Canyon: Rare in spring and summer; recorded at Evolution Lake, Sapphire and Martha Lakes, Lake Marjorie, and Sally Keyes Lake (just north of the parks).

PIGEONS AND DOVES *(Family Columbidae)*

There is no technical difference between "pigeons" and "doves," and both words are applied to these stocky, fast-flying birds with small heads and bills. North American pigeons and doves eat mainly seeds and nuts, and they produce a unique food called pigeons' milk, which they regurgitate into the gullets of their young. Secreted by specialized cells in the crop (the expanded lower portion of the esophagus), this substance resembles closely the creamy milk of rabbits. Members of this family drink in a manner unusual among birds: instead of lifting their heads to tip water down the throat as other birds do, they immerse their bills and suck.

Rock Dove *(Columba livia)*

Almost everyone knows the Rock Dove, or Domestic Pigeon. Apparently the first bird to be domesticated, it is famous for its fast flight and accurate homing abilities. It is native to Eurasia, but has become naturalized throughout the world, adapting to a free-living existence in cities and rural agricultural areas. These introduced populations clearly depend on humanity, as they rarely expand into undisturbed habitats. In the Sierra, a few small populations have become established in foothill communities such as Auburn. Usually foraging on the ground, Rock Doves eat seeds, grains, tender shoots, and some berries, as well as table scraps like bread crumbs. They usually nest on sheltered ledges of buildings, bridges or other equivalents to the rocky ledges of Eurasia. A few sticks and twigs suffice for a nest, preventing the eggs from rolling off.

Rock Doves come in an amazing diversity of colors and patterns, but almost always have white rumps. This visible and consistent mark reliably distinguishes them from their native relative, the Band-tailed Pigeon.

Where Found:
Yosemite: Recorded several times in Yosemite Valley; noted west of the park in Big Oak Flat.
Sequoia-Kings Canyon: Occasionally seen at Three Rivers and Ash Mountain.

Band-tailed Pigeon *(Columba fasciata)* Plate 9

Aside from water birds, raptors and ravens, the Band-tailed Pigeon is the largest Sierran bird that commonly makes long flights above the treetops. This habit may explain its appeal to Peregrine Falcons, which prey mainly on flying birds. It is also a popular target of hunters and was nearly extirpated in California before hunting was regulated.

Berries, other fruits and small seeds are important summer foods to Band-tailed Pigeons, but during all other seasons they depend on acorns, which form almost half their annual diet. They pick acorns from trees or out of forest litter, and swallow them whole. Like many seed-eating birds, they swallow gravel, which is stored in their muscular gizzards and used to grind up acorns and seeds.

Because they depend on acorns, Band-tails usually live around oaks. During late spring and summer they breed in ponderosa pine and mixed-conifer forests where black or golden oaks are common. After breeding, some wander as high as the subalpine zone, but they descend to winter below the heavy snows, even reaching the Central Valley in exceptional years. Once a local acorn supply is exhausted, flocks wander nomadically in search of other foods. Like other pigeons, Band-tails need a dependable water supply, which they usually visit in mid-morning and late afternoon. They also seek out mineral water, at least during fall and winter. They frequent traditional watering spots, mineral springs and roosting areas year after year.

Even during the breeding season, Band-tailed Pigeons feed and drink in flocks, and they reportedly nest colonially in the Southwest. In California, pairs typically defend separate nesting territories of several acres or more. They build rather rickety nest-platforms on sturdy limbs in dense groves of trees. Each male advertises his claim and courts a female with an owl-like "hoo hooo," the second note lower than the first. Once the one or two eggs are laid, the male abruptly stops cooing.

Sometimes a Band-tail may be confused with its close relative, the introduced Rock Dove. They have similar body shapes, predominantly grayish plumage and direct, rapid flight, making loud flapping noises when they take off. The Band-tail's broad, pale gray band across the end of its tail and lack of white on its rump distinguishes it from Rock Doves. Unlike them, it lives in wooded habitats and commonly perches in trees.

Where Found:
Yosemite: Yosemite Valley, Mariposa Grove, Big Oak Flat Road near Foresta turnoff, Crane Flat.
Sequoia-Kings Canyon: Between Ash Mountain and Giant Forest on the Generals Highway; Government Corrals at Cedar Grove.

Mourning Dove *(Zenaida macroura)* Plate 9

Streamlined in form and swift in flight, the familiar Mourning Dove frequents Sierran towns and ranches as well as wild areas. Its smaller size and long pointed tail readily distinguish it from both Band-tailed Pigeons and Rock Doves. The male's plaintive cooing in spring and summer earned it its popular name, but is motivated by territoriality rather than mood. He repeats his owl-like "hoo-ee hoooo hoo" tirelessly throughout the day. The loud, whistling sound made by Mourning Doves erupting into flight is produced by their wings and may serve as an alarm call.

Mourning Doves are common year-round in open foothill woodlands and sparse chaparral, but nest less frequently in open forests of the ponderosa pine and mixed-conifer zones. They need open ground for foraging but prefer trees for nesting. Also essential is a source of water, which they visit twice a day, often by travelling great distances. A few individuals wander to high elevations in late summer and fall, but all move down to the foothills for the winter.

Barely clearing the ground with their stubby legs, Mourning Doves walk back and forth over barren areas, searching for food. They feed almost exclusively on small seeds, supplemented with occasional insects and snails during the nesting season.

Their nests are flimsy platforms of sticks on crotches or horizontal branches of trees, at almost any height; where trees are scarce they may even be built on the ground. Some are built on top of old nests of other species. At least in some localities, Mourning Doves defend small territories around their nests, but they regularly feed in outlying areas. They typically raise from two to as many as five families per year. After nesting and through the winter, they gather into flocks, sometimes numbering fifty birds or more.

Where Found:
Yosemite: El Portal and below Foresta; widespread west of park.
Sequoia-Kings Canyon: Ash Mountain and lower half of Mineral King Road.

CUCKOOS AND ROADRUNNERS *(Family Cuculidae)*

Greater Roadrunner[1] *(Geococcyx californianus)*

This large, brownish ground-dwelling cuckoo, with its shaggy crest and long, cocked tail, inspired the famous "Beep-Beep" cartoons. Although not really as speedy as Beep-Beep, the Roadrunner may reach 15 miles per hour

[1]*Formerly, Roadrunner.*

or more on the ground. It can fly from danger, but usually sprints instead.

Fairly common in deserts of the Southwest, Roadrunners are rare and seldom seen residents of the Sierra foothills, occurring regularly north to Shasta County. They live in open, arid chaparral where good-sized thickets of large shrubs are separated by ample open ground. Pairs inhabit territories year-round and nest in shrubs or small trees. Their varied diet includes large insects, birds' eggs and young, rodents, lizards and snakes, including rattlers. Roadrunners are wary and easy to overlook. The best time to locate them is in spring when males reveal their presence with a short series of whiny, cooing notes, rather like a descending whimper of a puppy. They call most frequently around sunrise.

Where Found:
Yosemite: Not in park; observed in Sonora and along Highway 49 south of Coulterville.
Sequoia-Kings Canyon: Recorded at Shepherd Saddle, Ash Mountain and west of parks near Slick Rock (Lake Kaweah). Not recorded recently in the parks.

OWLS *(Order Strigiformes)*

Fearsome hunters of the night, owls hold a mysterious fascination for humans. Their direct stare and stolid upright posture when perched have earned them a reputation for wisdom. Because most species are nocturnal, casual observers only rarely see more than their silent, fleeing silhouettes. Owls usually reveal their presence by calls, distinctive for each species. Of all Sierran birds, only the owls, poorwills, nighthawks and certain aquatic species regularly feed at night.

A daytime encounter with a roosting owl is an unforgettable experience. With its large eyes, accentuated by surrounding facial discs, an owl's gaze can be piercing and intimidating. Owls have excellent vision, not only at night, but also in daytime. Both eyes point straight ahead, permitting depth perception for capturing prey. The facial discs aid in collecting and focusing sound for their extraordinarily acute ears, which can sense distance and direction precisely. Other adaptations for hunting include soft, velvety feathers permitting silent flight, powerful feet and talons for capturing prey, and strong, hooked beaks for tearing flesh.

Owls and other raptors regurgitate pellets consisting of indigestible residues such as bones, fur, and feathers (Figure 8). These provide ornithologists with valuable evidence of their food habits. Hawks and falcons tear apart their prey to get at the edible parts, but owls swallow their victims whole or in large pieces and so produce a greater volume of pellets. Their pellets contain more bones because they are less efficient at digesting those hard tissues than hawks and falcons.

There are two families of owls in the Sierra: Tytonidae, represented only by the Common Barn-Owl, and Strigidae, with ten other species. All are nocturnal, but several also hunt by day, especially the Short-eared, Pygmy, Burrowing and Great Gray.

BARN-OWLS *(Family Tytonidae)*

Common Barn-Owl[1] *(Tyto alba)* Plate 11
At dusk the light, ghost-like forms of Barn-Owls may appear flying softly and mothlike overhead. Many foothills residents know these owls because they nest and roost in old barns, silos, church towers and other buildings. Such artificial nest sites apparently have allowed their numbers to increase in recent decades. In the Sierra, Barn-Owls also roost in densely foliaged trees; they nest on protected ledges in cliffs or, rarely, in cavities in oak trees or streambanks. Unlike most Sierran owls, they regularly raise two broods per year.

Though more common in the foothills, some Barn-Owls live around mountain meadows of the ponderosa pine zone. Besides eating rats and mice in barnyards, they hunt for rodents and other small animals in open fields and meadows. Experiments conducted in total darkness have shown that they can locate prey entirely by sound. Their calls, usually given in flight, include long, piercing, raspy screeches and a series of clicks, five or ten seconds apart at first, but more frequent and softer toward the end. Unlike other owls, they have distinctly heart-shaped facial discs.

Where Found:
Yosemite: Recorded in Yosemite Valley. Probably breeds at Ackerson Meadow (just west of park) and at Paper Cabin Ridge (east of Don Pedro Reservoir).
Sequoia-Kings Canyon: Recorded at Buckeye Sewage Pond area; also west of the parks around Lemoncove and Allen Gap and below Terminus Dam (Lake Kaweah); seldom recorded above Lake Kaweah.

TYPICAL OWLS *(Family Strigidae)*

Flammulated Owl *(Otus flammeolus)* Plate 10
This diminutive and mysterious owl was long regarded as a rare species because of its irregular calling, secretive behavior and poorly known

[1]*Formerly, Barn Owl.*

habitat needs. Even when calling, the Flammulated Owl is hard to locate and, due to its quiet, ventriloquial hoots, may be closer than it sounds. It usually perches next to a tree trunk, deep within the canopy, where its matching coloration blends with bark and branches. Surprisingly, recent surveys based on a better understanding of its habits revealed that in local areas of optimal habitat, the Flammulated occurs in higher densities than any other Sierran owl.

Flammulated Owls favor stands of ponderosa or Jeffrey pines mixed with oaks. They generally avoid the dense, moist forests favored by Spotted Owls.

The Flammulated is the only small North American owl with dark eyes. Unlike most owls, it migrates long distances, spending the winter in southern Mexico and Guatemala. It returns to the Sierra by mid-April, but rarely calls before late May or after mid-June. The call is a single or double mellow hoot, given every two to three seconds.

In the Sierra, Flammulateds almost always nest in old flicker nest-cavities. They are particularly fond of moths, but also eat other insects and spiders, often capturing them in midair. The lack of flying insects in Sierran pine forests during winter probably explains why Flammulated Owls do not remain year-round. By late October, all have departed to the south, making their journey in the dark of night.

Where Found:
Yosemite: Merced Grove, Henness Ridge, and near Peregoy Meadow.
Sequoia-Kings Canyon: Deer Ridge, Potwisha.

Western Screech-Owl[1] *(Otus kennicottii)*   Plate 10

Screech-Owls were poorly named, for none of their typical calls even remotely resembles a screech. The call of the Western Screech-Owl is a short series of low, whistled notes on one pitch, speeding up like a bouncing ball at the end. This call is most common in late summer but is given throughout the year. It utters several other calls, but less frequently. In the Sierra, Screech-Owls are the only small owls with conspicuous ear tufts, and all individuals are gray, although there are different color phases elsewhere.

Fairly common in the Sierra foothills throughout the year, Screech-Owls prefer groves of oaks or riparian cottonwoods and willows. Less frequently, they occupy similar habitats in the ponderosa pine zone. Some Screech-Owls, especially juveniles, move upslope into the mixed-conifer zone after the nesting season. Many of these wanderers fall prey to the

[1]*Formerly this species and the Eastern Screech-Owl were combined in a single species, the Screech Owl.*

much larger Spotted Owl.

Strictly nocturnal, Screech-Owls begin searching for food shortly after dusk. Those in the Sierra feed mainly on large insects, but also eat mice, shrews, and other small animals. They nest in old holes of flickers and other woodpeckers and in natural cavities in trees.

Where Found:
Yosemite: Recorded in mid-summer at Hodgdon Meadow and during fall and winter in Yosemite Valley. Mostly occurs west of the park, as at El Portal, Tuolumne River canyon (near the North Fork), Groveland, and Ackerson Meadow.
Sequoia-Kings Canyon: Lower half of Mineral King Road, Potwisha, and Ash Mountain.

Great Horned Owl *(Bubo virginianus)*   Plate 11

The ferocious Great Horned Owl feeds primarily on rodents and rabbits but will kill almost any animal it can carry, including birds, snakes, fish and even porcupines, skunks, and house cats! It can fly away with prey as much as three times its own weight. This magnificent bird weighs more than any other owl in the Sierra, and only the Great Gray exceeds it in length.

Great Horned Owls occur commonly in the Sierra foothills, but less commonly in the coniferous forests above. Some live year-round as high as the subalpine zone. They can be found in almost any habitat with large clearings or open forests for foraging and sheltered roosting and nesting sites in trees or cliffs.

Like other owls, Great Horneds do not build their own nests. Instead, they raise their young in old nests of Red-tailed Hawks and other large birds or, less often, in caves, cliffs or cavities in trees. They are one of the earliest-nesting birds of the Sierra, beginning courtship in winter and laying eggs as early as January. During the nesting period, Great Horned Owls vigorously drive away other raptors attempting to nest in their territories, and often kill the young. They have even been known to kill adult Red-tailed Hawks and Great Gray Owls.

Great Horned Owls call most frequently at the beginning and end of the night, when they hoot in near-darkness from dead treetops or other prominent perches. They call most often in winter, while courting, but can be heard at any time of year. The typical call consists of four to seven unevenly spaced, resonant hoots. After they leave the nest, the young make loud, shrieking cries to maintain contact with their parents, which continue to feed them for several weeks. The only other Sierran owl that resembles the Great Horned is the Long-eared, which has prominent ear tufts but is smaller in size.

Yosemite: Yosemite Valley, Wawona, Foresta, Hodgdon Meadow, Crane Flat, White Wolf, Tuolumne Meadows.
Sequoia-Kings Canyon: Three Rivers, Ash Mountain, Potwisha, Buckeye Flats, Three Rivers, Cedar Grove; also recorded at Moro Creek Corrals, Lower Crabtree Meadow, and Lewis Creek Trail.

Northern Pygmy-Owl[1] *(Glaucidium gnoma)* Plate 10

With its small head and body and long tail, often cocked upward, the Northern Pygmy-Owl could be mistaken at a distance for a chunky songbird. It is the smallest Sierran owl by weight, only about as heavy as a blackbird.

Unlike most owls, Pygmies often hunt in daylight as well as at night, and they may pluck feathers or remove fur rather than eating their prey whole. They feed on mice, large insects and a variety of other animals, but are particularly fond of small birds. These fearless hunters occasionally attack birds as large as quail. For this reason no other owl, not even the Great Horned, gets mobbed so fiercely and frequently by songbirds. By calling and diving at it, flocks of small birds can drive an owl from their neighborhood entirely, or at least disrupt its hunting.

Pygmy-Owls are fairly common but localized in the foothills, with smaller numbers in the ponderosa pine zone and even higher. Resident year-round, they live in open woodlands and in forests bordering meadows and other large openings. They nest in medium-sized cavities like those left by Hairy Woodpeckers and Northern Flickers. Their usual call, a single mellow whistled note, is repeated every one or two seconds, most often early or late in the day. It might be confused with the higher-pitched note of a Townsend's Solitaire or with the distant call of a Mountain Quail, which is more like a sharp hoot. Occasionally Pygmy-Owls produce an emphatic, accelerating series of notes all on the same pitch, usually followed by one to three single notes.

Where Found:
Yosemite: Between El Portal and Foresta, in Yosemite Valley, and above Crane Flat; west of the park near Wards Ferry (lower Tuolumne River).
Sequoia-Kings Canyon: Ash Mountain, Elk Creek, Potwisha, Oak Grove, Silver City.

Burrowing Owl *(Athene cunicularia)*

People unfamiliar with Burrowing Owls may be startled to see these small raptors disappear into holes in the ground. Burrowing Owls often

[1]*Formerly, Pygmy Owl.*

perch by their burrows all day, making them easy to spot. They hunt mainly in the early evening and at night, hawking insects in midair and attacking rodents from a perched or hovering position. Sometimes they alight and hop after prey on the ground, making good use of their unusually long legs.

Rather than dig their own holes, Burrowing Owls take over burrows abandoned by ground squirrels or other animals and enlarge them. Colonies of up to 12 families live at the same site year after year unless disturbed. Their underground homes are used for both roosting and nesting.

Burrowing Owls prefer large expanses of relatively level, treeless country, avoiding dense ground cover and cultivated areas. They often colonize abandoned fields, however, and make use of artificial levees and berms. In the Sierra, they live mostly in the lower foothills. Although still fairly common in scattered localities, they have declined due to habitat loss, destruction of ground squirrels and their burrows, and ingestion of poisons used in rodent control.

Where Found:
Yosemite: Foothills west of the park, as along Tim Bell Road (northeast of Waterford) and along Highway 120 west of Chinese Camp.
Sequoia-Kings Canyon: One record from Ash Mountain; seldom recorded above San Joaquin Valley floor.

Spotted Owl (Strix occidentalis) Plate 12

Strictly nocturnal and confined to tall, dense forests, the mysterious Spotted Owl is known to most observers as an elusive shadow with an impressive array of calls. Most common is the four-hoot series, similar in rhythm to that of the Great Horned Owl, but higher and sharper, somewhat like the bark of a dog. Both sexes make this call, but the male's is lower in pitch. Other calls include a longer series of sharp hoots and a long whistle that rises in pitch toward the end. The former may be confused with a similar call made at night by pine martens (members of the weasel family) from high in the trees. Spotted Owls call most often during windless nights from March through June but may be heard at any time of year.

Although fairly common in suitable forests of the Sierra, Spotted Owls are vulnerable to habitat disturbance. Each pair requires several hundred acres of mature forest, and such large stands are rapidly succumbing to logging. They breed almost exclusively in mixed-conifer, ponderosa pine and Douglas-fir forests, especially moist stands where black oaks or other hardwoods form a well-developed understory. Sensitive to overheating, they seek shady stands for daytime roosting in summer. They usually hunt from an elevated perch, feeding primarily on small mammals, especially wood rats and flying squirrels, but also on bats, birds and insects.

Spotted Owls nest in natural hollows in trees and rocky cliffs and occasionally in nests deserted by hawks or ravens. The parents defend large breeding territories from February through September. The young disperse to other areas and sometimes wander into atypical habitats such as younger, second-growth forests. Recent studies in El Dorado County have shown that many adults descend to foothill woodlands in October to spend the winter.

Where Found:
Yosemite: Yosemite Valley, Wawona, Henness Ridge, Foresta, Hodgdon Meadow and west of the park at Hardin Flat and Ackerson Meadow.
Sequoia-Kings Canyon: Cedar Grove, Grant Grove area, Big Baldy, Giant Forest, Redwood Meadow, Silver City (on Mineral King Road). Winter records from Potwisha and Ash Mountain.

Great Gray Owl *(Strix nebulosa)* Plate 12

Its grandeur and extreme rarity south of Canada make the Great Gray Owl one of the most eagerly sought birds in the Sierra. Gazing at close range into its penetrating yellow eyes, accentuated by huge facial discs, is a memorable and enchanting experience. Although the Great Horned Owl is heavier, no other North American owl rivals the Great Gray in overall length and wingspan.

Primarily a denizen of the boreal forests of Canada and Alaska, the Great Gray Owl also occurs in southward extensions of suitable habitat in the Rocky Mountains and the Sierra Nevada. It is classified as endangered by the State of California, and a recent survey estimated that only 30 to 40 individuals remain in the state. Most of these live in or near Yosemite National Park. There is no evidence that they nest in Lassen or Sequoia-Kings Canyon National Parks, although they have been observed at least once in each area.

Great Gray Owls breed in ponderosa pine, mixed-conifer and red fir forests, and some move up into the subalpine zone in late summer and fall. In winter they move down into the ponderosa pine zone. They require moist meadow systems of 20 acres or more to feed in — another compelling reason to preserve these teeming centers of biological activity whenever possible.

When hunting, Great Grays watch and listen for prey from low perches along meadow edges, flying distances of a few feet to more than 50 yards to make a kill. In the Sierra their victims are usually gophers or voles. Great Grays have been observed diving for gophers through a foot of snow, and they sometimes catch them underground by breaking through tunnels near the surface. Unlike most owls, they sometimes forage in daylight, usually early or late in the day. More often they hunt at night; the remains of nocturnal flying squirrels have been found in their pellets (Fig. 8).

A recent study suggested that Great Grays in the Sierra nest successfully only in years when there is an above average density of prey such as voles to feed their young. Apparently none of the Sierran pairs even attempt to breed in some years. The few nests found in California have all been in the tops of large, broken-off snags, but elsewhere many pairs have used abandoned hawk nests.

In the Sierra, Great Gray Owls call most frequently after 1:00 a.m. but may be heard at any time of night or in late afternoon. They advertise breeding territories from April through August, making low double hoots or 5 to 12 low-pitched, evenly spaced "whoo's."

Where Found:
Yosemite: Crane Flat, Peregoy Meadow, Westfall Meadow, McGurk Meadow and west of the park at Ackerson Meadow.
Sequoia-Kings Canyon: One immature bird recorded on road to Wolverton; no evidence of breeding.

Long-eared Owl *(Asio otus)*   Plate 11

Few other Sierran birds are so poorly known as this quiet, secretive species. Long-eared Owls rarely call except during the spring breeding season, and few observers are familiar with their dialect in this region. A varied repertoire of calls has been heard in the Sierra, including a low, mellow, prolonged hoot, a series of five or six hoots (resembling those of the Great Horned Owl, but higher) and cat-like meows and screeches.

Figure 8. Regurgitated pellets reveal the presence of owls and certain other birds and provide samples of their diets. The pellet portrayed here is from a Great Gray Owl, which preys on rodents such as gophers, flying squirrels and voles.

Although seldom recorded in the Sierra, Long-eared Owls are fairly common in some localities in the foothills and the ponderosa pine zone. They apparently have declined in numbers due to human impacts on their preferred habitats — the tall cottonwoods, willows and live oaks that border streams and wet meadows. Many such areas have been cleared for cultivation, inundated by reservoirs or dried up by water diversions.

Like Great Horned Owls, Long-ears nest in vacant nests of other birds, especially hawks, magpies and crows. When not incubating eggs or brooding young, they roost in dense foliage of trees, willow thickets or even shrubs. They need an open area for hunting near their nest or roost and a sufficient supply of food, especially mice and voles. They also eat other small mammals and, rarely, frogs, snakes, insects and birds. Long-ears always hunt at night, silently flying low above the ground and listening for their prey.

This medium-sized owl can be confused with the much larger Great Horned Owl. Its ear tufts are unreliable as distinguishing marks, as their apparent size, angle and distance apart vary with the owl's mood. The Great Horned Owl, however, has fine horizontal barring on its underside, while the Long-eared has strong lengthwise streaking. When a Long-eared flies, its ear tufts are depressed, and it can easily be mistaken for a Short-eared Owl. Both species have dark "wrist" patches on their underwings, but the Short-eared can be recognized by its tawny brown coloration. Unlike the Short-eared, the Long-eared is rarely abroad in daylight.

Where Found:
Yosemite: West of the park at Ackerson Meadow and at Paper Cabin Ridge (east of Don Pedro Reservoir); apparently no longer inhabits the park itself.
Sequoia-Kings Canyon: One record from Bearpaw Meadow and an old record from Ash Mountain; probably occurs west of the parks.

Short-eared Owl (Asio flammeus)

Probably the most diurnal of Sierran owls, the Short-eared Owl usually hunts in late afternoon and early evening. It flies slowly over open country with shallow, floppy wingbeats, keeping near the ground and sometimes stopping to hover before dropping on its prey. By far its most common victims are meadow voles, but parents feeding young capture other small mammals and birds as well.

Short-eared Owls inhabit broad, relatively treeless expanses, especially marshes and tall, moist grasslands. Those in the Sierra are mostly post-breeding wanderers and winter visitors from the north. They are rare in the foothills and even scarcer at higher elevations but have been seen as high as 11,000 feet in late summer. Short-eared Owls nest very locally in the

Central Valley and possibly in the low Sierra foothills. They lay their eggs on the ground in slight depressions, sparsely lined with grasses and feathers. Habitat destruction by cultivation, heavy grazing and marsh drainage, as well as illegal shooting, has caused California's nesting and wintering populations to decline.

Care should be taken in identifying this species, as a Long-eared Owl depresses its ear tufts in flight and can be mistaken for a Short-eared. An owl hunting in the daytime is probably the latter, as the Long-eared is strictly nocturnal.

Where Found:
Yosemite: Recorded at Yosemite Valley, Mt. Clark, and Isberg Pass; no breeding records.
Sequoia-Kings Canyon: One record from Elizabeth Pass; no breeding records.

Northern Saw-whet Owl[1] *(Aegolius acadicus)*   Plates 10, 26

Like other small owls, Saw-whets must keep constant watch for their greatest enemies, the larger owls. Because these talented little ventriloquists usually call from dense cover, they are difficult to find, even when perched close by. During the day they roost in holes or in dense foliage, where their speckled plumage provides good camouflage. Despite their secretive habits, they are remarkably tolerant of people in daylight, often letting observers approach within a few feet.

Little is known of Saw-whet Owls in the Sierra because they are silent much of the year and have not been studied systematically. During spring and summer they occur mainly in the ponderosa pine and mixed-conifer zones, but in winter they may desert higher elevations where snow is heavy and move down to the foothills. Saw-whet Owls eat insects, small mammals, frogs and birds in proportions that vary with local availability. They nest in holes vacated by flickers or other woodpeckers.

Saw-whet owls call primarily from March to early May in the Sierra, and few other owls make such a wide variety of sounds. The most common is a mellow whistled note, repeated in a long, monotonous series, at about two notes per second. When imitated, the Saw-whet sometimes responds by changing the call's pitch and tempo.

Where Found:
Yosemite: Recorded at Yosemite Valley (one nest record), Merced Grove, Crane Flat, and six miles east of Coulterville.
Sequoia-Kings Canyon: Recorded at Florence Lake, Paradise Valley,

[1]*Formerly, Saw-whet Owl.*

Whitaker Forest (near Redwood Mountain), Little Baldy, Lodgepole, Long Meadow (near Wolverton), Giant Forest, and Moro Rock.

NIGHTJARS *(Family Caprimulgidae)*

Like owls, which may be their closest relatives, nightjars are primarily nocturnal and have unusually soft feathers that permit silent flight. They have small, weak feet, short bills and broad, gaping mouths for catching insects in midair. The two Sierran nightjars give rather pleasing calls, but a European species makes a jarring nocturnal cry — hence the family name.

Common Nighthawk *(Chordeiles minor)*   Plate 13

Darting erratically through the air in pursuit of high-flying insects, Common Nighthawks fill the role of swallows at night. They feed mostly between sunset and sunrise, taking prey ranging in size from mosquitoes to large moths. In midsummer nighthawks come out during the daytime as well, perhaps because they need extra food for their young. They announce their presence with a peculiar, loud, nasal "beeer," frequently uttered in flight. This species was formerly known as the "Booming Nighthawk" because when males are courting, defending eggs or protecting young, they perform steep power dives, pulling out with a loud "whoof." This startling, unforgettable sound is produced by air rushing through their wings.

Common Nighthawks usually forage over open habitats such as meadows, ridgetops, lakes and forest clearings. Uncommon in the Sierra, they nest mostly in the mixed-conifer zone and above, even as high as 10,750 feet in Sequoia National Park. They also breed in the northern foothills in scattered locations from Yuba to Tehama Counties. Rather than build nests, they lay their eggs directly on bare rocky or gravelly ground and rely on their mottled gray-brown coloration for camouflage. The few nesting sites found in the Sierra have been on rocky outcrops and other habitats with little ground cover and few, if any, trees. In some parts of the United States, heavily burned forests especially attract nighthawks, but such nest-sites have not yet been noted in the Sierra. Common Nighthawks migrate, and by early September most have departed for South America, not to return again until June.

The Common Nighthawk can easily be confused with its smaller relative, the Lesser Nighthawk, which breeds in the Central Valley but only rarely wanders up into the foothills in late summer. The Lesser, however, makes different calls, and the white or buffy crossbars in its wings are noticeably closer to the wingtips. Another relative, the Common Poorwill, has shorter, rounded wings with no crossbars. The female Common Nighthawk resembles the male but does not have a white band across her tail.

Where Found:
Yosemite: Rare but widespread; Yosemite Valley, Wawona, Merced Lake, Tuolumne Meadows and Vogelsang Lake.
Sequoia-Kings Canyon: Uncommon; Moraine Lake (Chagoopa Plateau), Crescent Meadow, Blossom Lakes, and Lloyd Meadows Basin (Sequoia National Forest).

Common Poorwill[1] *(Phalaenoptilus nuttallii)* Plate 13

It is difficult to get a good look at these nocturnal insect-eaters of the chaparral. They may be glimpsed along back roads at night, fluttering up like giant moths in the glare of headlights, or resting on the ground, their eyeshine glowing pink or orange. Like owls, poorwills are more easily heard than seen. On warm summer nights, beginning at dusk, they utter a mellow whistled "poor-will-o," the second note pitched higher than the first, and the lower, third note audible only at close range. Sometimes several birds call back and forth at once, creating a beautiful, haunting chorus.

In contrast to the high-flying Common Nighthawks, poorwills flit silently just above bushes or low over openings, roads and trails. Often they pick insects from the ground or fly up to capture them in midair.

Poorwills build no nest but lay their eggs on bare ground or in a shallow scrape matted with pine needles, usually in the shade of a rock, shrub or low plant. Most common in the foothills, they nest in brushy habitats, with or without scattered trees, up to the mixed-conifer zone. After breeding, a few wander to higher elevations, even to tree line.

In winter some poorwills go into torpor, a state of inactivity characterized by lowered body temperature, reduced metabolic rate and extremely slow heartbeat and breathing. Such measures conserve their energy at a time when food is scarce, permitting survival for long periods on energy stored as body fat. A few other birds, including swifts and hummingbirds, enter torpor for short periods, but only poorwills are known to enter a prolonged state of dormancy (also known as hibernation when it occurs during the winter). One wild bird was torpid for 88 days, maintaining a body temperature of 65 °F, 41 degrees below the normal temperature of an active poorwill.

Only a few torpid poorwills have been reported in northern California, but because they are difficult to find, it is conceivable that many spend the winter here. In some areas they appear regularly in winter, but only on warm evenings. Most poorwills probably migrate to southern California and Baja California for the months of October through March.

[1]*Formerly, Poor-will.*

Where Found:
Yosemite: Yosemite Valley, Foresta, near Hetch Hetchy, Henness Ridge (nests); more common in foothills west of the park.
Sequoia-Kings Canyon: Canyons of all four branches of the Kaweah River, as high as Sunset and Beetle Rocks at the edge of Giant Forest. One late summer record from tree line near Pinchot Pass.

SWIFTS *(Family Apodidae)*

Even those aerial gymnasts, the swallows, cannot match the speed and darting maneuvers of the swifts. With their highly streamlined bodies and long, pointed wings, these aptly named birds resemble cigars with crescents for wings. Swifts and swallows both spend the daylight hours on the wing snatching insects, but the two groups are only superficially similar. Swallows are passerines, or perching birds; swifts are closely related to hummingbirds, sharing similar internal wing structures and tiny feet. Swifts feed, drink, gather nesting material, court each other and even copulate in the air! In Europe one species has been observed to spend the night on the wing soaring at great heights. Their weak feet make it nearly impossible to land on branches or the ground; instead they cling with long claws to vertical rock faces or hollow trees. Most swifts glue their nests with saliva onto inaccessible cliff walls. Both parents incubate and rear the young, which depend on them for a long time before leaving the nest. After fledging, however, the young usually require no further adult care.

Black Swift *(Cypseloides niger)*   Plate 14

Few birds are so limited in their choice of nesting sites as Black Swifts or have preferences so grand and majestic. Only a few nesting colonies of 5 to 15 pairs have been found in the Sierra, and all are on moist cliffs near or behind great waterfalls such as Yosemite and Bridalveil Falls in Yosemite and Hamilton and Marble Falls in Sequoia National Park. They may also nest at Feather Falls on the Feather River and possibly elsewhere along remote rivers and moist canyons of the Sierra, particularly at elevations between the ponderosa pine and red fir zones. Due to their inaccessibility Black Swift nests were not examined closely until 1901. The discoverer was surprised to find only one large egg in a simple nest, and later searches of other nest sites confirmed that they never lay more than one. The single egg is large—about three times the size of a White-throated Swift's!

Black Swifts utter high-pitched musical notes as they skim rapidly through the mists. These sooty-black acrobats are larger and fly with slower, less erratic wingbeats than the White-throated Swifts that often cruise with them. Black Swifts may spiral thousands of feet into the air pursuing clouds of insects. They may soar up to the Sierra crest, especially after nesting is completed in late summer. Though uncommon, they range widely and might be seen almost anywhere in the Sierra, including the foothills in spring. Most Black Swifts depart the Sierra by the end of August.

Where Found:
Yosemite: Yosemite Falls, Bridalveil Fall and Tenaya Canyon (first Sierran nests found there); observed over Wawona Meadow.
Sequoia-Kings Canyon: Lookout Peak, Ella Falls, Watchtower, Alta Peak, Hamilton Falls, Moro Rock, Marble Falls.

Vaux's Swift *(Chaetura vauxi)* Plate 14

These smallest of Sierran swifts are also the plainest. With cigar-shaped bodies and tiny tails, Vaux's Swifts look a little like bats as they twist and spin after aerial insects. They spend the daylight hours cruising in wide arcs above natural forest clearings, recent burns or mountain meadows, sometimes swinging high above the treetops. They favor tree-lined lake-shores and streams as hunting grounds, probably because this habitat harbors abundant insects.

Vaux's Swifts migrate uncommonly through foothill woodlands and mid-elevation meadows of the western Sierra from May through August. They also breed regularly in the region, but their secretive habits make nests hard to find. Unlike their cliff-nesting relatives, Vaux's glue their saucer-like creations to the insides of tree cavities—especially in large, hollow conifer trunks. They favor burned-out snags; forest fires probably favor these swifts by creating nest sites.

Where Found:
Yosemite: Yosemite Valley, Wawona Meadow, Hodgdon Meadow, Crane Flat (nesting); west of the park at Hardin Flat.
Sequoia-Kings Canyon: Giant Forest (meadows in area); also Ash Mountain along Middle Fork Kaweah River in autumn.

White-throated Swift *(Aeronautes saxatalis)* Plates 6, 14

Crossbow-shaped silhouettes darting over sheer Sierra cliffs are likely to be White-throated Swifts. Much more common in the region than other swifts, they can be seen above almost any habitat, especially rocky bluffs overlooking river gorges or other open terrain. They are most numerous from Yosemite south to the Kern River. Present from May until late August, they breed from the foothill grasslands at least up to the red fir zone. In late summer they may cruise above the highest ridges in search of insect swarms. To nest they select inaccessible crannies on sheer cliff faces and build shallow saucers of feathers, using saliva for glue. Nests can be from ten to thousands of feet above the ground.

These gregarious birds often forage in the company of other swifts and Violet-green Swallows. Violet-greens have entirely white flanks and underparts, while the swifts have bold patterns of white on their throats, breasts and flanks, separated by black side patches. These markings are particularly noticeable when viewed against a cliff or other dark background. Silhouetted against the sky high overhead, these swifts often appear entirely dark like Black Swifts. As they whirl by on long, pointed wings, White-throateds often utter a series of musical, descending, high-pitched notes. Few species can match their velocity or aerial virtuosity. One bird was seen to outrace a Peregrine Falcon stooping down at a speed estimated at more than 175 miles per hour!

Where Found:
Yosemite: Yosemite Falls, Bridalveil Fall, Vernal and Nevada Falls, Cloud's Rest, Hetch Hetchy, lower gorges of Merced and Tuolumne Rivers; in fall up to Tuolumne Meadows, Mt. Dana and Mt. Conness.
Sequoia-Kings Canyon: Lookout Peak, Park Ridge, Buck Rock, Big Baldy, Little Baldy, Watchtower, Moro Rock.

HUMMINGBIRDS *(Family Trochilidae)*

With their whirring wings and shimmering iridescent greens and reds, these tiny aerial wizards bring a sense of magic to Sierran meadows, rock gardens and brushfields. Both hummers and the flowers they visit have coevolved characteristics that enhance their mutualistic relationship. Their small size, long bills and tongues and ability to hover enable hummers to feed efficiently on nectar and pollen as well as on insects and spiders found in flowers. Many "hummingbird flowers" have evolved internal structures that facilitate pollination by hummers. Some, such as penstemon and paintbrush, keep their nectar from insects deep in tubular "throats" which effectively reserve it for hummingbirds. Others, like manzanita, have small flowers with narrow openings and no landing places for bees. Hummingbird flowers are often red, explaining the well-known attraction of hummers to red hats, shirts and other objects.

Hummingbirds have the fastest wingbeat of all birds and are the only ones capable of backward flight. To sustain such exertion over long periods, they have evolved one of the highest metabolic rates of any creature; consequently they must conserve energy whenever possible. On cold nights, rather than deplete their fat reserves to stay warm, many hummingbirds enter a state of torpor, like a brief hibernation, with greatly lowered body temperatures and metabolic rates.

Male hummingbirds are admired by people, and presumably by female hummers, for their colorful "gorgets," or throat feathers, and for their spectacular diving displays, used during aggression and courtship. Females exclude the males from their nesting territories and raise the young without help. Sierran species line their tiny, deep cup-nests with plant down and wrap them in spiderwebs.

Black-chinned Hummingbird *(Archilochus alexandri)*   Plate 15

Every male Sierran hummingbird has a jewel on his throat, but the Black-chin's is hard to see. Under most conditions his throat simply looks black, but the proper lighting and angle reveal a stunning blue-violet band below the truly black chin.

Black-chinned Hummingbirds nest in deciduous streamside woodlands lining the bottoms of warm foothill canyons as well as in irrigated orchards and gardens. In general they prefer moister habitats than the Anna's, the most common foothill hummingbird. Females usually build their nests in low foliage over a stream or dry creek bed. Males occupy nearby sites, typically upslope in tall, broken chaparral mixed with live oaks. When displaying to intruders or potential mates, they "swing" back and forth through the air in wide, shallow arcs.

Black-chins arrive in the Sierra foothills in April and depart for Mexico by September. Each July and August a few move up into the ponderosa pine zone or even higher. Rather uncommon in the northern Sierra, they may be more numerous in the southern part of the range.

Where Found:
Yosemite: Foothills west of the park, as at El Portal, Dudley and Snelling; most often seen at feeders. A few postbreeding records in Yosemite Valley.
Sequoia-Kings Canyon: Three Rivers, Ash Mountain; most often seen at feeders.

Anna's Hummingbird *(Calypte anna)*   Plate 15

The male Anna's Hummingbird displays his aerial prowess to the fullest when intimidating a trespassing hummingbird that does not flee at his approach. First he hovers about ten feet above the intruder, orienting toward the sun to display his brilliant red crown and throat feathers. He sings a few buzzy notes before mounting slowly in a wavering vertical path to a height of 60 feet or more. Suddenly he drops into a steep power dive at the other hummer, pulling out just in time with a sharp, loud "peek", and looping up to his starting point to hover and buzz again. Air rushing through his specially adapted tail feathers makes the startling sound at the base of the dive, which resembles a Beechey ground squirrel's alarm note. The male may repeat his J-shaped dive several times in sequence, directing it at all intruders, males and females alike. Apparently fearless, he attacks birds many times his size, even the usually truculent Scrub Jay.

More Anna's breed in the Sierra than any other hummer, and they are the only hummers to remain year-round in the foothill woodlands and chaparral. They thus require good supplies of winter-blooming flowers such as manzanita, gooseberry and currant. Perhaps more than other Sierran hummingbirds, they need large numbers of small insects and spiders as well.

Anna's Hummingbird is one of the few California birds that begins nesting in midwinter; egg-laying begins as early as December! Females prefer dense stands of live oaks, where they build tiny nests in shrubs or trees and camouflage them with lichens. Meanwhile, males establish territories in open woodlands or chaparral and advertise them with a distinctive song of squeaky and buzzy notes, uttered from a perch. A female initiates courtship by entering a male's territory to feed. Several chases and displays ensue, eventually ending up in the female's nesting area, where the pair may copulate. The male soon departs, leaving the female to raise the family alone.

From April to September, after breeding, Anna's Hummingbirds regularly move up to the mixed-conifer zone or even higher, usually choosing arid brushy habitats, but also meadows. The females and young have throats more heavily spotted with red than other Sierran hummers and lack the rufous tail patches and buffy sides of the female Calliope and Rufous Hummingbirds.

Where Found:
Yosemite: Widespread in foothills; uncommon upslope after breeding; in park, occurs at Yosemite Valley, Foresta and Crane Flat.
Sequoia-Kings Canyon: Three Rivers, Ash Mountain, Hospital Rock, Potwisha; noted upslope after breeding, as at Crescent Meadow, Emerald Lake and Mineral King.

Calliope Hummingbird *(Stellula calliope)*　　　　　Plate 15

Despite its tiny size, smaller than any other bird north of Mexico, the Calliope Hummingbird somehow survives the chilling temperatures of summer nights in the High Sierra. Males probably conserve energy by reducing their body temperature at night (see p. 98), but females on the nest must maintain normal temperatures to protect their eggs and young. Females stay warm by snuggling down in their thick nest insulation and by situating their nests strategically; they place them on branches directly beneath other limbs or sprays of foliage, thus reducing radiation of heat to the cold night sky.

In spring the Calliope migrates in small numbers through the Sierra foothills. It is the only hummer that regularly breeds above the foothills, nesting mainly from the ponderosa pine to the red fir zone. Rather uncommon, it prefers open forests near streams, seeps or meadow edges with good supplies of "hummingbird flowers" such as gooseberry, currant, manzanita, penstemon and paintbrush. Often it takes sap from sapsucker drillings or feeds in rock gardens amid scattered Jeffrey pines and junipers on sunny slopes and ridges.

In May and June the male defends a select patch of flowers and chases away other intruding hummers. He makes an impressive flight display in the form of a broad, vertical "U," with a power dive down one side, a short, quiet buzz at the bottom, and a gradual ascent up the other side. Often directed at a female, the display probably plays a role in both courtship and aggression. By early July most males have departed for their wintering grounds in Mexico. The females and young follow later and are mostly gone by mid-August.

Since both females and young are difficult to identify, their status in late summer is uncertain. They look much like the female Rufous but have smaller bodies, shorter bills and shorter tails with less rusty coloration. Unlike the Anna's, they have a buffy wash on their sides.

Where Found:
Yosemite: Yosemite Valley, Chinquapin, Mono Meadow, Yosemite Creek (above Valley rim), Hardin Flat (west of park).
Sequoia-Kings Canyon: Crescent Meadow, Moro Rock, Wolverton, Mineral King.

Rufous Hummingbird *(Selasphorus rufus)* Plate 15

Because Rufous Hummingbirds are so common in the summer, when other hummingbirds are breeding, early ornithologists naturally assumed they nested in the Sierra. Further study revealed that they only pass through in migration between their breeding grounds, which extend from Alaska south to Oregon, and their wintering areas in Mexico. In spring they travel northward through the foothills and the Central Valley, straying rarely up to the ponderosa pine zone. By June some head back, and by early July the southward migration is in full swing.

Though common at all elevations in summer, Rufous Hummingbirds are most numerous above the ponderosa pine forests, as they follow the later bloom of flowers at high elevations. Outnumbering all other hummers, these tiny migrants linger in meadows, brushfields and rocky slopes with plenty of favored blooms, up to well above tree line. On the east slope of the Sierra, some have been noted defending patches of penstemons from other hummers.

The southbound migration is led by a wave of males, for they do not help with nesting and thus are free to leave the breeding grounds early. By

August, males have become rare, but females and young are abundant.

The similar and closely related Allen's Hummingbird (*S. sasin*) has been recorded in the Sierra several times during the spring and summer, from the ponderosa pine up to the alpine zone. The green back of the adult male Allen's distinguishes it from the adult male Rufous, whose back is typically a solid rusty color but may display a fair number of green feathers. Unfortunately the female and immature Allen's cannot be distinguished from the Rufous in the field. Thus, Allen's Hummingbirds may be more common than the few records indicate.

Where Found:
Yosemite: Widespread from the foothills up to the alpine zone; park locations include Yosemite Valley, Wawona, Crane Flat, Porcupine Creek, Tuolumne Meadows, and Lyell Canyon.
Sequoia-Kings Canyon: In summer, common at Farewell Gap (above Mineral King); also recorded at Grant Grove, Wolverton, Round Meadow, Crescent Meadow, and Log Meadow. During spring migration noted at Ash Mountain.

KINGFISHERS *(Family Alcedinidae)*

Belted Kingfisher *(Ceryle alcyon)*   Plate 1
A harsh, grating rattle announces the passage of a Belted Kingfisher as it flies with irregular wingbeats above a Sierran lake or stream. When it lands, its double-crested head and massive bill seem out of proportion to its short tail and tiny feet. In contrast to most birds, the female is the more brightly colored of the two, with a broad chestnut band across her breast and flanks.

As their name suggests, Kingfishers hunt for fish by flying over water and scanning from exposed limbs, bridges and wires. They attack aquatic prey with dramatic dives from perched or hovering positions, often disappearing briefly underwater before returning to a favorite spot to kill and eat their catch. Adults consume small fish, crayfish and bullfrog tadpoles, but feed mostly insects to their nestlings. They prefer to hunt over clear, shallow water, where they can see prey easily.

Although solitary for most of the year, mated kingfishers remain together during the breeding season, from April to early August. They excavate their own nesting holes in steep stream banks of clay or sand. These holes are about three feet below the tops of banks and may be six or seven feet deep. Both parents participate in the digging, which may take up to three weeks.

Fairly common in the western Sierra, Belted Kingfishers nest from the

Central Valley up to the ponderosa pine zone. A few birds follow streams up to tree line after breeding. Kingfishers move downslope and southward in winter when Sierran waters begin to freeze. Although a few occur year-round along the whole length of the Sierra, Kingfishers breed primarily from Kings Canyon northward and winter mostly to the south of this region.

Where Found:
Yosemite: Merced and Tuolumne River drainages from the lowlands up to Tuolumne Meadows; often noted near El Portal, Yosemite Valley and Wawona; also recorded at Lake Eleanor, Benson Lake, Merced Lake and Harden Lake.

Sequoia-Kings Canyon: Kings, Kaweah and Kern Rivers and their major tributaries; recorded near Evolution Creek, Grouse Meadow, Cedar Grove, Zumwalt Meadows, Lodgepole, Potwisha, Ash Mountain and Mineral King.

WOODPECKERS *(Family Picidae)*

As their name suggests, woodpeckers are admirably equipped for drilling in wood. They excavate nest cavities and winter roosts with their large, powerful bills and drill holes or flake off bark in search of insects. Special cushioning protects their brains from shock, and unusual bone structures support their extremely long barb-tipped tongues, used to extract insects or sap from holes (see Fig. 9). With their strong feet and stiff tail feathers, they can brace themselves vertically on trees while pecking.

Woodpeckers' bills are also used for "drumming" — pecking loudly in specific patterns to communicate with mates or territorial rivals. In some species drumming is more important than vocalizing and is equivalent to the singing of other birds. Woodpeckers generally peck in rapid-fire patterns when drumming and much more slowly when feeding.

Western Sierran forests support ten nesting species of woodpeckers, with up to seven co-occurring in the middle elevations. Most species are nonmigratory, and several remain to brave the fierce winters in the high Sierra.

Lewis' Woodpecker *(Melanerpes lewis)*   Figure 10
Lewis' Woodpecker is a stunning but peculiar-looking woodpecker, with its rose-pink belly and dark, iridescent back and wings. Unlike other Sierran woodpeckers, which fly in an undulating, up-and-down pattern, it proceeds on a steady, level course, more like a small crow. It comes and goes less predictably than other woodpeckers, perhaps responding to changes in local food supplies.

a

b

Keith Hansen 1984

Figure 9. Williamson's Sapsucker (a) probing a hole for insects with its long, sticky tongue, which may be protruded more than three times the length of its bill! Such extensions are made possible by a tongue bone divided into two cartilaginous pieces (hyoid apparatus) that wrap around the skull and anchor in the right nostril (b).

In spring and fall Lewis' Woodpeckers migrate across the Sierra between their breeding grounds in open forests east of the crest and their wintering areas in the western foothills and beyond. Others move in from the Cascades. Usually they keep to the foothills, but in exceptional years many reach higher elevations during late summer and fall. Migrants numbering in the thousands were sighted in September of 1925 crossing an 11,000-foot pass near Foerster Peak in Yosemite and again in the fall of 1932 passing through Yosemite Valley.

Curiously, Lewis' Woodpeckers nest in the interior coast ranges and (at least formerly) in the Central Valley, but not in similar habitats in the Sierra foothills. They winter in open oak woodlands with good crops of acorns, their staple food at that season. Like Acorn Woodpeckers, they store acorns, but Lewis' use natural crevices rather than drill their own holes. They defend acorn caches individually rather than in groups, and may spend more than 40% of their time guarding these stores. They also relish insects, capturing them in midair or swooping down to snatch them from shrubs and grasses. Sometimes they act like large swallows, chasing one insect after another in long acrobatic flights before returning to a perch.

Where Found:
Yosemite: Irregular. Recorded at Yosemite Valley, Big Meadow, near Smoky Jack, at Foerster's Peak, and west of the park at Cathey's Valley, Snelling, La Grange, and 20 miles east of Oakdale.
Sequoia-Kings Canyon: Irregular migrant, sometimes common; most often reported in the Middle Fork Kaweah River canyon, as at Deer Ridge; also at Hotel Creek, Lewis Creek, Cherry Gap, Muir Grove, Giant Forest, Ash Mountain, and Milk Ranch Peak. Occasionally winters in the Springville area, southwest of the parks.

Acorn Woodpecker *(Melanerpes formicivorus)* Plate 16
Perhaps the most familiar of Sierran woodpeckers, these clamorous, clown-faced birds have a habit of caching acorns, which are central to their individual and social existence. They prefer areas with two or more species of oak, because the acorn supply is more dependable. Each kind of oak has bad acorn years, but it is unlikely that several species will have crop failures the same year. Unless the acorn supply is exhausted, Acorn Woodpeckers remain on their territories year-round. They are most common in open oak woodlands of the foothills, but large numbers also live in ponderosa pine and mixed-conifer forest stands where oaks are abundant.

The tight-knit social groups of Acorn Woodpeckers are unique among Sierran birds. Others nest in colonies or feed in flocks, but only this species forms cooperative breeding groups of three or more adults. Group members defend a mutual territory and ordinarily only one pair in each group raises a family. Other adults serve as helpers, bringing food to the young birds and sometimes helping excavate the nest. After fledging, the young remain on the territory for at least a year, and some never leave.

A central feature of each territory is the granary, usually a huge old oak or conifer, but sometimes a telephone pole or group of fenceposts, which group members stock with acorns and defend against squirrels, jays and

Figure 10. Lewis' Woodpecker.

Acorn Woodpeckers from other colonies. A single granary may contain more than 10,000 acorn-sized holes drilled by the woodpeckers and stuffed with acorns in the autumn. Although acorns are the main food from late summer through winter, insects and sap are more important in spring and early summer. Unlike most woodpeckers, Acorns rarely drill for insects, but take them on the wing instead, flying up like oversized flycatchers from the tops of oaks.

Where Found:
Yosemite: Yosemite Valley, below Foresta, lower Alder Creek (near Wawona); recorded in late summer at Hodgdon Meadow, Crane Flat, and near Tuolumne Grove; more widespread west of the park, as at El Portal and Groveland.
Sequoia-Kings Canyon: Common at Three Rivers, Ash Mountain, Potwisha, Hospital Rock and the lower part of Mineral King Road.

Red-breasted Sapsucker[1] *(Sphyrapicus ruber)*   **Plate 16**

Despite their vivid colors, Red-breasted Sapsuckers are relatively inconspicuous. They drill quietly, call infrequently and only occasionally produce their distinctive, irregular drumming signal. They do, however, leave an unmistakable sign of their presence: small holes drilled in neat horizontal rows on living trees (see Plate 16). After drilling holes, sapsuckers return at frequent intervals to eat the oozing sap and any insects attracted to it. Some of their hard-earned food is "stolen" by hummingbirds, warblers and other forest birds which have learned that sapsucker holes provide a free lunch. Sapsuckers also eat considerable quantities of cambium, the soft, growing tissue under the bark. They return repeatedly to a favored tree until it is riddled with holes, occasionally girdling one to death. Still, serious damage is usually limited to a few trees. In the nesting season, these woodpeckers supplement their diet by hawking insects in midair over meadows and forest openings.

In the Sierra, Red-breasted Sapsuckers nest in the mixed-conifer zone and less commonly in the red firs. Usually they occupy rather open forests near streams or wet meadows. Although it is often said they prefer hardwoods, they feed extensively on conifers, including giant sequoias and incense cedars. Many are attracted to the historic fruit orchards planted in Yosemite Valley during the 1860's. Their need for living trees distinguishes them from other montane woodpeckers such as the Hairy, Black-backed, and Pileated, which prefer dead or dying tree parts.

Red-breasted Sapsuckers excavate nesting cavities in dead trees or in live ones with rotten heartwood. After nesting, some disperse up to subalpine

[1]*Formerly, Yellow-bellied Sapsucker (in part).*

forests and down to the ponderosa pine zone, but by October most have departed. No one knows whether these Sierran birds migrate south or simply move downslope. Members of their species winter in the foothills and Central Valley and south to Baja California, where warmer temperatures keep the sap flowing.

Recently the Red-breasted and Yellow-bellied Sapsuckers were recognized as two distinct species, having formerly been lumped as one. The Red-naped race (*S. varius nuchalis*) of the Yellow-bellied Sapsucker appears rarely on both slopes of the Sierra in fall and winter and has nested on the east slope. Unlike the Red-breasted, it has strong black and white stripes on its face and a broad black chest band.

Where Found:
Yosemite: Mariposa Grove, Peregoy Meadow, Foresta, Hodgdon Meadow, Tuolumne Grove, Crane Flat, Gin Flat, Porcupine Creek. Moves down to Yosemite Valley and up to high elevations after breeding.
Sequoia-Kings Canyon: Grant Grove, Wolverton Meadow, Giant Forest, Mineral King. Occurs occasionally in winter at Ash Mountain and other low-elevation sites.

Williamson's Sapsucker *(Sphyrapicus thyroideus)* Plate 17, Figure 9

Unlike other woodpeckers, male and female Williamson's Sapsuckers differ strikingly in appearance, so much that from 1855 to 1875 they were classified as separate species. One ornithologist even placed them in separate genera! These sapsuckers prefer subalpine forests, especially those dominated by lodgepole pines. They generally breed at higher elevations than the Red-breasted, but both species nest in the red fir zone. Even there most Williamson's Sapsuckers stick to forests where lodgepoles are numerous, as around meadows and on rocky slopes and ridgetops.

The Williamson's Sapsucker drums in a characteristic pattern—an opening roll of taps followed by 3 to 5 double or single taps: "tttttt-tt-tt-tt-tt." Like the Red-breasted it eats sap and cambium, but the Williamson's drills holes in irregular rather than neatly-aligned rows. While feeding young, it specializes almost exclusively on ants gleaned from trees, logs and the ground. In the winter, when sap is barely flowing in Sierran conifers, it probably feeds on dormant bark insects.

In the Sierra, Williamson's Sapsuckers often nest in old, living lodgepole pines with rotten heartwood, but they also use red firs and other conifers. Unlike most woodpeckers, which take circuitous routes to their nests to deceive predators, Williamson's usually fly directly to their holes, making nests relatively easy to find.

The winter whereabouts of this species are a mystery, partly because it is so quiet at that season. The few Sierran records come mostly from ponderosa pine and mixed-conifer forests, suggesting a downslope migration. The paucity of sightings at higher elevations, however, may merely reflect the lack of winter observers there. Another possibility is that Sierran populations move south for winter; some Williamson's Sapsuckers migrate south as far as northern Baja California and the Sierra Madre of northern Mexico.

Where Found:
Yosemite: Westfall Meadow, Peregoy Meadow, White Wolf, Porcupine Flat, Tuolumne Meadows. Winter records at Tuolumne Grove, Yosemite Valley and Foresta.
Sequoia-Kings Canyon: Sugarloaf Meadow, Hockett Meadows, Lloyd Meadows Basin (Sequoia National Forest), Troy Meadows (Kern Plateau). Winter records at Grant Grove.

Nuttall's Woodpecker *(Picoides nuttallii)* Plate 16

Nuttall's Woodpeckers are small but hard to overlook, with their frequent and unmistakable calls and their resonant drum-rolls in spring. Like their close relative, the Downy Woodpecker, they use their small bills to probe in crevices and pry off bark in search of insects and only occasionally drill as the larger woodpeckers do. They usually concentrate on tree trunks and large branches, however, while the Downy prefers small branches and twigs. Sometimes Nuttall's Woodpeckers capture insects on the wing and even eat seeds and berries.

While nesting, this species confines itself to the foothills and Central Valley, an elevation range lower than any other Sierran woodpecker. Within this zone it frequents almost all wooded habitats except pure stands of willows, a domain claimed exclusively by Downy Woodpeckers. Most individuals reside year-round at low elevations, but during the nonbreeding season a few venture upslope along watercourses into the mixed-conifer zone. Given a choice, the Nuttall's prefers to forage on oaks and to nest in riparian hardwoods such as willows, cottonwoods and sycamores. Thus it is most common where both habitat types are available, frequently near streams. It usually excavates its nest cavity in dead trees or limbs.

The Ladder-backed Woodpecker of southwestern deserts closely resembles the Nuttall's but has more white on its face and a different call. The ranges of the two species overlap slightly at the southern end of the Sierra, in the South Fork of the Kern River Valley.

Where Found:
Yosemite: Widespread year-round in foothills west of the park, exceptionally breeding up to Mather (4500 feet). Winters fairly regularly in Yosemite Valley.

109

Downy Woodpecker *(Picoides pubescens)*   Plate 16

Smallest of North American woodpeckers, the Downy is almost identical in coloration to the Hairy but has black barring on its white outer tail feathers and a tiny bill, less than half the length of its head. More than any other woodpecker, it sticks to streamside groves of willows, alders and other hardwoods for feeding and nesting. Less often it uses nearby oaks or, rarely, conifers. Orchards, especially apple, often substitute for its natural habitat. This little woodpecker resides fairly commonly year-round in the foothills and ponderosa pine zone and occasionally wanders up to the mixed-conifer belt after breeding.

The Downy Woodpecker usually excavates its small nest- and roost-holes in heavily decayed dead trees or limbs, perhaps because firmer wood offers too formidable a challenge for its small bill. When feeding, it usually searches for insects by flaking off bark or probing into woody crevices with its bill, rather like a large but upright nuthatch. It typically works on small branches and twigs, preferring live trees over dead ones. The Downy's quiet single-note call, and even its hole-drilling, can be heard only from a short distance. It also makes a noisy rattle call, like the Hairy Woodpecker's but higher in pitch and descending at the end, and a loud, regular drumming pattern, also like the Hairy's. The Downy produces these louder signals infrequently, however, making it a difficult species to track down.

Where Found:
Yosemite: Yosemite Valley, Foresta and occasionally higher after breeding.
Sequoia-Kings Canyon: Uncommon at Three Rivers, Ash Mountain and Potwisha.

Hairy Woodpecker *(Picoides villosus)*   Plate 16

From the gray pines of the upper foothills to the lodgepoles of subalpine forests, Hairy Woodpeckers relentlessly chisel away the bark of conifers and riparian hardwoods in pursuit of their prey. Even during harsh Sierran winters, when most birds have deserted higher elevations, these hardy generalists remain. They prefer older forests or recent burns because swarms of bark- and wood-boring beetles lay their eggs in the dead or weakened trees. Like Black-backed Woodpeckers, they move in to feast on the abundant larvae, or "grubs," which they obtain, along with other wood-boring insects, by drilling vigorously or chipping off bark. Pine seeds supplement this diet in winter.

In the eastern United States, Hairy Woodpeckers usually nest in live trees with rotted cores, but in the Sierra most pairs select dead trees. Unlike most woodpeckers, they often nest in small trees, 15 inches in diameter or less. They tend to remain close to their nesting territory for life unless food becomes too scarce.

The Hairy is a noisy, conspicuous woodpecker, often making a sharp single-note call or a loud rattle. Both sexes drum frequently, in a loud, regular, rapid roll. This woodpecker is larger than the similarly plumaged Downy, but size is often difficult to judge; a better mark is the Hairy's larger bill, well over half as long as its head.

Where Found:
Yosemite: Yosemite Valley, Mariposa Grove, Peregoy Meadow, Big Meadow, Tuolumne Grove, Crane Flat, White Wolf, Tuolumne Meadows.
Sequoia-Kings Canyon: Cedar Grove, Williams Meadow, Grant Grove, Tokopah Valley, Wolverton, Giant Forest, Mineral King.

White-headed Woodpecker *(Picoides albolarvatus)*   Plate 17

This striking woodpecker often feeds and nests low on the trunks of giant conifers. Though a familiar and characteristic inhabitant of giant sequoia groves, the White-headed abides, perhaps more than any other Sierran woodpecker, among large pines, especially ponderosa, sugar and Jeffrey. In other parts of its range, studies have shown that more than half of its fall and winter diet consists of pine seeds, extracted mainly from cones still hanging on trees. Near Lake Almanor in the eastern Sierra, White-headed Woodpeckers attacked more than 30% of 1656 sugar pine cones studied, leaving deep vertical trenches and cleaning out most seeds before the cones had opened. In the western Sierra, however, these woodpeckers must need additional winter foods, for all the common pines in their habitat shed their seeds in late summer and fall.

During the nesting season White-headed Woodpeckers feed heavily on insects and spiders, obtained by prying and chipping off bark and searching among clusters of conifer needles. Although they seem to favor pines, they also feed on firs and giant sequoias and may prefer incense cedars in winter. Unlike Pileated and Hairy Woodpeckers inhabiting the same forests, they usually select live trees for feeding and do not drill as much for food. In recently burned forests, however, they join Hairy and Black-backed Woodpeckers to feast on the abundant bark beetle larvae in dead and weakened trees.

White-headed Woodpeckers nest from the ponderosa pine zone up sparingly to the red fir forests. For nest cavities they prefer large, dead, broken-off pines with wood partially decayed to permit excavation, but not so rotten that the nest hole will lose its shape. Compared to other Sierran woodpeckers, they show a tendency to nest low on the trunk, averaging only eight feet above the ground and even using large fallen logs

111

on occasion. In the southern Sierra White-headeds apparently desert red fir and mixed-conifer forests in fall and winter, probably moving down into the ponderosa pine zone.

This woodpecker makes a rapid, even drum-roll sound similar to that of the Hairy. Its sharp two- or three-note call, similar in tone to the Hairy's single harsh note, is quite distinctive. It sounds much like a stronger, sharper version of the Nuttall's call, which is more commonly heard at lower elevations.

Where Found:
Yosemite: Yosemite Valley, Mariposa Grove, Bridalveil Creek, Foresta, Tuolumne Grove, Crane Flat, Gin Flat.
Sequoia-Kings Canyon: Lewis Creek, Cedar Grove, Grant Grove, Lodgepole, Giant Forest, Mineral King.

Black-backed Woodpecker[1] *(Picoides arcticus)*   Plate 17

Like the Pine Grosbeak and Great Gray Owl, the Black-backed Woodpecker's rarity and limited range in the United States make it a treasured find to birdwatchers in the Sierra. These birds occur primarily in cold-climate coniferous forests of Canada and Alaska and in fingerlike southward extensions of these boreal forests in the Rocky Mountains and Sierra Nevada. There all three species reach the southern limits of their ranges.

This woodpecker has only three toes on each foot instead of the usual four but appears just as agile on vertical surfaces as other woodpeckers. The males and immature females sport yellow caps, unique among Sierran woodpeckers save for an occasional freak immature Hairy. Surprisingly bold for a woodpecker, the Black-backed often tolerates close approach. It busily drills and chisels off bark with its unusually long, stout bill, gobbling up grubs, mostly beetle larvae.

Black-backs prefer to forage low on the trunks of dead or dying conifers and choose stands infested with bark- or wood-boring beetles. Although rare in the Sierra, they are fairly common in recently burned forests at higher elevations. Standard forestry practices that prevent forest fires and reduce infestations of boring insects thus deprive this species of prime feeding habitat. Apparently most individuals remain in subalpine and red fir forests, their preferred habitats, through the winter, but some move down to the mixed-conifer and ponderosa pine zones.

The Black-backed makes a harsh, gurgly, descending rattle, an unmistakable call like no other Sierran bird's. It also produces a harsh "chip" call, somewhat like that of the Hairy Woodpecker but more metallic. Like the Hairy, it drums in a regular, rolling pattern. Although often quiet, this

---

[1]*Formerly, Black-backed Three-toed Woodpecker.*

Plate 1

Belted Kingfisher, female
Common Merganser, male
Common Merganser, female

Harlequin Duck, male
Harlequin Duck, female
American Dipper

Plate 2

Wood Duck, male
Eared Grebe, nonbreeding
Pied-billed Grebe, breeding

Great Blue Heron
Mallard, male

Plate 3

Osprey

Bald Eagle

Plate 4

Northern Goshawk, immature

Cooper's Hawk, immature   Sharp-shinned Hawk, immature

Northern Goshawk, adult   Cooper's Hawk, adult

Sharp-shinned Hawk, adult,
with White-crowned Sparrow

Plate 5

Turkey Vulture

Common Raven
Red-tailed Hawk
Golden Eagle

Plate 6

Prairie Falcon
White-throated Swifts | Peregrine Falcon, immature
Peregrine Falcon, adult | American Kestrel, female
American Kestrel, male

Plate 7

California Quail, male
Mountain Quail, male
Blue Grouse, female
Blue Grouse, male

Plate 8

California Gull

Killdeer

Spotted Sandpiper, breeding

American Coot

Plate 9

Mourning Dove

Band-tailed Pigeon

Plate 10

Western Screech-Owl

Northern Pygmy-Owl

Flammulated Owl

Northern Saw-whet Owl, adult

Northern Saw-whet Owl, juvenile

Plate 11

Great Horned Owl

Long-eared Owl

Common Barn-Owl

Plate 12

Spotted Owl

Great Gray Owl

Plate 13

Common Poorwill, male

Common Nighthawk, male

Common Nighthawk, female

Common Poorwill

Plate 14

Black Swift

White-throated Swift

Vaux's Swifts

Plate 15

Anna's Hummingbird, male
Anna's Hummingbird, female
Calliope Hummingbird, male
Calliope Hummingbird, female

Rufous Hummingbird, male
Rufous Hummingbird, female
Black-chinned Hummingbird, male
Black-chinned Hummingbird, female

Plate 16

Downy Woodpecker, male   Hairy Woodpecker, male
            Downy Woodpecker, female
                    Nuttall's Woodpecker, male
            Red-breasted Sapsucker   Acorn Woodpecker, male

Plate 17

White-headed Woodpecker, male   **Pileated Woodpecker,** male
Black-backed Woodpecker, male   **Pileated Woodpecker,** female
    Williamson's Sapsucker, male
Northern Flicker, male   **Williamson's Sapsucker,** female

Plate 18

Olive-sided Flycatcher

Hammond's Flycatcher   Western Wood-Pewee

Plate 19

Western Kingbird   Say's Phoebe
Ash-throated Flycatcher   Black Phoebe

Plate 20

Western Meadowlark
Loggerhead Shrike
Water Pipit
Horned Lark

Plate 21

Violet-green Swallow, male   **Tree Swallow,** male

Northern Rough-winged Swallow

Barn Swallow, male   **Cliff Swallow**

Plate 22

Steller's Jay   Clark's Nutcracker

Scrub Jay

Yellow-billed Magpie

Plate 23

Plain Titmouse

Chestnut-backed Chickadee

Mountain Chickadee   Bushtit

Plate 24

Red-breasted Nuthatch, male
Pygmy Nuthatch

Brown Creeper
White-breasted Nuthatch, male

Plate 25

House Wren

Bewick's Wren

Winter Wren

Canyon Wren

Marsh Wren

Rock Wren

Plate 26

Warbling Vireo Solitary Vireo

Hutton's Vireo

Northern Saw-whet Owl, with Dark-eyed Junco Ruby-crowned Kinglet

Ruby-crowned Kinglet, male, with crest raised

Golden-crowned Kinglet, male

Golden-crowned Kinglet, female

Plate 27

Black-chinned Sparrow, male   Black-chinned Sparrow, female
Lazuli Bunting, male
Lazuli Bunting, female
Blue-gray Gnatcatcher, male
Wrentit   Blue-gray Gnatcatcher, female

Plate 28

Townsend's Solitaire   **Western Bluebird,** male

Western Bluebird, female

Mountain Bluebird, female

Mountain Bluebird, male

Plate 29

Varied Thrush, male

American Robin, male

Swainson's Thrush

Hermit Thrush

Plate 30

Northern Mockingbird   Phainopepla, male
California Thrasher

Cedar Waxwing

Plate 31

Nashville Warbler, male
Nashville Warbler, female

Common Yellowthroat, male
Common Yellowthroat, female

Orange-crowned Warbler
Wilson's Warbler, male
Wilson's Warbler, female
MacGillivray's Warbler, female
MacGillivray's Warbler, male

Plate 32

Hermit Warbler, male	**Yellow-rumped Warbler**, nonbreeding
Hermit Warbler, female	**Yellow-rumped Warbler**, breeding male
	Black-throated Gray Warbler, male
Townsend's Warbler, male	**Black-throated Gray Warbler**, female
Townsend's Warbler, female	**Yellow Warbler**, male
	Yellow Warbler, female

Plate 33

Evening Grosbeak, male

Black-headed Grosbeak, male

Black-headed Grosbeak, female

Northern Oriole, male   Western Tanager, female

Northern Oriole, female   Western Tanager, male

Plate 34

Rufous-sided Towhee, male
Rufous-sided Towhee, female
Brown Towhee
Green-tailed Towhee

Plate 35

Lark Sparrow

Chipping Sparrow, adult
Chipping Sparrow, immature

Sage Sparrow

Rufous-crowned Sparrow

Plate 36

Grasshopper Sparrow

Vesper Sparrow
Savannah Sparrow

Song Sparrow
Lincoln's Sparrow

Fox Sparrow

Plate 37

Golden-crowned Sparrow, immature   White-crowned Sparrow, adult
Golden-crowned Sparrow, adult   White-crowned Sparrow, immature
Dark-eyed Junco, Slate-colored
Dark-eyed Junco, Oregon
House Sparrow, female   House Sparrow, male

Plate 38

Red-winged Blackbird, male

Brown-headed Cowbird, male

Brewer's Blackbird, male

European Starling, breeding

Plate 39

Red Crossbill, male

Pine Grosbeak, male   **Red Crossbill**, female

Pine Grosbeak, female

Rosy Finch, female   **Rosy Finch**, male

Plate 40

Cassin's Finch, female   **Cassin's Finch**, male
Purple Finch, female   **Purple Finch**, male
House Finch, female   **House Finch**, male

Plate 41

Lawrence's Goldfinch, female
   Lawrence's Goldfinch, male   Lesser Goldfinch, male
                                        Lesser Goldfinch, female
   Pine Siskin   American Goldfinch, male
                             American Goldfinch, female

Plate 42

Vegetation Zones of the Western Sierra Nevada

STEVE GRANHOLM

Foothill grassland

STEVE GRANHOLM

Foothill chaparral

JOHN HARRIS

Foothill woodland

Plate 43

E.C. BEEDY

Ponderosa pine

E.C. BEEDY

Red fir

Mixed-conifer

E.C. BEEDY

Plate 44

STEVE GRANHOLM

Subalpine

E.C. BEEDY

Alpine

Special Habitats

E.C. BEEDY

Wet meadow

E.C. BEEDY

Riparian deciduous

woodpecker can be noisy near its nest, particularly when disturbed. It excavates a cavity in a live or dead conifer, usually below 20 feet. Nest trees are often small, sometimes less than ten inches in diameter.

Where Found:
Yosemite: Peregoy Meadow, Siesta Lake, White Wolf, Porcupine Creek, Mt. Watkins. A few winter records at lower elevations such as Crane Flat, Hodgdon Meadow and Yosemite Valley.
Sequoia-Kings Canyon: Has nested at Sugarloaf Valley and Lodgepole Campground; also recorded at Blaney Meadow, Crown Valley, Rattlesnake Creek (Middle Fork Kings River), Weaver Lake, Twin Lakes and Mineral King.

Northern Flicker[1] *(Colaptes auratus)* Plate 17

Until recently the three races of the Northern Flicker were considered separate species. The western race, the Red-shafted Flicker, was named for the colorful underlinings of its wings and tail. Native Sierran peoples highly valued these bright salmon-red feathers and wove the stiff wing and tail quills along with abalone shells and other ornaments into their elaborate ceremonial robes and headdresses. Using traps, snares, nets and small arrows, they took flickers and other birds for both feathers and meat.

Flickers' red underwings, polka-dot breasts and red "whiskers" (males only) set them apart from all other Sierran woodpeckers. Also remarkable is their cosmopolitan taste in habitats, equalled by no other woodpecker and few other birds in the Sierra: they nest in all forest types from the Central Valley up to tree line! Flickers prefer open forests with large, scattered trees and open ground for feeding, and most of them retreat below the heavy snows for the winter. At this season they may gather in small groups to feed.

Flickers avoid snow-covered areas because, unlike other woodpeckers, they obtain most of their food on the ground. They eat mainly ants, but also other insects, seeds and fruits. Although they sometimes take bark-dwelling insects, most flickers pecking on trees are engaged in other pursuits. They communicate by drumming on trees in loud, regular patterns, and they excavate holes in dead or live trees for nests and winter roosts. Except for Pileated Woodpeckers, flickers are the largest Sierran woodpeckers and drill the biggest nest cavities, which may be of great importance to small owls, kestrels, and other wildlife that cannot use the holes of smaller woodpeckers.

The Northern Flicker makes a loud "ca-ca-ca-ca...," slowing at the end, often mistaken for a Pileated Woodpecker, but more constant in pitch. In

[1]*Formerly, Common Flicker; before that, Red-shafted Flicker.*

fall and winter an occasional Yellow-shafted Flicker shows up in the Sierra. This eastern form of the Northern Flicker has yellow underlinings in its wings and tail, different head coloration than the Red-shafted, and black rather than red mustache marks (on males). Some of the Sierran records are probably of hybrids between the Red-shafted and Yellow-shafted forms.

Where Found:
Yosemite: Yosemite Valley, Wawona, Mariposa Grove, Chinquapin, Hodgdon Meadow, Tuolumne Grove, Crane Flat, Gin Flat, Tuolumne Meadows.
Sequoia-Kings Canyon: Ash Mountain, Potwisha, Elk Creek, Hospital Rock, Giant Forest, Grant Grove, Cedar Grove; has nested as high as 10,000 feet at Silliman Creek.

Pileated Woodpecker *(Dryocopus pileatus)*   Plate 17, Title Page

As large as a crow, with a jet-black body and flaming red crest, the Pileated Woodpecker is as spectacular and unforgettable as any bird in the Sierra. Although seldom seen, it can be heard at great distances, calling loudly or drumming a rolling tattoo. One call, a repeated "kak-kak-kak-kak...," closely resembles that of the Northern Flicker but is louder and often rises and falls slightly in pitch. The Pileated may be shy or surprisingly fearless, sometimes allowing a close approach.

This largest of Sierran woodpeckers finds its optimal habitat in the most majestic stands of trees: the giant sequoias and towering pines and firs of the mixed-conifer zone. Less commonly it lives in ponderosa pine and red fir forests. Not migratory, it remains near its nesting territory year-round. Because each pair requires several hundred acres of fairly dense, mature forest, Pileated Woodpeckers in the Sierra have undoubtedly declined due to logging, especially recent clearcutting. They also suffer from forestry "sanitation" practices, which remove the dead trees and logs they use for feeding and nesting.

With powerful, deliberate blows, Pileated Woodpeckers chisel into dead wood or strip away loose bark to extract carpenter ants and beetle larvae, their preferred prey. These deep, massive excavations, often roughly rectangular, provide unmistakable evidence of their presence in an area. In late summer and fall they supplement their diet with berries and nuts. They have been seen hanging like oversized chickadees from the slender branches of dogwoods and elderberries, pecking at berries and flapping awkwardly to change positions.

Most nests found in the Sierra have been in large dead conifers or live aspens. The oval or triangular nest holes, about four to five inches across, provide homes for many of the larger hole-nesting birds and are the only woodpecker cavities large enough to accommodate Wood Ducks and Common Mergansers.

Where Found:
Yosemite: Yosemite Valley (e.g. Mirror Lake), Wawona Meadow, Mariposa Grove, Westfall Meadow, Hodgdon Meadow, Tuolumne Grove, Crane Flat, Gin Flat.
Sequoia-Kings Canyon: Zumwalt Meadows, Giant Forest, Huckleberry Meadow, Crystal Cave Road, Colony Mill Road.

TYRANT FLYCATCHERS *(Family Tyrannidae)*

Called tyrants for their aggressive territorial behavior, these flycatchers vigorously drive away intruders of their own species and potential predators like jays and hawks. Although their vocal apparatus is less complex than that of other members of the order Passeriformes, each species produces a simple but distinctive song. Tyrannids capture insects in midair, and their broad bills, slightly hooked at the tips, are well adapted for this "hawking" or "flycatching" habit. Prominent rictal bristles around the bill were once thought to aid in capturing insects, but recent experiments suggest that these stiff modified feathers serve primarily to protect their eyes from insects that are missed. Almost entirely insectivorous, flycatchers of several species nevertheless eat a few berries in late summer.

Except for the two phoebes, tyrannids all migrate long distances southward for the winter, departing by August or September and not returning until April or May.

Olive-sided Flycatcher *(Contopus borealis)* Plate 18

Olive-sided Flycatchers lead enviable lives, singing and hunting from the tallest treetops, overlooking broad Sierran landscapes. From such commanding viewpoints these large, stocky flycatchers make long acrobatic flights in pursuit of flying insects. They build their bowl-shaped nests at great heights as well, usually on horizontal branches more than 40 feet above the ground.

Their easily imitated song, "hic-three-beers," consists of three rapid, whistled notes, the middle one the highest. Once learned, it makes the Olive-sided easy to find, for it can be heard at great distances, as can the "pip-pip-pip" calls.

Olive-sided Flycatchers breed in coniferous forests of all but the highest subalpine types, preferring forest clearings and edges. They generally avoid dense stands except where scattered giant conifers tower over thick growths of younger trees. During spring and late summer, migrants appear sparingly in streamside hardwoods and foothill oak woodlands.

115

An Olive-sided might be mistaken for a Western Wood-Pewee but has a larger head and bill, a shorter tail and a sharp white line down the center of its dark olive-brown breast, creating a distinct "vested" appearance.

Where Found:
Yosemite: Yosemite Valley, Mariposa Grove, Wawona, Peregoy Meadow, Foresta, Hodgdon Meadow, Crane Flat, Porcupine Creek, Olmsted Point.
Sequoia-Kings Canyon: Grant Grove, Wolverton, Giant Forest, High Sierra Trail, Crystal Cave Road, Mineral King.

Western Wood-Pewee *(Contopus sordidulus)* Plate 18

No other flycatcher and few other birds are so widespread in the Sierra as the Western Wood-Pewee. This versatile species nests in all wooded habitats except for the densest forests, from the Central Valley up to the subalpine zone. It feeds in forest clearings, often in burned and selectively logged areas, but especially along the edges of moist meadows and boggy lakes where insects are plentiful. In such locations the pewee's buzzy, downslurred "pee-er" is a frequent and familiar accompaniment to the more melodious bird songs around it. At dawn, and occasionally during the day, pewees produce a more musical call, reminiscent of the "dee-hic" of the Dusky Flycatcher.

Larger than *Empidonax* flycatchers, pewees also make longer flights in pursuit of insects. They hunt from exposed perches, typically at moderate heights, that afford them broad views of the surrounding airspace. They build compact cup-nests on horizontal branches or forks, often in plain view.

Easy to mistake for the smaller *Empidonax*, the pewee can be distinguished by its darker, brownish coloration, lack of eye rings, peaked rather than rounded head, slimmer appearance and distinctly longer wings, reaching well beyond the base of the tail; also, the pewee rarely flicks its tail as the *Empidonax* species do (but note that one *Empidonax*, the Willow Flycatcher, is brownish and often lacks eye rings).

Where Found:
Yosemite: Yosemite Valley, Wawona, Peregoy Meadow, Glacier Point, Foresta, Hodgdon Meadow, Crane Flat, Porcupine Flat, Tuolumne Meadows.
Sequoia-Kings Canyon: Cedar Grove, Lodgepole, Giant Forest, Colony Mill, High Sierra Trail, Kern Canyon, Mineral King.

Empidonax flycatchers

The five small, active flycatchers of the genus *Empidonax* that occur in the Sierra Nevada look so much alike that even experienced ornithologists have difficulty distinguishing them in the field. Nevertheless, they are distinct species, rarely interbreeding in nature, and each occupies a different habitat while nesting. Birds show up in the "wrong" places often enough, however, to make identification based on habitat alone risky. Four of the five species definitely breed in the western Sierra. The Gray Flycatcher nests along the base of the east slope; it occurs west of the crest as a rare spring migrant through the foothills and is a possible breeder on the Kern Plateau.

Figure 11. Although no single mark is entirely reliable for distinguishing the look-alike Hammond's (a) and Dusky (b) Flycatchers in the field, the following pointers are useful in good viewing conditions. The Hammond's sits with its tail almost vertical and has an overall "dumpier" appearance, being larger-headed, shorter-billed, shorter-tailed and longer-winged. It has more contrast between its face and throat and a crisper, more distinct eye ring than the Dusky. Hammond's breast is somewhat darker, forming a broad band suggesting a "buttoned vest." The Dusky often sits with the tail at a 45° angle, appears sleeker overall, and has a less distinct chest band that often does not meet in the center. Finally, Dusky has a darker tail that contrasts subtly with its rump, while Hammond's shows little or no contrast.

On the nesting grounds the surest way to distinguish these small fly-catchers is by voice, but behavioral clues and subtle differences in coloration also help. The Gray, Willow and Western Flycatchers produce distinctive songs that are best learned by listening to singing males in typical habitats during the nesting season. The Gray pumps its tail downward instead of upward as the other four species do. Willow Flycatchers show only faint eye rings, if any, and are brownish above; they are often confused with Western Wood-Pewees (see p. 116). Only the Western Flycatcher has a yellow throat, and its back is a brighter greenish-olive than other Sierran *Empidonax*.

With their olive-drab backs and whitish throats, Hammond's and Dusky Flycatchers differ only subtly in appearance (see Fig. 11). Their songs are also similar but can be told apart after some practice. While most of the Dusky's notes are clear-toned, many of the Hammond's have a rough, burry quality. Typically the Dusky seems less nervous than the Hammond's and seldom flits its wings except when calling or first landing on a perch.

During migration (in spring and late summer) field identification of *Empidonax* is even more difficult. Not only are most individuals silent at such times, but the species overlap widely in habitats. Serious birders should consult the more complete discussions of *Empidonax* identification by McCaskie et al. and Farrand (see Bibliography).

Willow Flycatcher[1] *(Empidonax trailii)*

No name could be more appropriate for this small brownish flycatcher that nests almost exclusively in patches of shrubby willows. Few other Sierran birds are so specialized in their choice of habitat. Willows in wet meadows and beside streams and lakes provide foraging lookouts and roost sites as well as concealment for nests.

Willow Flycatchers have declined seriously throughout California in recent decades. Formerly common up to the ponderosa pine zone and higher, they have completely disappeared as a nesting species in the foot-hills, except along the Kern River, and are quite rare at higher elevations. This alarming decline almost surely derives in large part from human impacts on their habitats. Willow patches have been flooded by reservoirs, dried up by water diversions, overbrowsed by cattle and cleared for recreational developments. Willow Flycatchers are also especially vulnerable to nest parasitism by Brown-headed Cowbirds, which have increased dramatically at low elevations since 1940. Growing numbers of cowbirds now invade the higher mountains in summer, posing a serious threat to the

[1]*This species and the Alder Flycatcher formerly were combined as a single species, Traill's Flycatcher.*

118

remaining Willow Flycatchers that nest there.

Willow Flycatchers still nest in scattered locations in the ponderosa pine and mixed-conifer zones. They are most numerous in broad river valleys such as the South Fork Kern River Valley east of Lake Isabella. In late spring and late summer moderate numbers of nonbreeders migrate through these middle elevations and the foothills. Because spring migrants often linger well into June and occasionally sing, they may easily be mistaken for breeding birds. They can also be difficult to distinguish from Western Wood-Pewees and from other *Empidonax* (see p. 116-118).

Where Found:
Yosemite: Recent breeding at Hodgdon Meadow, Wawona, and Ackerson Meadow (just west of the park), probably at Crane Flat and Peregoy Meadow and possibly at Westfall Meadow; apparently no longer breeds in Yosemite Valley, where it once was common.
Sequoia-Kings Canyon: Grant Grove Meadow, Zumwalt Meadow and (at least formerly) meadows in Giant Forest.

Hammond's Flycatcher *(Empidonax hammondii)* Plate 18, Figure 11

A small, nervous flycatcher in tall, shady groves of white or red fir is most likely a Hammond's. This species is notoriously difficult to distinguish from the Dusky Flycatcher (see p. 116-118), which overlaps it in habitat use, particularly during migration. According to many accounts, the Hammond's Flycatcher feeds high in the trees, while the Dusky frequents lower levels, but this distinction is less consistent than their differences in breeding habitat. The Dusky inhabits sunny, open forests and forest edges, while the Hammond's chooses shady spots beneath dense canopies. In such cool environments it nests, sings and forages at low levels as well as high. It makes short aerial forays after insects, only rarely venturing far from the sheltering foliage or branchwork of trees.

Hammond's Flycatchers are most common in mixed-conifer and red fir forests, but they also nest sparingly in shady forests of the subalpine and ponderosa pine zones. In the latter habitat they may breed side by side with Western Flycatchers, especially near streams. Migrating Hammond's Flycatchers occur rarely in foothill oak woodlands, broadleaved riparian stands and even up nearly to tree line.

Where Found:
Yosemite: Mariposa Grove, Glacier Point area, Tuolumne Grove, Crane Flat, Porcupine Flat.
Sequoia-Kings Canyon: Grant Grove, Zumwalt Meadow, Giant Forest, Mineral King.

Dusky Flycatcher *(Empidonax oberholseri)* Figure 11

The Dusky Flycatcher is the sun-loving counterpart of the confusingly similar, shade-dwelling Hammond's. Both species nest from the ponderosa pine zone up to subalpine forests, but the Dusky chooses more sunny, open stands. Dusky Flycatchers are equally at home on brushy slopes or rocky ridges with scattered trees, in open lodgepole pine forests with grassy understories or along the edges of denser forests. Of all the Sierran flycatchers, only the Dusky weathers harsh subalpine conditions to nest in the highest stands of gnarled pines. Unlike the Hammond's it is widespread on the east slope.

Dusky Flycatchers build their nests on low branches of trees or shrubs, usually below seven feet. They typically sing and sally for insects from low exposed perches but also perch higher up. Less nervous than the Hammond's, they rarely flit their wings except when calling or just after landing on a perch (see p. 116-118).

Where Found:
Yosemite: Hodgdon Meadow, Mariposa Grove, Henness Ridge, Crane Flat Lookout, White Wolf, Tuolumne Meadows.
Sequoia-Kings Canyon: Cedar Grove, Giant Forest, Kern Canyon, Redwood Meadow, Lloyd Meadows (Sequoia National Forest).

Western Flycatcher *(Empidonax difficilis)*

Although drab by most standards, the Western Flycatcher is the most showy Sierran *Empidonax;* it is greener above and brighter yellow below than the other four species. It also chooses the most luxuriant habitat—lush, streamside forests of hardwoods such as maples, alders and oaks, often mixed with conifers. Rather uncommon while breeding, it is mostly confined to the ponderosa pine zone at that season but also occurs sparsely in the foothills and mixed-conifer zone. Only rarely does it co-occur with the Hammond's Flycatcher, in dense, moist conifer forests. In late summer, after nesting, it occasionally reaches higher elevations, sometimes nearly to tree line, and in spring it migrates fairly commonly through foothill woodlands.

The Western Flycatcher is easily recognized by its distinctive call, a sharp, rising, whistled "su-wheet," which also serves as one of the three short phrases in its song. This species is more readily identified by its coloration than other Sierran *Empidonax* (see p. 116-118).

Western Flycatchers build nests in a remarkable variety of sites, including crotches of small trees; holes in cliffs, banks or tree trunks; and occasionally in old buildings or the undersides of bridges.

Where Found:
Yosemite: Mirror Lake (Yosemite Valley), below Foresta, below Tuolumne Grove and west of the park at El Portal and Hardin Flat.
Sequoia-Kings Canyon: Zumwalt Meadows, Wolverton, Mineral King.

Black Phoebe *(Sayornis nigricans)* Plate 19

Even a small pond, irrigation ditch or water trough may provide sufficient moisture to attract a breeding pair of Black Phoebes. Their energetic calls and crisply contrasting plumage grace the banks of foothill streams and lakes and rarely up to the ponderosa pine forests. No other Sierran flycatcher is so closely associated with water. Fairly common in the foothills, these small flycatchers prefer areas shaded by canyon walls or trees, but use open, sunny areas as well. They are not shy and will forage from rooftops and garden shrubbery.

Black Phoebes fly out from low perches to catch insects and even snatch small fish from the water surface. For nest-building they need a source of mud, which they plaster along with plant fibers onto rough vertical rock walls or structures such as bridges, buildings or culverts. A pair once nested on top of a spotlight at the Cedar Grove amphitheater in Kings Canyon.

Unlike other Sierran flycatchers, Black Phoebes generally remain year-round on their nesting range, and some even winter above the foothills. After breeding, a few occasionally wander as high as the subalpine zone.

Where Found:
Yosemite: Yosemite Valley, Wawona, Foresta, Hodgdon Meadow; west of the Park at El Portal and Hardin Flat.
Sequoia-Kings Canyon: Common at Three Rivers, Ash Mountain, Potwisha and Cedar Grove.

Say's Phoebe *(Sayornis saya)* Plate 19

While Black Phoebes need water, Say's Phoebes shun it. These dry-country flycatchers nest chiefly in the high deserts east of the Sierra but also in the San Joaquin Valley and adjacent Sierra foothills. In their arid environment, they can hardly build mud-nests like the Black Phoebe. Instead they seek out rock walls or earthen banks with crevices or ledges to support their nests. They frequently nest under bridges and in deserted buildings and sometimes in tree cavities.

Say's Phoebes inhabit open terrain with few if any trees or shrubs. From perches on fences, shrubs or rocks, they scan for low-flying insects, sometimes hovering like bluebirds before snapping their prey in mid-air, off low plants or even from the ground. Occasional migrants may be seen in the ponderosa pine zone or even higher, especially during March and

April. In winter, however, Say's Phoebes confine themselves to the lower foothills and Central Valley.

Where Found:
Yosemite: Rare spring migrant in Yosemite Valley. Winters west of the park in the lower foothills around Snelling and La Grange.
Sequoia-Kings Canyon: Rare in winter around Lake Kaweah, west of the parks. Breeds at the southern end of the Sierra in the South Fork Kern River Valley and foothills of the Greenhorn Mountains.

Ash-throated Flycatcher *(Myiarchus cinerascens)* Plate 19

With its subtle blend of ashy gray, pale yellow and rufous, the Ash-throated is perhaps the most beautiful of Sierran flycatchers. Its most frequent call resembles the rolling warble of a softly-blown referee's whistle. Like the Western Kingbird it inhabits the arid foothills, often far from water, and flycatches from low perches. The Ash-throated, however, lives in areas with more shrubs and is the only breeding flycatcher of the foothill chaparral. It seems to prefer open oak woodlands with brushy understories, and because it nests in woodpecker holes and other cavities at least one tree must be present. Like many cavity-nesters that do not excavate their own holes, the Ash-throated Flycatcher builds a substantial nest within.

Many flycatchers return to the same perch after pursuing an insect, but the Ash-throated often moves on to a new one and thus feeds over a broader area. Sometimes it picks insects off of foliage as well as in flight. After breeding, individuals occasionally wander up to the mixed-conifer zone or even higher before departing for the winter.

Where Found:
Yosemite: Very rare in the park after breeding; recorded at Big Meadow, Hodgdon Meadow, Yosemite Valley and the north shore of Hetch Hetchy. Breeds west of the park at El Portal, below Foresta, and around Moccasin and Coulterville.
Sequoia-Kings Canyon: Three Rivers, Ash Mountain, Elk Creek, Potwisha, Hospital Rock, Buckeye Flats.

Western Kingbird *(Tyrannus verticalis)* Plate 19

In Sierra foothill grasslands and sparse woodlands a large, yellow-bellied flycatcher often attracts notice as it perches on roadside fences or engages in twisting, turning flight, pursuing insects. This is the Western Kingbird, the largest and most brightly-colored of Sierran flycatchers. Kingbirds prefer dry, open habitats with scattered trees, fences, telephone lines, or other lookouts for hunting insects. They usually avoid landscapes dominated by shrubs and trees.

When trees are present, they build nests on horizontal branches, but otherwise structures such as telephone poles, barns, and even fenceposts suffice. Unlike most flycatchers, Western Kingbirds coexist peacefully with others of their species nesting nearby, even in the same tree. They are highly aggressive, however, toward hawks, crows and ravens and may drive away other birds as well; hence the name kingbird.

During migration, especially in May and August, Western Kingbirds appear rarely in open habitats above the foothills, up to the subalpine zone. Like most flycatchers they winter in Mexico and Central America, where more insects are available at that season.

Where Found:
Yosemite: Postbreeding records at Big Meadow and Yosemite Valley. Breeds west of the park at Snelling, La Grange, Coulterville, Chinese Camp, El Portal and below Foresta.
Sequoia-Kings Canyon: Three Rivers, Ash Mountain, Elk Creek, Potwisha, Hospital Rock, Buckeye Flats.

LARKS *(Family Alaudidae)*

Horned Lark *(Eremophila alpestris)*   Plate 20
Despite their small black "horns," golden throats and bold face and breast markings, Horned Larks are easily overlooked. Flocks walk or run across open terrain, and the sandy browns of their backs blend in with dirt clods and tussocks of grass. They pick up insects, weed seeds and other foods from the ground with their short, slender bills. These skittish birds take flight if approached too closely, usually give a shrill "zee" when flushed, and continue with tinkling notes as they depart in low undulating flight. As they fly away, their blackish tails flash white at the outer feathers.

Like Song Sparrows, Horned Larks come in many races across our continent, and four or five of these occur in the western Sierra. These races fall into two categories: residents of the Central Valley and west slope foothills, and those of the Great Basin, which range up the east slope to the alpine zone and spill over the crest in scattered locations. Horned Larks rarely show up in mid-elevation habitats on the west slope. Lowland larks favor short, sparse grasslands or cultivated fields on level ground or gentle hillsides; they avoid trees and shrubs. The alpine races breed rarely in large, open fell-fields and mountain meadows of short sedges and grasses. Although Horned Larks occur at high elevations in the northern Sierra during late summer, nesting on the west slope has been confirmed only in central and southern portions of the range. A few birds remain in the high country each winter, as do Rosy Finches, but most move down to open habitats east of the Sierra. Horned Larks form flocks during the nonbreeding season, but from March until July they pair off, voicing cheery "see-see-di" songs and nesting in simple depressions on bare ground.

Where Found:
Yosemite: Low elevations—probably in open grasslands along Highways 120 and 140 east of Oakdale and Planada, noted up to Yosemite Valley. High elevations—Ten Lakes, Roosevelt Lake, Mono Pass and just east of the park at Dana Plateau.
Sequoia-Kings Canyon: Low elevations—probably in open grasslands along Highways 180 and 198 east of Centerville and west of Three Rivers; noted historically at Ash Mountain. High elevations—Upper Basin, Kern Basin, Mitre Basin. Recorded up to 9600 feet near Pear Lake in February.

SWALLOWS *(Family Hirundinidae)*

Swallows spend much of their day diving and turning at exceptional speeds as they pursue flying insects and take them in midair with gaping mouths. Their small, weak feet are not suited to walking but do allow them to perch securely on branches, rooftops or telephone wires.

Most swallows nest in some kind of cavity, either found or of their own making. Some colonial species, such as Cliff Swallows, nest together by the thousands. When autumn chills diminish the summer's horde of flying insects, most swallows leave for warmer southern quarters.

Tree Swallow *(Tachycineta bicolor)* Plate 21

Unlike other members of their family, Tree Swallows regularly overwinter in small numbers in the lowlands of central California. These sleek, iridescent blue-green birds are often the first swallows to arrive in the western Sierra in spring and among the last to leave in fall. This hardiness may in part derive from their vegetarian tendencies. They eat berries and seeds when insects are sparse and so can sustain themselves when exclusively insect-eating swallows might starve.

Tree Swallows make sweet, musical twitterings as they forage above lakes, marshes and damp meadows. Although they regularly nest up to the ponderosa pine zone, they are uncommon and unpredictable, possibly due to a shortage of nesting sites. They prefer to nest near water and often seek out holes in trees and stumps in recently flooded areas.

Adult Tree Swallows may be confused with the similarly colored Violet-greens; the former are a greenish-blue on their backs and wings, while the latter are a lime-green. More significantly, Tree Swallows lack the large white cheek and rump patches of the Violet-greens and have longer tails and wings.

Where Found:
Yosemite: West of the park at Don Pedro Reservoir, lower canyons of the Tuolumne and Merced Rivers and Hardin Flat; Yosemite Valley; unusually high-elevation nesting at Tuolumne Meadows.
Sequoia-Kings Canyon: Kern Canyon near Whitney Creek; Ash Mountain.

Violet-green Swallow *(Tachycineta thalassina)*   Plate 21

Darting through the mists above Sierran waterfalls or cruising in wide arcs above mountain lakes and meadows, Violet-greens are the most abundant Sierran swallows. They breed commonly in open oak woodlands of the foothills and fairly commonly in the coniferous forest zones up to the subalpine. Definite evidence of nesting has been found at Granite Basin (10,000 feet) in Fresno County and possibly higher. Violet-greens are less selective in their choice of breeding sites than the other swallows. They nest high or low on rocky cliffs above river gorges and in holes in bridges, dams, buildings and trees. Recently burned forests attract insects and also provide abundant nest-sites in hollow trees. Some Violet-greens nest in small colonies, but others nest alone. Peak breeding occurs from April to July, and by late August they begin their southward migration.

Violet-green Swallows sometimes mingle with Tree Swallows or White-throated Swifts. The swifts have longer, more pointed wings, but the two swallows are harder to separate. Violet-greens have white semicircles on their flanks that nearly meet on their rumps, and white face patches that entirely surround their eyes. They also have shorter tails and wings.

Where Found:
Yosemite: El Portal, Yosemite Valley, Wawona Meadow, Chinquapin, Big Meadow, Hodgdon Meadow, Crane Flat, Tuolumne Meadows.
Sequoia-Kings Canyon: Zumwalt Meadows, Roaring River Falls, Cedar Grove, Grant Grove Meadow, Moro Rock, Potwisha, Ash Mountain.

Northern Rough-winged Swallow[1] *(Stelgidopteryx serripennis)*
Plate 21

Compared to the rich rusts and metallic blues and greens of other swallows, the modest browns and grays of the Rough-winged's plumage seem drab indeed. Though other swallows surpass them in beauty, rough-wings are equally adept in flight. They forage low over water or marshy

[1]*Formerly, Rough-winged Swallow.*

habitats, skillfully darting around shrubs and vine-tangles, rarely mounting high in the air like other swallows. Rough-wings are fairly common in the foothills of the western Sierra and occasionally nest up to the ponderosa pine zone. Unlike most other swallows, they forage frequently over arid grasslands and chaparral, as well as over rivers, lakes and wet meadows.

Rough-winged Swallows usually arrive in the lower foothills by March. They search out nest holes in low banks of sand or clay, often beside lakes or languid streams. They do not require water at the nesting site, but only within cruising range. The nest is usually an abandoned rodent or kingfisher burrow, but may be dug out by the swallows themselves. They will nest alone, or several pairs may nest in close proximity on the same earthen bank. By late July and early August, most pairs have completed rearing their young and begin their southward migration.

The pale dusky-browns of Rough-wings resemble Bank Swallows, but the former lack clearly defined breast bands and have longer wings.

Where Found:
Yosemite: West of the park along the Merced and Tuolumne Rivers and at El Portal and Hardin Flat; in park at Big Meadow and Yosemite Valley; a few records from Wawona.
Sequoia-Kings Canyon: Three Rivers, Ash Mountain, Potwisha.

Cliff Swallow *(Hirundo pyrrhonota)* Plate 21

Cliff Swallows are one of the few native birds that have benefited from human activity. The cement faces of dams, undersides of bridges, eaves of buildings and walls of deserted stone quarries readily substitute for their natural nesting sites on canyon walls. A single colony of these swallows may contain thousands of nests. Like Barn Swallows, parents build their nest from mud. Cliff Swallows search for just the right puddle edge, usually the nearest one with suitable mud, then form it into pellets with their bills. They fly endlessly back and forth from nest site to puddle, swarming and fluttering frantically as if the mud were in short supply. Construction of the flask-shaped nests may take up to two weeks. They build synchronously, and neighbors crowd in upon each other, often squabbling and stealing mud pellets.

Females lay their three or four eggs before completing the roofs of their mud homes. Although Cliff Swallows no doubt derive some protection from predators by nesting colonially high on walls, they are also vulnerable to prolonged spring storms that batter their exposed homes and to humans who sometimes hose these creations off buildings. Perhaps their worst enemies, however, are the introduced House Sparrows that drive Cliff Swallows from their homes after completion.

Cliff Swallows feed over smooth water, grasslands and chaparral of the Central Valley and Sierra foothills and can be abundant in places. At higher elevations, however, they are rare and intermittent breeders up to the ponderosa pine zone, occurring particularly on dams that block Sierran streams. One high-elevation outpost of about 30 pairs nested in Amador County at 8400 feet.

Cliff Swallows' range in the Sierra overlaps broadly with that of Barn Swallows. While the two species often consort while feeding, the nearly square tails, buff-colored rumps and creamy-white foreheads of Cliff Swallows make it easy to recognize them.

Where Found:
Yosemite: Has nested on the O'Shaugnessy Dam on the Tuolumne River, and west of the park at Groveland and Hardin Flat; also recorded at El Portal and in Yosemite Valley.
Sequoia-Kings Canyon: Bridges along the Middle Fork Kaweah River at Three Rivers; also at Ash Mountain, Elk Creek and Marble Falls.

Barn Swallow *(Hirundo rustica)* Plate 21

Like Cliff Swallows, Barn Swallows are expert masons. They form their cup-shaped nests by painstakingly alternating layers of straw and mud pellets. They choose bridges, beams or barn rafters for the foundations of their homes.

By early March, Barn Swallows begin to arrive in California, but usually they do not start nest construction until April. During the breeding season they are common in the Central Valley and the Sierra foothills and are fairly common up to the ponderosa pine zone. Though uncommon higher, nesting birds have been noted at Lake Van Norden (6700 feet) in Nevada County and as high as 6000 feet in Tehama, Butte and Plumas Counties. They feed over open ponds, slow-moving streams, grasslands and wet meadows. Their nesting and foraging preferences draw Barn Swallows to farms with irrigated pastures.

Picking out Barn Swallows in a mixed swarm of whirling swallows is easy even if colors are not visible, because their tails are unique. They are deeply forked when fanned out, but long and needlelike when closed. Barn Swallows sing a high-pitched chatter with a finale of deeper, guttural notes.

Where Found:
Yosemite: El Portal, Yosemite Valley, Wawona, Big Meadow, Hodgdon Meadow.
Sequoia-Kings Canyon: Common below Terminus Dam (Lake Kaweah); also recorded at Marble Falls Bridge and surprisingly in Muir Hut on Muir Pass (12,000 feet) during a summer storm.

CROWS AND JAYS *(Family Corvidae)*

These raucous songbirds are often disparaged for "camp-robbing," eating garbage and carrion and scolding human trespassers with loud, harsh cries. Many bird students, however, are fascinated by the corvids' superior learning abilities, keen memories and complex vocal repertoires. These large, bold birds have strong legs and long, stout bills. Highly omnivorous, they feed on small animals, carrion, seeds, and fruit; they search over large areas, quickly exploiting new sources of food. They often forage along roads, eating animals killed by vehicles.

Steller's Jay *(Cyanocitta stelleri)* — Plate 22, Cover

Noisy, bold and inquisitive, these striking black and blue jays are among the best known birds of the Sierra. Steller's Jays, miscalled Blue Jays by some, actually are the western counterparts of those similarly crested eastern birds.

Steller's Jays' impressive intelligence is demonstrated by their rapid exploitation of new food resources. In the absence of humans, they subsist largely on seeds, insects and fruit, but will readily feed on small animals, birds' eggs and young and on carrion. Around houses, farms and campgrounds, they soon learn to seek garbage and handouts. Unfortunately, the thriving populations of Steller's Jays around human settlements no doubt reduce the numbers of less aggressive songbirds by destroying nests.

Steller's Jays are widespread throughout Sierran conifer forests up to the red fir zone, and occur much higher around stables, campgrounds and other developed areas. Strangely, they seem to avoid lodgepole pine forests, even the large groves that occur within the red fir zone, except where humans have enhanced the food supply. Many of them remain at high elevations throughout the winter, but in most years a substantial number move down into foothill woodlands and riparian forests to feed on acorns and berries.

Despite their otherwise conspicuous behavior, Steller's Jays are among the most secretive nesters in the Sierra. They hide their large bowl-shaped nests in the foliage of conifers, often below 15 feet. Parents keep extremely quiet around the nest and vary their routes to and from feeding areas, perhaps to confuse potential predators.

Steller's Jays employ a complex vocabulary of calls when interacting socially and aggressively or warning against predators. They are superb mimics, frequently imitating the screams of Red-tailed Hawks, but the benefit to the birds of such vocal virtuosity is unknown.

Where Found:
Yosemite: From Yosemite Valley and lower boundaries of the park up to Glacier Point, Porcupine Flat, and even higher around developed areas

such as Tuolumne Meadows and Tioga Pass.

Sequoia-Kings Canyon: Cedar Grove, Grant Grove, Giant Forest, Wolverton, Mineral King.

Scrub Jay *(Aphelocoma coerulescens)* Plate 22

The lives of Scrub Jays, like those of Acorn Woodpeckers, are intimately linked to oak trees. A central feature of their annual cycle is the storage of acorns, a staple food that they harvest in the fall and hide singly in small holes dug in the ground with their bills. Some forgotten acorns germinate into seedlings, thus benefiting the subsequent generations of both oaks and jays. Pine nuts, almonds and large seeds are cached in a similar fashion. These stores form the bulk of their diet through the winter, but insects become important during the nesting season. Like other members of their family, Scrub Jays eat a variety of foods: berries, birds' eggs and young, other small animals and garbage. They often pick acorns directly from trees but, unlike Steller's Jays, take most other foods on the ground.

Scrub Jays build bulky nests, usually low in the foliage of trees, vines or shrubs, and often near water. As with Steller's Jays, they stay extremely quiet around nests to avoid attracting predators. Elsewhere, however, these crestless jays habitually perch in plain view and may approach human visitors to investigate. Both sexes make a great variety of strident calls, among the most familiar and characteristic sounds of the foothills, and both sing soft, musical "whisper" songs. They nest in oak woodlands, chaparral and riparian forests, just barely up into the ponderosa pine zone. Unlike many foothill birds, they seldom travel above their breeding elevations. The occasional birds that occur near the Sierran crest in late summer and fall are probably wanderers from the Great Basin.

Where Found:
Yosemite: Below Foresta and around El Portal, Mariposa, Groveland and Big Oak Flat; also recorded at Yosemite Valley, Hodgdon Meadow and Tuolumne Grove.
Sequoia-Kings Canyon: Three Rivers, Ash Mountain, Potwisha, Hospital Rock.

Clark's Nutcracker *(Nucifraga columbiana)* Plate 22

Pine nuts are the staff of life for these ubiquitous corvids of the high Sierra. In late summer and fall, a single Clark's Nutcracker may harvest and store more than 30,000 pine seeds, which then serve as its main food supply until the following summer.

Nutcrackers harvest pine seeds in subalpine forests by prying them from cones hanging on trees or lying on the ground. They seek out large-seeded pines like whitebarks and Jeffreys, bypassing the small seeds of lodgepoles and western white pines. Some seeds may be eaten immediately, but as many as 150 are stored at a time in a "sublingual pouch" at the base of the tongue. Like a chipmunk's, these pouches facilitate the transport of seeds to special storage areas. Nutcrackers studied at Tioga Pass and Mammoth Lakes had two widely separated caches, one in a subalpine forest and one in a lower-elevation Jeffrey or pinyon pine forest, sometimes eight miles or more downslope. Seeds are cached secretively in small holes dug with the bill, a few seeds per hole, and are subsequently located by memory. Nutcrackers have been seen digging through four feet of snow to recover hidden seeds!

In the fall, most descend to the vicinity of a lower-elevation storage area, usually east of the Sierran crest, where they continue to harvest and cache large pine seeds. They remain to breed, beginning as early as February. Nutcrackers nest at various heights amidst the foliage of conifers and feed the nestlings almost exclusively on stored seeds. By late May, most young birds have fledged, and by late June they move up to subalpine forests with their parents. Until the next crop of pine seeds ripens, they feed mainly on insects and on seeds stored the summer before, but also take berries, carrion, eggs and nestling birds of smaller species.

Although a few nutcrackers have been found nesting on the west slope, most winter and breed at middle elevations east of the crest. On the west slope in summer and fall, they are common in subalpine forests, with moderate numbers occurring above tree line and down to the mixed-conifer zone. In exceptional years, probably due to a shortage of pine nuts at high elevations, many descend to the lower pine forests, and a few desert the Sierra to search for food in the surrounding lowlands.

Where Found:
Yosemite: Mt. Dana, Tioga Pass, Tuolumne Meadows, Olmsted Point, May Lake. No recent nesting records.
Sequoia-Kings Canyon: Evolution Lake, Alta Peak, Upper Kern Basin, Rock Creek, Mineral King. No recent nesting records.

Yellow-billed Magpie *(Pica nuttalli)* Plate 22

Exotically attired for a corvid, with blue, violet, and green iridescence and long, graceful tails, Yellow-billed Magpies stream overhead at sunset to their communal winter roosts. These common inhabitants of the Sacramento and northern San Joaquin Valleys range up into the lower foothills in parts of the central and southern Sierra where grasslands are interspersed with scattered oaks or bordered by belts of trees. By day they disperse from their roosting trees to feed in small flocks on the ground, searching for insects and other invertebrates, often in agricultural fields. Like other corvids, these omnivores also feed on carrion, small animals, acorns and fruit.

In spring they nest in loose colonies, with each pair defending a small territory. Their conspicuous, bulky stick nests, high in the canopy of oaks, cottonwoods or sycamores, commonly serve nesting American Kestrels, Long-eared Owls and other species after the magpies abandon them. The Yellow-billed Magpie is one of the few birds that nests only in California and the only species never recorded outside its native state. It is highly sedentary, and individuals rarely wander more than a few miles from their nesting territories.

The Black-billed Magpie, almost identical except for its bill color and somewhat larger size, lives along the eastern base of the Sierra and very rarely appears on the west slope.

Where Found:
Yosemite: Lower foothills, as at Hornitos and east of Oakdale.
Sequoia-Kings Canyon: May not occur regularly in foothills below parks.

American Crow[1] *(Corvus brachyrhynchos)*   Figure 12

This lowland species, most common in the Central Valley, resides sparsely in the lower Sierran foothills. In spring and fall, it may reach mountain meadows in the ponderosa pine and mixed-conifer zones, but rarely. Considerably smaller than a Common Raven, the American Crow makes higher-pitched cawing calls and has a rounded rather than wedge-shaped tail (see Fig. 12).

Crows range over large, open grasslands and cultivated areas, stopping to feed on a wide assortment of plant and animal materials, including carrion. They require trees for nesting and roosting. In the winter, crows gather in large flocks, sometimes numbering in the thousands, and roost communally in dense groves of trees. They often travel long distances daily to and from suitable feeding areas. Communal roosting decreases the possibility of surprise attacks by predators and may enable individuals to learn the location of productive feeding areas from each other.

Where Found:
Yosemite: Recorded at Snelling in the lower foothills; occasionally as high as Yosemite Valley and Crane Flat in migration.
Sequoia-Kings Canyon: Recorded at Ash Mountain and Three Rivers, but more regular at lower elevations; common below Lake Kaweah.

Common Raven *(Corvus corax)*   Plate 5, Figure 12

Largest of the "songbirds," Common Ravens look like raptors at first

[1]*Formerly, Common Crow.*

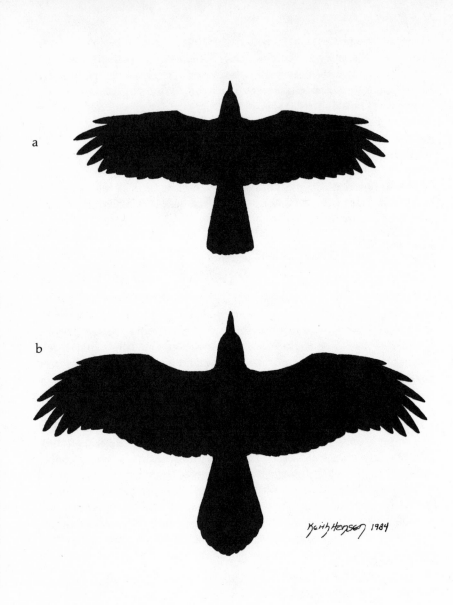

a

b

Figure 12. American Crows (a) and Common Ravens (b) are easiest to identify in flight. The crow is considerably smaller overall, with a squarish tail. The raven has a more massive head and bill, and its tail is "wedge-shaped," terminating in a rounded point.

glance and resemble them in many of their habits. With wingspans of four feet or more, they approach the size of Red-tailed Hawks and often soar overhead. Ravens range widely over large open spaces, searching for carrion. In some areas, carcasses of livestock form a principal food item. Although they lack the strong, sharp talons of hawks and owls, ravens occasionally pursue small birds and mammals, knock them down and peck them to death. In the foothills east of Fresno, some ravens were seen plucking White-throated Swifts off their perch sites on the face of Pine Flat Dam and devouring them on top of the structure. They also relish large insects as well as grains, fruit and garbage.

Courting pairs of ravens make breathtaking dives and spectacular, tumbling falls in perfect formation. Solitary birds also perform such stunts, seemingly just for the fun of it. The favorite sites for their bulky stick-nests are ledges on rocky cliffs, sheltered by overhangs or trees. Peregrine or Prairie Falcons occasionally re-use these cliff nests. Sometimes ravens use a tall tree, typically the largest one in the vicinity with sufficient foliage at the top to obscure the nest from the ground. They may even nest in deserted barns or similar structures.

The raven resembles a crow but can be distinguished by its shaggy throat feathers, heavier bill, deeper croaking cries and a much larger "wedge-shaped" tail, terminating in a rounded point (see Fig. 12). Its much larger size is not always evident in the field. Unlike crows, it shuns settled areas, and the two species seldom co-occur.

In the Sierra, ravens live mainly in the foothills, especially in the southern part of the range, though uncommonly even there. They are very rare in the central and northern Sierra from Butte to Calaveras Counties, but their numbers have increased since 1950 in Tehama County and in the vicinity of Yosemite National Park. Perhaps they have benefited from new food supplies such as garbage and road-kills. They occasionally nest in the conifer forest zones, and some range up above tree line in summer and fall. In midwinter of 1979, they were seen commonly at Rae Lakes, Rock Creek and Crabtree Meadow in the high eastern portion of Sequoia National Park.

Where Found:
Yosemite: Mariposa Grove, Badger Pass area, Foresta, Hodgdon Meadow, Crane Flat (nesting) and occasionally higher.
Sequoia-Kings Canyon: Ash Mountain, Potwisha, Hospital Rock, Colony Mill Road, Giant Forest, Alta Peak, Siberian Outpost, Little Baldy, Big Baldy, Cedar Grove.

CHICKADEES AND TITMICE (Family Paridae)
These small, lively, inquisitive birds readily flock to backyard feeders

and seem surprisingly unafraid of humans. They flock together during the nonbreeding season, often with kinglets, nuthatches or woodpeckers. The sexes are similar, and many species, such as chickadees, show boldly patterned plumages. Sierran species all reside in the region year-round, but some move short distances up and downslope.

Mountain Chickadee *(Parus gambeli)* Plate 23, Cover

The delicate appearance of Mountain Chickadees is deceptive, for they endure the snowy winters of the Sierra's middle and higher elevations in greater numbers than any other bird. These engaging mountaineers live year-round from the ponderosa pine zone up to the highest subalpine forests. In fall, winter and spring, small numbers sometimes descend into the foothill woodlands.

Winter survival presents an enormous challenge to birds so small. Soft, thick plumage and warm roosting holes in trees enable them to live through frigid winters at high elevations. They require great quantities of food to stay warm, however, and many birds may die during heavy winters. Between storms, they search ceaselessly for eggs, larvae, and adult insects and spiders, as well as conifer seeds hidden within crevices of bark or sprays of foliage. During past outbreaks of the lodgepole needle miner at Tuolumne Meadows in Yosemite, Mountain Chickadees were the primary predators of these destructive moths. Although they glean insects from the tops of foliage and branches, they often swing below a twig or cone and hang upside down, looking for prey they might have overlooked from above. In the nonbreeding season, chickadees generally forage in small flocks with Red-breasted Nuthatches, Golden-crowned Kinglets or other forest birds. Flocking together provides more eyes to watch for predators.

Mountain Chickadees maintain contact while foraging in loose flocks by uttering lisping "tsee-tsee-tsee" notes or "chick-a-dee-a-dee." Their song, given during the nesting season, is a sweet, whistled "dee-do-do," with the identical second and third notes lower than the first. These extremely curious birds often drop down to low branches to inspect passing humans or other animals. When alarmed they scold with a sharp "tsik-a" call and harass the object of their fears.

Winter flocks begin to disintegrate as breeding pairs form in late April or early May. Though they forage in all kinds of forest, chickadees usually nest in large trees, either in natural cavities or abandoned woodpecker holes. Occasionally they excavate their own nests in rotten wood or fallen logs. They make the holes comfortable by forming a base of wood chips, lining them with fur, feathers or, often, animal feces. Seven eggs are the norm, but clutches of twelve have been recorded. The female incubates the eggs, but both parents share the heavy task of feeding their large, hungry brood.

Where Found:
Yosemite: Yosemite Valley, Chinquapin, Wawona, Mariposa Grove, Tuolumne Grove, Crane Flat, White Wolf, Porcupine Flat, Tuolumne Meadows.
Sequoia-Kings Canyon: Cedar Grove, Grant Grove, Giant Forest, Crystal Cave Road.

Chestnut-backed Chickadee *(Parus rufescens)* Plate 23

These common Coast and Cascade Range residents were not discovered in the Sierra Nevada until 1937, when one was collected at an elevation of 2700 feet along the North Fork Feather River. Chestnut-backed Chickadees were not observed in Yosemite Valley until 1958, and have not penetrated much farther south. Today they reside regularly, but locally, year-round in the ponderosa pine and mixed-conifer zones from the Yosemite area northward. Typically they frequent moist stands of mature conifers such as Douglas-firs and incense cedars, mixed with hardwoods such as alders and willows.

These highly social birds flock while foraging, at least during the non-breeding season. They glean small insects, conifer seeds and fruits from terminal limbs, often by dangling or hovering to inspect surfaces hidden from above. Their calls resemble those of the far more abundant Mountain Chickadees. The Chestnut-backs, however, have a more nasal, buzzy quality, and do not produce a whistled song.

Where Found:
Yosemite: Happy Isles (Yosemite Valley), Tuolumne Grove; west of the park at Hardin Flat.
Sequoia-Kings Canyon: No records.

Plain Titmouse *(Parus inornatus)* Plate 23

The clear, whistled melodies of the Plain Titmouse sound confusingly similar to those of the Bewick's Wren, another common resident of the foothill woodlands. To make matters worse, its complex repertoire includes frequent wheezy "tcick-a-dee-dee," calls resembling those of the Mountain and Chestnut-backed Chickadees.

In the Sierra, titmice are common inhabitants of the foothills where they frequent riparian forests and woodlands dominated by blue, live or valley oaks. While they clearly prefer the sunny hillsides of the foothills, small numbers also live upslope in black oak and conifer forests. Titmice do not breed above the ponderosa pine zone, but rare individuals have been found up to the red fir forests in late summer.

Unlike most songbirds, pairs of titmice remain mated for several years. They defend their nesting territories at all seasons and are quick to scold trespassers. Titmice eat a varied fare, preferring insects while breeding and seeds and fruits in winter. They pluck insects from foliage and flowers, but like other members of their family, they also dangle from twigs, probe into bark crevices or drop to the ground to feed. They will pry off bark or pull apart lichens and leaf galls to expose insects, and often hammer open acorns and fruits. Titmice nest in cavities or occasionally in woodpecker holes, most often in oaks. In the Sierra, nesting takes place from March until about mid-July, and the females incubate the eggs while the males feed them.

Where Found:
Yosemite: Widespread in lower drainages of the Tuolumne and Merced Rivers including La Grange, El Portal, Coulterville and near Don Pedro Reservoir; recorded up to Yosemite Valley, Wawona and White Wolf.
Sequoia-Kings Canyon: Three Rivers, Ash Mountain, Potwisha Campground, Hospital Rock and lower section of the Mineral King Road.

BUSHTITS *(Family Aegithalidae)*

Bushtit[1] *(Psaltriparus minimus)*   **Plate 23**
These long-tailed, grayish mites, scarcely larger than most hummingbirds, like to socialize during the nonbreeding season. Loose flocks of up to 50 individuals, all in continuous motion, float like slowly advancing waves through the foliage of trees and shrubs. Scattered birds maintain contact through their high-pitched, "tsee-tsee-tsee" calls. Bushtits forage like chickadees, gleaning small insects from foliage and hanging effortlessly to scrutinize the undersides of leaves and twigs. Occasionally they eat seeds or even nectar, but insects are the mainstay of their diet.

Bushtits are common in the Sierra foothills, where they frequent live and blue oaks, as well as evergreen shrubs. Toward the end of summer, small flocks drift upslope along stream courses, feeding along meadow edges and in open shrub fields up at least to the red fir zone. Most return to the foothills by about October before the heavy snows set in, but small flocks sometimes remain in open conifer and oak forests through the winter.

Winter flocks, possibly composed of related individuals, break up around March as they begin to pair off for breeding. Adult females can be told from adult males (and all immatures) by their light golden rather than dark eyes.

Although undistinguished in plumage and song, Bushtits create exquisite and remarkable abodes: long, soft pouches woven from lichens,

[1]*Formerly, Common Bushtit.*

mosses, spider webs, willow down or feathers and often decorated with flower blossoms or moth wings. Construction may take up to six weeks. These splendid nests, suspended from twigs, seem overly large for their tiny white eggs. Bushtit nests frustrate four-footed predators by design and by their placement at least fifteen feet above the ground, but Scrub Jays take a heavy toll by tearing pouches open and devouring eggs or nestlings.

Until recently Bushtits were put with titmice and chickadees in the family Paridae. Due primarily to differences in nesting behavior, they are now considered members of the family Aegithalidae, along with similar European species.

Where Found:
Yosemite: Recorded near Don Pedro Reservoir, Big Oak Flat, Mariposa, El Portal, Yosemite Valley and Big Meadow; in fall up to Little Yosemite Valley, Wawona, Crane Flat and White Wolf.
Sequoia-Kings Canyon: Three Rivers, Ash Mountain, Potwisha, Hospital Rock; in fall up to Grant Grove and Giant Forest.

NUTHATCHES *(Family Sittidae)*
Early English birdwatchers observed small tree-climbing birds wedging nuts into tree crevices and hacking them open with their stout, upturned bills. First called "Nuthacks," they finally became known as "Nuthatches." These agile little climbers use their sharp claws to travel up, down or sideways along bark surfaces. In this fashion they can examine crevices for food overlooked by woodpeckers and Brown Creepers, which always travel upward. Nuthatches fly with relatively slow wingbeats that can be heard as they flutter between trees. The three Sierran species all have gray backs and short, square tails with white spots on the outer feathers. Females usually appear slightly paler than the males. Some nuthatches nest in abandoned woodpecker holes, while others excavate their own cozy nests in trees or snags.

Red-breasted Nuthatch *(Sitta canadensis)*   Plate 24
The nasal "ank-ank-ank" calls of Red-breasted Nuthatches are seldom forgotten once learned. These horn-like sounds are surprisingly loud and penetrating for such small birds. Red-breasted Nuthatches often chatter sociably in the tops of conifers but sometimes drop to lower branches to forage or inspect intruders to their woods.

In the western Sierra, Red-breasted Nuthatches range from the ponderosa pine forests up to tree line, but are most abundant at mid-elevations deep in shady groves of white or red firs. They also work over deciduous trees such as cottonwoods, aspens and black oaks. They gather seeds and acorns for winter food caches that, along with insects and spiders, sustain them through the long, freezing winters. Even on the coldest days, they actively feed with other winter residents, such as Mountain Chickadees, Brown Creepers and Golden-crowned Kinglets. Every other winter or so, a few Red-breasted Nuthatches abandon coniferous forests for the more productive lowlands of the Central Valley. Whether these birds come from the Sierra or down from northern latitudes remains undiscovered.

Red-breasted Nuthatches excavate their own nests in large trees or, rarely, take over abandoned woodpecker holes and natural cavities. For unknown reasons they smear pitch at the entrances to their feather-lined nests.

Where Found:
Yosemite: Yosemite Valley, Mariposa Grove, Chinquapin, Hodgdon Meadow, Tuolumne Grove, Crane Flat, Gin Flat, Porcupine Flat.
Sequoia-Kings Canyon: Cedar Grove, Grant Grove, Scaffold Meadow, Big Baldy Trail, Little Baldy Trail, Wolverton, Giant Forest, Alta Meadows.

White-breasted Nuthatch *(Sitta carolinensis)* Plate 24

Most birdwatchers associate White-breasted Nuthatches with oak forests, for they are most abundant there. Oak trees provide acorns, a staple they cache in crevices for winter use. They do not depend solely on oaks, however, for where acorns are not available, they will harvest pine seeds. Fairly common in the foothills, White-breasted Nuthatches are rare in ponderosa pine and mixed-conifer forests. A Great Basin race of this species winters and breeds regularly at least up to 10,000 feet on the east slope, and a few spill over the Sierra crest where they live in subalpine and red fir forests. Cross-country skiers occasionally surprise these hardy mountaineers when travelling through the highest forests. Whether in oaks, pines or firs, White-breasted Nuthatches prefer open forests with large, well-spaced trees.

Although larger than other nuthatches, White-breasted Nuthatches forage upside down on tree trunks or hang under branches just as agilely as the smaller ones. They voice a frequent nasal "yank-yank" or "keer" while picking insects or spiders from bark surfaces. With the approach of spring, they find abandoned woodpecker holes or natural cavities in snags and line them with feathers. Only occasionally do they excavate their own nest holes in decayed wood.

Where Found:
Yosemite: West of the park at Big Oak Flat, Groveland and El Portal; in park at Wawona, Porcupine Creek and Tuolumne Meadows; just east of

the park at the Hall Natural Area (Inyo National Forest). **Sequoia-Kings Canyon:** Three Rivers, Ash Mountain, Elk Creek, Potwisha and Hospital Rock; high elevations at Sugarloaf Meadow, Bighorn Plateau, Crabtree Ranger Station, Mt. Guyot, Siberian Pass, Chagoopa Plateau and below Mineral Peak.

Pygmy Nuthatch *(Sitta pygmaea)* Plate 24

Pygmies are the smallest, rarest and most social of the Sierran nuthatches. They prefer open forests of large ponderosa, sugar or Jeffrey pines, but flocks occasionally feed in Douglas-firs and giant sequoias. They eat mostly pine seeds except in the breeding season, when adults and young feed primarily on insects and spiders. In the western Sierra their occurrence is irregular and discontinuous, but most populations have been noted in ponderosa pine and mixed-conifer forests. They tend to be more common in the southern Sierra.

In contrast to other nuthatches, Pygmies often move in flocks and forage out to the ends of the smallest twigs. Preferring to remain high in the trees, they are most easily detected by their "det-de-de-det" calls, reminiscent of the Red Crossbill's, but less forceful.

Pygmy Nuthatches lay eggs in holes they excavate themselves, or less commonly in existing tree cavities. They often roost communally in holes to share body heat during freezing winter nights. Up to 150 birds have been found snuggling together in one cavity.

Where Found:
Yosemite: Principally recorded in Yosemite Valley near Happy Isles, Vernal and Nevada Falls and along the Yosemite Falls trail; just west of the park along Ackerson Creek near Evergreen Road.
Sequoia-Kings Canyon: Cedar Grove, Grant Grove, Sugarloaf Valley; often found in pinyon pines around the rim of Kings Canyon; Florence Lake (Sierra National Forest); Lloyd Meadows (Sequoia National Forest); Chimney Creek and the Kern Plateau (south of the parks).

CREEPERS *(Family Certhiidae)*

Brown Creeper *(Certhia americana)* Plate 24

Though common, Brown Creepers blend in well against conifer bark with their streaky brown heads, backs and wings, making them difficult for beginning birdwatchers to find. Those familiar with their "see-see-see" calls or distinctive whistled songs, however, have little trouble locating them. Distinguishing their calls from those of Golden-crowned Kinglets can be a challenge, but the Brown Creeper's calls tend to be more forceful and clear-toned.

Unlike the omnivorous nuthatches that often head downwards, creepers seek only insects and spiders and always move upwards along trunks or large branches. After spiralling to the top of one tree, probing bark crevices with their down-curved bills, they flit to the bottom of another and hitch their way up again, using their long, stiff tail feathers as props.

Brown Creepers are common residents in every type of coniferous forest of the western Sierra. Most abundant in dense, old-growth stands, they prefer trees with deeply furrowed bark, including giant sequoias and incense cedars. Loose strips of bark from such trees form ideal supports for their hammock-like nests of moss and twigs. In winter, Brown Creepers are usually solitary, but a few may flock together or join small groups of nuthatches, kinglets and chickadees, spending most of their time feeding to store energy to survive the night. Although primarily associated with conifers in the western Sierra, Brown Creepers sometimes retreat to low-elevation oak and riparian forests in small numbers during winter.

Where Found:
Yosemite: Yosemite Valley, Mariposa Grove, Peregoy Meadow, Merced Grove, Tuolumne Grove, Crane Flat, Gin Flat, White Wolf, Porcupine Flat.
Sequoia-Kings Canyon: Cedar Grove, Grant Grove, Giant Forest, Mineral King; seen during winter in Sugarloaf Valley.

WRENS *(Family Troglodytidae)*

The sprightly, engaging wrens are small, chunky birds and typically hold their tails upright, especially when alarmed or agitated. Although dressed in subtle browns and grays, they have exceptionally beautiful, complex songs, embellished with chirps, trills and energetic chatters. Wrens make a living by picking insects or spiders from foliage, leaf litter or rock surfaces. Most are cavity nesters, hence the name Troglodytidae, meaning "cave-dweller." Females incubate the eggs, but both parents care for the nestlings. In the Sierra, wrens occur in a great variety of habitats, from rocky jumbles to moist forest glades. Of six species occurring in the region, all but the House and Marsh Wrens stay year-round.

Rock Wren *(Salpinctes obsoletus)*   Plate 25

The Rock Wren is marvelously adapted for life among rock outcroppings, talus slopes and dry earthen banks. Its long, sharp-clawed toes allow it to scamper up the sides of sheer cliffs in search of insects and spiders. It has a rather flattened body and long, slender head and bill that facilitate exploring narrow crevices for hidden prey. Although Rock Wrens require rocky or hard-earth slopes for breeding, they are less fussy about the requisite climate and elevation. They have been recorded nesting 250 feet below sea level in Death Valley and up to 12,500 feet on the slopes of Mt. Langley, Tulare County. In the western Sierra they are most common below the montane conifer forests and amidst the windswept slopes above tree line. Birds in the high country move downslope below the snow line in winter. The scarcity of Rock Wrens at middle elevations is mysterious, as much seemingly suitable habitat is available. For example, few have ever been seen on the rocky talus and canyon walls of Yosemite Valley. Rock Wrens hide their nests in rock crannies or in abandoned rodent burrows. One nest at Hetch Hetchy was in a large log overhanging the reservoir; the entire nest cavity was paved with small granite chips. For unknown reasons, Rock Wrens often construct pebble pathways near their nests.

Both Rock and Canyon Wrens inhabit rock outcrops and boulder piles and occasionally occur in the same areas. In general, though, Rock Wrens prefer drier sites, while Canyon Wrens like shade and moisture. They are easy to tell apart; the drabber Rock Wren lacks the clear white throat and breast of the Canyon Wren, and its ample fan-shaped tail is buffy at the corners. Its songs combine harsh, tinkling phrases and rapid trills—beautiful, but not as inspired as those of the Canyon Wren.

Where Found:
Yosemite: Resident west of the park in Merced and Tuolumne River Canyons; nests along north shore of Hetch Hetchy Reservoir; in summer observed at Wawona Point, Inspiration Point (west end of Yosemite Valley) and up to Tuolumne Meadows, Vogelsang Lake, Mono Pass and Mt. Dana.
Sequoia-Kings Canyon: Low elevations—Potwisha area and along the Generals Highway in the foothills. High elevations—Granite Basin, Cedar Grove, Rae Lakes, Mt. Whitney, Boreal Plateau, Farewell Gap and Coyote Creek.

Canyon Wren (*Catherpes mexicanus*)   Plate 25

Steep-walled gorges of Sierran rivers echo the bell-like songs of Canyon Wrens. Their penetrating notes descend in pitch as if tumbling down the canyon walls themselves.

In the Sierra, Canyon Wrens nest fairly commonly on steep, rocky canyon walls and talus slopes from the foothill grasslands up at least to the mixed-conifer zone. Rarely they range as high as alpine fell fields in summer and fall, but most retreat to the lowlands for winter. One hardy bird spent an entire winter at 6,000 feet in Placer County feeding on spider eggs found under porches and old buildings; between storms it hopped around on deep snow drifts, picked at entombed insects and occasionally burst forth in full song.

Both Canyon and Rock Wrens select rocky jumbles for foraging and nesting, and their ranges overlap. Canyon Wrens, however, prefer shade and water nearby while Rock Wrens have no aversion to aridity and often live on parched hillsides. Both species scuttle confidently over steep rock walls and piles, darting into crannies in search of insects, and occasionally stopping to bob up and down as does their distant relative the Dipper. It is not difficult to tell the two wrens apart, as the clear white throat and chest of the Canyon Wren distinguish it from the drabber, buff-colored Rock Wren.

Canyon Wren nests are sequestered in crevices or caves in talus slopes or on rocky cliff-faces, far above most ground predators. These solitary songsters are confined to their rocky homes even after breeding; they have few seasonal movements. They are fairly common in the cathedral-like setting of Yosemite Valley where rock climbers encounter them thousands of feet above the floor. Canyon Wrens move across polished rock faces using a sideways "crab-crawl" technique, similar to the climbers, to maintain their grip at such steep angles.

Where Found:
Yosemite: Resident west of the park in gorges of the Merced and Tuolumne Rivers and at El Portal; in park at Yosemite Valley and Hetch Hetchy; a few fall records just east of the park at Hall Natural Area (Inyo National Forest).
Sequoia-Kings Canyon: Tehipite Valley, Cedar Grove, Zumwalt Meadows, Moro Rock, Crystal Cave (nesting), Ash Mountain.

Bewick's Wren *(Thryomanes bewickii)* — Plate 25

With heads thrown back and long tails dropped, Bewick's Wrens voice their rich, varied songs, filled with bold trills and hissing phrases. Their brown plumage resembles that of their relative, the House Wren. Bewick's are easily identified, however, by their clear white underparts and eyebrow stripes.

Bewick's Wrens are common year-round in foothill oak and riparian woodlands and in chaparral; they breed there and sparingly up to the ponderosa pine zone. Within these elevations, they prefer habitats with scattered trees, dense patches of shrubs, vine tangles and dead branches where they forage for insects. Their nesting sites are as varied as their songs. Nests have been found in clefts on dry, rocky hillsides, in tree cavities in moist, deciduous groves, and in crevices of bridges or buildings; nearly all are within a few feet of the ground. Although some upslope movement has been noted in fall, Bewick's Wrens rarely travel above the mixed-conifer zone.

Yosemite: West of the park in canyons of Merced and Tuolumne Rivers and at Mariposa, El Portal, Old Priest Grade (Highway 120), Big Oak Flat and Groveland. In fall noted up to Crane Flat.
Sequoia-Kings Canyon: Three Rivers, Ash Mountain, Potwisha, Hospital Rock.

House Wren *(Troglodytes aedon)* Plate 25

This plainest of North American wrens is so named for its habit of building nests in or around houses, barns or other structures. It is the eastern race of the House Wren, however, that is so inclined; in the Sierra and throughout the west, House Wrens usually nest in tree cavities. Abandoned woodpecker holes suit them well and almost any sized cavity will do—if it is too large they fill the excess space with sticks. They forage and nest in deciduous trees such as oaks, willows and alders but rarely use conifers. Male House Wrens may build several nests in their staunchly defended territories before the female selects her favorite. A mated pair may produce two or three broods per season.

House Wrens are abundant along the eastern slope of the Sierra where their complex, gurgly music pours forth from riparian groves. In the western Sierra they nest commonly in the foothills and fairly commonly up to the ponderosa pine zone where they frequent streamside thickets, deciduous woodlands and meadow edges. While foraging for insects, they usually keep to low undergrowth and avoid higher foliage, but males often emerge to sing from prominent perches. From July until September, these diminutive birds travel along stream courses and mountain meadows up to tree line. Rarely, they forage in brushy habitats far from water. Unlike most of their relatives, House Wrens are rare in the Sierra foothills during winter, preferring the warmer climates of southern California and Mexico.

Where Found:
Yosemite: Breeds in El Portal and Yosemite Valley. Post-breeding birds noted at Crane Flat, Mt. Watkins, Merced Lake, Snow Creek and Tuolumne Meadows.
Sequoia-Kings Canyon: Three Rivers, Ash Mountain, Crescent Meadow, Wolverton, Grant Grove.

Winter Wren *(Troglodytes troglodytes)* Plate 25

Intruders who chance upon the nesting territory of a pair of Winter Wrens will find themselves confronted energetically by a protesting male. With his minute stump of a tail cocked at a jaunty angle, he scolds with emphatic ticks. His alarm notes are entirely different from his lovely song—a long, lively sequence of high-pitched trills. A single Winter Wren has been recorded singing more than 30 different songs.

This tiny wren, smallest of its family, is inconspicuous in the Sierra because of its localized distribution and reclusive tendencies. It can be fairly common, however, in dense ponderosa pine and mixed-conifer forests where it prefers moist, shady undergrowth, especially near streams and small seeps. The enormous roots of giant sequoias are among its favorite haunts. Like all wrens it skulks near the ground in active search for its insect prey.

During courtship, males often build several "dummy nests" before the female decides which one finally to use. They typically hide nests on or near the ground in tangles of roots from fallen trees, crevices under logs, or cavities in trees or banks.

Resident in the Sierra, Winter Wrens increase in numbers during fall and winter. Between August and October they occasionally venture up to the red fir and subalpine forests, but they usually descend below the heavy snows for winter.

Where Found:
Yosemite: Happy Isles, Vernal Falls Trail (Yosemite Valley), Mariposa Grove, Merced Grove, Tuolumne Grove, El Portal (winter).
Sequoia-Kings Canyon: Cedar Grove, Giant Forest, Crescent Meadow, Crystal Cave, Sequoia Creek. In winter recorded up to 8,500 feet on Cunningham Creek in the Roaring River drainage.

Marsh Wren[1] *(Cistothorus palustris)*   **Plate 25**

A series of clicks, sputters and chattery trills rising from the marshy edge of a Sierran lake or boggy meadow betrays a Marsh Wren's hideaway. This reclusive noisemaker thrives in tule and cattail marshes of the Central Valley but is rare in the western Sierra. East of the crest, it has been recorded nesting only at Lake Tahoe. Surprisingly, this tiny bird is an important nest predator of other birds such as House and Bewick's Wrens and even Red-Winged Blackbirds—it destroys nesting efforts by pecking eggs.

After nesting, Marsh Wrens occasionally venture as high as the mixed-conifer zone in late summer and fall. During this period, they may be found in almost any kind of low, lush vegetation in standing water or wet meadows.

A streak of white above the eye and black and white stripes on the back distinguished the Marsh Wren from House and Winter Wrens, which might occur in the same habitats.

[1]*Formerly, Long-billed Marsh Wren.*

Where Found:

Yosemite: A few records from Yosemite Valley and Wawona Meadow; west of the park, recorded six miles east of Coulterville and at La Grange.

Sequoia-Kings Canyon: A few records from below Terminus Dam (Lake Kaweah) and one historical record from Cedar Grove.

DIPPERS *(Family Cinclidae)*

American Dipper[1] *(Cinclus mexicanus)*   Plate 1, Figure 13

Sharp chatters rise above the thundering noise and mists of Sierran headwater streams as dippers flit nervously from rock to rock. When flying, they skim low over the water, forsaking all shortcuts over land. These plump, sooty-gray birds bob incessantly up and down on bended knees while flashing their white eyelids. When feeding, they cling to precipitous rock faces, dive beneath foaming waters and pop to the surface some distance downstream. Their powerful legs, long toes and streamlined bodies allow them to walk with ease over mossy boulders or beneath cascading rapids. They do not have webbed feet but occasionally swim across still pools like tiny ducks. Dippers have evolved many adaptations to aquatic living: enlarged oil glands for waterproofing outer feathers, a thick undercoat of down and specialized flaps over their nostrils and eyes (nictitating membranes) to protect them from pounding spray. On deep dives they "fly" under water using their short rounded wings as flippers and their flattened, stubby tails as rudders.

Dippers occur year-round at all elevations above the foothills. They frequent swift, rocky-bottomed streams and occasionally lakeshores. The surrounding landscape can be buried by snow and empty of bird life, but dippers will frolic in their icy waters. Only when high mountain streams freeze solid in winter do dippers move downslope. Although solitary during most of the year, males and females pair for the breeding season, between March and June. The males sing long, mournful courting songs in early spring. These songs are unfamiliar to most birdwatchers because they usually cease before the spring snowmelt and are hard for human ears to hear above the water's roar. The females, which look just like the males, build nests of mosses and grasses, usually cradled in inaccessible rock ledges above streams or behind waterfalls where mist keeps the moss green, providing good camouflage (see Fig. 13). Both parents feed their spot-breasted young. Dippers prefer fresh, unpolluted waters that support caddisflies, other aquatic insects and their larvae, snails and fish fry.

---

[1]*Formerly, Dipper; before that, Water Ouzel.*

Figure 13. American Dipper nest.

Where found:
Yosemite: Merced River from well below El Portal up to Yosemite Valley; Little Yosemite Valley, Yosemite Creek, Bridalveil Creek and Snow Creek; entire length of the Tuolumne River from Pate Valley up to Lyell Canyon and from Hetch Hetchy Reservoir downstream to Don Pedro Reservoir. **Sequoia-Kings Canyon:** Kern, Kings and Kaweah Rivers and major tributaries; recorded near Paradise Valley, Cedar Grove, Lodgepole, Potwisha and as low as Three Rivers in winter. Found at about 9600 feet on Rock Creek in February when the water was half covered by snow.

MUSCICAPIDS *(Family Muscicapidae)*
This large, diverse family of insectivores is represented in the Sierra by three subfamilies. All are so distinct that until recently they were considered separate families, and therefore they are discussed separately below.

KINGLETS AND GNATCATCHERS *(Subfamily Sylviinae)*
Delicate, active birds that flit fairy-like among twigs and leaves, members of this group have slender, pointed bills for capturing insects. Although kinglets have bright, regal crowns, most species are drably colored in olives, grays or browns. The sexes are quite similar but not identical. Most species reside in cold northern latitudes all year rather than migrate south like many Sierran songbirds. Their unusually fluffy, thick plumages keep them warm on long winter nights. Members of this family sing complex songs and call frequently.

Golden-crowned Kinglet *(Regulus satrapa)*   Plate 26
Faint whispering calls of Golden-crowned Kinglets may be lost to human ears when breezes rustle the treetops. Their calls are a rapid series of "see-see-see" notes, much like the Brown Creeper's, which are usually longer, clearer and more forceful. During their breeding season, kinglets also produce a song that begins with the usual high-pitched notes and descends into a chickadee-like chatter. Kinglets are among the smallest of Sierran birds, only slightly larger than Bushtits and hummingbirds. Like those species, they are highly active. They flit quickly between thick sprays of conifer foliage or flutter up to pick off insects, caterpillars and other delicacies from terminal needles. Their affinity for the high canopy makes Golden-crowned Kinglets difficult to see. They occasionally drop to lower foliage to feed and sometimes reveal their crown jewels: the males have bright crimson patches bordered by gold, black and white, while the females have similar patterns, but lack the crimson.
During their 1914 to 1920 surveys of the Yosemite region, Grinnell and

Storer (see Bibliography) described Golden-crowned Kinglets as only "moderately common" and found them sparingly in the Transition, or mixed-conifer zone. Today they are abundant from the ponderosa pine to the red fir zone and uncommon in the subalpine forests. In dense stands dominated by white, red or Douglas-fir they often outnumber all other bird species. Fire control in national parks and forests in the past allowed shade tolerant trees to fill in the formerly park-like forests, thus making them attractive to these tiny insectivores. The National Park policy of conducting management burns to restore forests to their natural state may reverse this development. In the meantime Golden-crowned Kinglets enjoy the benefits.

Golden-crowned Kinglet nests are hidden amid the thickest foliage and so are seldom seen. The deep, thick cups are bound together with spider webs, mosses and lichens. These kinglets rarely nest in the subalpine zone, but a few birds appear there late in summer. When snows begin to blanket the Sierra in fall and winter, a few drop down to more hospitable climates in the foothill oak and riparian woodlands. Most birds, however, remain in their breeding haunts all year. Weather permitting, they forage almost continuously during winter days for eggs and larvae of spiders and insects concealed in foliage or under flakes of bark. Frequently they fall in with other overwintering species, such as Mountain Chickadees, Red-breasted Nuthatches, Brown Creepers and Hairy Woodpeckers. How all these birds survive sub-freezing temperatures is a mystery, especially for the kinglets, which, unlike the others, do not even roost in holes.

Where Found:
Yosemite: Yosemite Valley, Chinquapin, Mariposa Grove, Tuolumne Grove, Crane Flat, Gin Flat, Porcupine Flat; uncommon at Tuolumne Meadows.
Sequoia-Kings Canyon: Grant Grove, Big Baldy Trail, Little Baldy Trail, Wolverton, Giant Forest, Crescent Meadow.

Ruby-crowned Kinglet *(Regulus calendula)* Plate 26

When fighting or otherwise aroused, the male Ruby-crowned Kinglet erects his crown feathers, unveiling a stunning patch of scarlet that is hidden most of the.time. Although she looks nearly identical, the female lacks a ruby crown.

From fall into early spring, Ruby-crowned Kinglets abound in the Sierra foothills, frequenting all habitats with dense growths of trees and shrubs, including riparian forests, oak woodlands, chaparral and suburban gardens. Uncommonly, they range up to the mixed-conifer zone and visit meadow edges and open ridges with scattered trees. Ruby-crowns tend to be solitary in winter, but sometimes join small flocks of foraging birds.

They flit between branches to pick insects from twigs and leaves, or flutter out to catch them in midair. They sound harsh chatters most of the year, but males preparing to depart for their breeding grounds in February or March start singing territorial songs. The melody starts with a few faint whistles and ends with a rising crescendo of loud trills and sweet warbles. They continue to sing throughout the summer on their breeding grounds.

Although they winter among broadleaved trees and shrubs, they breed only in coniferous forests. A few nests have been discovered from the ponderosa pine to the red fir zone of the Sierra, but these kinglets breed primarily in subalpine forests, where they prefer open stands of lodgepole pines or mountain hemlocks near creeks or meadow edges. In these habitats they may be fairly common, but never as numerous as Golden-crowns in their optimal habitats—the fir-dominated forests of lower elevations. Ruby-crowned Kinglets breed in the Sierra from mid-May at least until late July and they position their deep cup nests high in conifer boughs. Small numbers of Ruby-crowns stray to the Sierra crest after breeding. The Sierra breeding populations may not be the same ones that winter in lowland California; rather, they probably migrate farther south.

Ruby-crowned Kinglets may easily be confused with Hutton's Vireos (see Plate 26) during winter when both occupy oak woodlands. The kinglets are more animated than the vireos and constantly flick their wings while hopping from perch to perch. They have whitish marks in front and behind their eyes (instead of spectacles broken at the top), as well as smaller heads, more delicate bills, and black wing bars directly behind the white wing bars.

Where Found:
Yosemite: In winter in the lower drainages of the Merced and Tuolumne Rivers and at El Portal, Yosemite Valley and Hetch Hetchy. In summer at Siesta Lake, White Wolf, Porcupine Creek, Tuolumne Meadows, Glen Aulin and Tioga Pass.
Sequoia-Kings Canyon: In winter at Three Rivers, Ash Mountain, Potwisha. In summer at Cedar Grove, Kern River Canyon, Giant Forest, Hockett Lakes region and Cyclone Meadows.

Blue-gray Gnatcatcher *(Polioptila caerulea)* Plate 27
Soft, nasal calls usually precede the emergence of these sprightly, feisty birds from thick tangles of shrubs or oak foliage where they feed and nest. Their long, black, cocked tails twitch constantly, and white outer feathers flash as they flutter between perches. Blue-gray Gnatcatchers feed much as kinglets do, picking small insects from foliage or flying out to seize them in midair.

Arid hillsides of scattered oaks and dense shrubbery serve as prime nesting habitat for Blue-gray Gnatcatchers. They may use riparian thickets on occasion, but only if chaparral or dry woodlands are near. They fix their intricate cup nests on horizontal limbs of small trees or shrubs where they are protected from direct sunlight by overhanging leaves. Gnatcatchers nest fairly commonly in the Sierra to the upper limits of the foothill chaparral. They warble their soft songs only during the peak breeding season, from April until early July. In late summer, a few travel up to montane chaparral of the mixed-conifer zone, but seldom much higher. During the winter they occur in the foothills, especially in the south, but are very rare; most migrate to warmer portions of the southwestern U.S.

Male and female gnatcatchers are similar, but breeding males have black lines on their foreheads and in front of their eyes.

Where Found:
Yosemite: West of the park in canyons of Merced and Tuolumne Rivers and at El Portal; noted up to Yosemite Valley in late summer and fall.
Sequoia-Kings Canyon: Shepherd Saddle Road, Elk Creek, Marble Falls Trail, Deer Ridge.

THRUSHES *(Subfamily Turdinae)*

With their long, moderately slender bills, thrushes take insects, worms and spiders from the ground and low plants or snatch them from midair. In late summer and fall, they feast on fruits and berries. Their young leave the nest with heavily-spotted breasts, but only two of the seven Sierran species retain their breast spots as adults. The vivid hues of the two bluebirds pose a striking contrast to the browns, grays and reds of other thrushes. Bluebirds seldom sing after dawn, and their soft warbled songs pale in comparison with their drabber relatives' complex melodies, widely praised for their beauty. Most thrushes build the familiar robin-like cup-nests in trees or on the ground, but the bluebirds use holes in trees.

Western Bluebird *(Sialia mexicana)*   Plate 28

Bluebirds perch on low branches or fences in open grassy areas when hunting and dart out to capture insects on the ground, on low plants or occasionally in midair. They often hover a few feet above the ground before dropping to seize their prey. Bluebirds nest in tree cavities, often old woodpecker holes. They will also use nest boxes or abandoned mud nests of Barn or Cliff Swallows. Often woodpeckers invade burned forests in large numbers and bluebirds follow, taking advantage of the abundant nest-sites, insects and open habitat.

The Western Bluebird, a classic "edge" species, typically inhabits the border between two markedly different habitats, woodlands and openings. Often a large diversity of animals inhabit such edges. Many simply live in one of the two habitats, but some, like the Western Bluebird, prefer the border itself. Such edge species may be attracted by the especially abundant or unique resources or by combinations not available in either habitat alone.

The Western Bluebird breeds most commonly in foothill woodlands but also in open conifer forests, usually at lower elevations than the Mountain Bluebird. Both species were found nesting, however, in a recently burned red fir-lodgepole pine forest at 7800 feet in Yosemite National Park.

In late summer and fall, Western Bluebirds form small flocks and become more common in the conifer belt, especially in oak groves and meadows up to the subalpine zone. They retreat below the snow line for the winter. Good crops of ripe mistletoe berries may determine in large part where they spend the postbreeding and winter seasons; they invade even the densest oak groves to feast on this favored food. Western Bluebirds often flock with Yellow-rumped Warblers but rarely with other species, although they sometimes mingle with waxwings and robins at good clumps of berries.

Where Found:
Yosemite: Yosemite Valley, Wawona, Foresta; more common west of the park, as at El Portal, Groveland and Wards Ferry (lower Tuolumne River). **Sequoia-Kings Canyon:** Cedar Grove, Grant Grove, Wolverton, Giant Forest, Three Rivers, Ash Mountain, Mineral King.

Mountain Bluebird *(Sialia currucoides)* Plate 28

In the visual wealth of high Sierran landscapes the stunning, sky-blue plumage of the male Mountain Bluebird stands out as a special gem. Even the grayish females and young show flashes of this intense blue in their wings, rumps and tails. Mountain Bluebirds typically occupy large meadows, dry grassy openings and rocky fell-fields from the red fir zone to above tree line. In these open landscapes they scan for insects from low shrubs or rocks and fly out to seize them on the ground or in midair. Often they hover 10 to 20 feet above the ground before dropping on their prey. Less dependent on trees than Western Bluebirds, they sometimes nest in rock crevices or human structures, though they prefer abandoned woodpecker holes when available. Competition for holes is keen and Mountain Bluebirds have been seen chasing chickadees, nuthatches and Violet-green Swallows away from potential nest-sites. Rarely, Western Bluebirds nest as high as the red fir zone, and fierce competition for nest-holes would be expected where the two bluebirds co-occur.

After young Mountain Bluebirds leave the nest, their parents lead them to nearby stands of dense vegetation, presumably to hide them from predators until they gain independence. Small flocks, perhaps family groups, form in the fall and linger at high elevations through September or later. By winter most Mountain Bluebirds have departed for the Central Valley, the lowlands east of the Sierra or more southern latitudes, but a few winter at high elevations. In spring and fall some migrate through middle elevations, in transit between their breeding and wintering areas.

Where Found:
Yosemite: Mt. Hoffman, Tuolumne Meadows, Tioga Pass, Mono Pass, Saddlebag Lake (just east of the park).
Sequoia-Kings Canyon: Charlotte Lake, Center Basin, Upper Kern Basin, Boreal Plateau.

Townsend's Solitaire *(Myadestes townsendi)*   Plate 28, Figure 14

Although no more solitary than many other forest birds, Townsend's Solitaire is a drab species whose quiet nature during the nesting season makes it seem less common than it really is. Solitaires fly out from perches to hawk insects in midair or pick them off bark, foliage or the ground. Some forage conspicuously over mountain chaparral, using tall scattered conifers as perches, but many stick to open understories of shaded forests. There only the flash of white tail edges and buff wing patches and the snapping of their beaks as they capture prey betray their ghostlike presence.

In exuberant contrast is the male's song, which though infrequently delivered, is extolled for its virtuosity. For this performance he selects a perch near the top of a tall conifer and utters a complex series of musical warbles and trills that may continue for half a minute. In tone the song has the clear flute-like quality of thrushes and robins, while its rapid, warbly pattern is reminiscent of Cassin's Finches. When establishing their fall-winter territories, solitaires may actually sing more often than in the spring. They also make a short, mellow whistle that may be mistaken for a Pygmy-Owl call, though higher in pitch.

Their simple nest is built on or near the ground, on a well-drained spot under a protecting overhang such as an exposed tree root, the edge of a log or a crevice in a bank, rock wall or road cut. Most solitaires nest in the mixed-conifer and red fir zones, typically on ridges or canyon slopes.

Because they prefer open forests and denser stands with sparse understories, solitaires stand to benefit from forest fires of low to moderate intensity. Such fires remove understory vegetation and thin out the overstory without destroying many mature trees.

After breeding, solitaires often gather into small flocks and disperse both up and downslope in search of ripening berries, their favored food during colder months. They remain wherever they find an abundant supply, and so their winter distribution varies from year to year. Their favorite foods at higher elevations are juniper berries, and they vigorously defend a good patch against others of their own kind. At lower elevations they prefer mistletoe berries, but eat the fruits of toyon, manzanita and elderberries as well.

Where Found:
Yosemite: Mariposa Grove, Henness Ridge, Merced Grove Trail, Crane Flat, Gin Flat, Siesta Lake, Tuolumne Meadows.
Sequoia-Kings Canyon: Lewis Creek, Paradise Valley, Redwood Canyon, Wolverton area, Crescent Meadow, Mineral King.

Figure 14. Townsend's Solitaire.

Swainson's Thrush *(Catharus ustulatus)*   Plate 29

The disappearance of the Swainson's Thrush from Yosemite Valley is one of the unsolved mysteries of Sierran ornithology. Considered rather common in the 1920's, it has not been reported there for over 40 years. Its decline could be due to the influx of Brown-headed Cowbirds, but there is little evidence that Swainson's Thrushes are common hosts to these brood parasites. Whether Swainson's Thrushes have declined in other parts of the Sierra is unknown. They do still occur throughout the length of the range but are restricted to widely scattered localities, as was the case in the early 1900's. They nest at Buck's Lake, Plumas County, and are quite common at Blodgett Forest, El Dorado County.

A Swainson's Thrush looks a good deal like its close relative, the Hermit Thrush. The Swainson's is best distinguished by the lack of contrast between its plain brown back and tail. Only the Swainson's has a buffy wash beneath its breast spots, and its conspicuous buffy eye ring extends to the bill, forming "spectacles." These marks can be missed under poor viewing conditions. A good behavioral clue is that the Swainson's is usually calm and demure, unlike the Hermit, which frequently flicks its wings and pumps its tail up and down.

In the Sierra, Swainson's Thrushes breed in the ponderosa pine and mixed-conifer zones in dense thickets of willows, alders or brushy forest undergrowth near streams, lakes and wet meadows. They nest in shrubs or small trees, usually below eight feet. This secretive species searches for insects and spiders on the damp forest floor and is more often heard than seen. It delivers an ascending series of short, clear-toned phrases, among the finest of Sierran birdsongs, and a distinctive "water-drop" call note. Swainson's Thrushes are occasionally sighted in the Sierra foothills during their northward spring migration from wintering grounds in Central and South America.

Where Found:
Yosemite: In recent decades, recorded in the park only near Tuolumne Grove, White Wolf and east of Harden Lake; historically nested in Yosemite Valley and near Bower Cave (west of the park).
Sequoia-Kings Canyon: Paradise Valley, Zumwalt Meadows, Grant Grove, Mineral King Valley.

Hermit Thrush *(Catharus guttatus)*   Plate 29

From May until July the clear, sweet songs of the Hermit Thrush echo throughout Sierran forests of middle and high elevations, the short liquid phrases alternating between higher and lower pitches. Despite its numbers, however, this elusive thrush is seldom seen. Trying to find such birds in dense stands of giant Sierran conifers can be a frustrating experience, and one reward of learning bird songs is being able to locate species like thrushes without even glimpsing them.

The Hermit Thrush probes for insects and spiders in grassy areas or forest litter, usually under shady canopies, where its brown plumage makes it easy to overlook. It nests as low as the ponderosa pine zone in dense, moist groves, but mostly occurs in the mixed-conifer zone and above. In the subalpine zone it often inhabits more open forests, suggesting that its choice of dense habitat at lower elevations may reflect a physiological need for cool temperatures. While breeding it avoids forests with dense, shrubby understories, and usually nests below 15 feet in a clump of saplings with a clear view of the nearby surroundings. There the female lays three to five turquoise eggs, like a Robin's but smaller.

The Hermit Thrush often flicks its wings while perched and pumps its tail up and down, unlike the much rarer Swainson's Thrush, which looks a lot like it. The Hermit's quiet, raspy call can be mistaken for a Rufous-sided Towhee. This thrush can be confused with the Fox Sparrow, which also has a brownish back, rusty-red tail and a spotted breast. But the Fox Sparrow, unlike thrushes, has a thick seedeater's bill and a habit of scratching for food with its large feet.

Most Hermit Thrushes breeding in the Sierra depart for Mexico by late August, and a smaller contingent from the north takes their place in September and October. These migrants prefer brushy and riparian habitats with good crops of fruit. They descend to the foothills for the winter but, as their name suggests, never gather into flocks like robins and bluebirds.

Where Found:
Yosemite: Mariposa Grove, Peregoy Meadow, Tuolumne Grove, Crane Flat, Tuolumne Meadows; rare breeder in Yosemite Valley.
Sequoia-Kings Canyon: Cedar Grove, Grant Grove, Wolverton, Giant Forest, Mineral King.

American Robin *(Turdus migratorius)* Plate 29

Wet meadows of the Sierra teem with bird activity, especially along their edges and in bordering trees and shrubs. The robin, however, is one of the few species that regularly forages in the open, far from shade and cover. Typically it dashes across a meadow, stops short and cocks its head to listen and peer at the ground ahead. After a momentary freeze it jabs its bill at an unsuspecting worm or insect. Robins also forage in moist forest understories, and in the fall and winter they feast on fruits of toyon, dogwood, mistletoe and elderberry. They nest throughout the Sierra, preferring moist, open coniferous forests. Human developments such as irrigated lawns and pastures benefit robins and have allowed them to extend their breeding range down into the foothills.

The male robin proclaims his territory with a simple warbling song, one of the first heard at dawn. His song is easily confused with those of the Black-headed Grosbeak and Western Tanager, common in his habitat. The female, drabber in color than the male, lays three or four exquisite light blue eggs. On leaving the nest, the young resemble their parents but for their speckled breasts and lack of red.

In the winter robins invade the foothills and Central Valley, sometimes flocking by the thousands. A flock seen in 1984 was spread out over a three-mile section of the Tuolumne River canyon and contained an estimated one hundred thousand birds! At night robins return from miles around to communal roosts that may encompass many acres of woodland. A few winter each year at higher elevations, but usually remain below the heavy snows. Doubtless many of the Sierra's wintering robins come from colder climes to the north, while some or all of its breeding robins probably migrate south for the winter, rather than downslope.

Where Found:
Yosemite: Yosemite Valley, Wawona, Glacier Point, Foresta, Crane Flat, Tenaya Lake, Tuolumne Meadows, Tioga Pass.
Sequoia-Kings Canyon: Breeds at Cedar Grove, Grant Grove, Lodgepole, Giant Forest and Mineral King. Winters at Three Rivers and Ash Mountain.

Varied Thrush (*Ixoreus naevius*) Plate 29

This flashy visitor from the north is one of the few Sierran songbirds that occurs in winter but does not remain to breed. Despite its bright colors, the Varied Thrush is easily overlooked, due to its quiet nature and affinity for deep, shaded forests and dense chaparral. Although it calls infrequently in winter, the first clue to its presence may be its vibrant, musical buzz, like someone whistling and humming at once.

From October to April, Varied Thrushes may appear locally in large numbers, but some years they are rare or absent. They concentrate where berries are plentiful, generally remaining below the heavy snows. They may form sizable flocks or mingle with robins, where they could go unnoticed due to similar shape and size. In flight Varied Thrushes can best be distinguished by their orange wing bars or by the male's black breastband. Besides eating toyon, manzanita, mistletoe and dogwood berries, they search for acorns and invertebrates in the damp forest litter. As the berry crop is depleted at higher elevations, they descend to the foothills for the winter.

Where Found:
Yosemite: Winters irregularly in Yosemite Valley, with records at Mariposa Grove, Chinquapin and west of the park, as at Ackerson Meadow, near Early Intake and at Wards Ferry on the lower Tuolumne River.
Sequoia-Kings Canyon: Winters irregularly at Ash Mountain. Observed in fall migration at Grant Grove and Mineral King.

WRENTITS *(Subfamily Timaliinae)*

Wrentit *(Chamaea fasciata)* Plate 27

More than any other sound, the ringing staccato notes of Wrentits express the spirit of the chaparral. Both males and females echo these "bouncing-ball" calls, but the latter do not trill at the end. Wrentits call in all seasons and are more often heard than seen. They stay near the ground in dense growths of chamise and other shrubbery and seem reluctant to expose themselves to view. When feeding they flit between twigs and leaves, picking insects, spiders and small berries from foliage. Wrentits mate for life and spend much of their time in close company with each other, foraging, preening and roosting. Males and females appear identical, with grayish-brown plumage, white eyes and wren-like uptilted tails.

Wrentits abound year-round on shrub-clad slopes of the Sierra foothills and breed sparingly up into the montane chaparral of the ponderosa pine zone. They may seem less common than they really are because they space themselves out uniformly. In truth, they are among the most abundant chaparral species. Pairs remain near their nest sites most of their lives and both parents share in building cup nests concealed in low shrubs. After the spring breeding season, a few individuals (mostly immatures) move up to forage amidst the snowberries, manzanitas and huckleberry oaks of the mixed-conifer zone, where they may remain until fall.

Where Found:
Yosemite: Alder Creek Trail near Wawona; Foresta; west of the park in canyons of Merced and Tuolumne Rivers and on slopes above El Portal, Old Priest Grade and New Priest Grade (Highway 120).
Sequoia-Kings Canyon: Ash Mountain, Elk Creek Trail, Potwisha, Marble Falls Trail, near Hospital Rock and as high as Hanging Rock, Giant Forest.

MOCKINGBIRDS AND THRASHERS *(Family Mimidae)*

Mockingbirds and thrashers are inspired singers and accomplished mimics, as their family name suggests. Most display patterns of gray or brown, identical for both sexes. These slender, long-tailed birds use their strong, down-curved bills to forage on the ground or in dense brush cover.

Northern Mockingbird[1] *(Mimus polyglottos)* Plate 30

The enchantingly varied songs of Northern Mockingbirds can be heard in the Sierra foothills at all times of year, save perhaps in late summer and early winter when they may be silent for a few weeks. They sing melodies composed of many motifs, each repeated several times before switching to a different tune. They imitate the sounds of lowland birds such as Scrub Jays, Acorn Woodpeckers, Plain Titmice and Northern Orioles, as well as toads, frogs, cats, dogs, squeaky doors or almost anything that strikes their fancy. At least 10% of their song is mimicry and the remainder, pure mockingbird. Frequently they sing long into the night, especially on warm evenings when the moon is out.

Prior to the arrival of Europeans in California, these birds were probably confined to low-elevation sagebrush, chaparral and deserts from the San Joaquin Valley south. As settlers moved into the state, mockingbirds gradually spread northward as far as Crescent City and Redding and eastward to Sierra foothill towns such as Auburn and Jackson. They strongly prefer farmlands, suburbs and country gardens with fruiting shrubs and trees and avoid heavily wooded areas. Although common in the Central Valley, they reside uncommonly in the Sierra foothills and rarely venture much higher.

Mockingbirds defend nesting territories vigorously against all intruders. With white wing patches and outer tail feathers flashing, they fly aggressively at other mockingbirds, Scrub Jays, cats, dogs and even humans. They nest from February until September, a very long breeding period compared to most birds. Both parents construct the nest with coarse twigs and weed stems in forked branches, usually near the ground. While young birds are in the nests they are fed protein-rich animal foods such as grasshoppers, beetles or spiders. During the nonbreeding season, however, mockingbirds depend largely on fruits and berries gleaned from plants or picked off the ground.

Where Found:
Yosemite: Snelling, Mariposa, Coulterville, Big Oak Flat and Groveland; recorded historically up to Yosemite Valley.
Sequoia-Kings Canyon: Three Rivers; rare at Ash Mountain.

California Thrasher *(Toxostoma redivivum)* Plate 30

Hidden deep beneath the cover of protective chaparral, California

[1]*Formerly, Mockingbird.*

Thrashers rake their long, curved bills sideways through leaf litter and probe in the soil for beetles, ants, wasps or spiders. These long-tailed, brownish birds also relish berries and seeds taken from bushes as well as on the ground. Males and females both sing from the tops of shrubs or low trees. Like their relatives, the mockingbirds, they sing richly varied songs, though their repertoires are not as extensive and they mimic less freely. Thrashers repeat themselves less, uttering each phrase only once or twice.

Thrashers avoid heavily forested areas but are fairly common on brushy slopes of the Sierra foothills. In dense growths of chamise or buckbrush their songs mingle with those of Wrentits and the similarly plumaged Brown Towhees. Less commonly, thrashers occur in brushy streamside thickets and rustic suburban gardens. Residents of the foothills, thrashers never wander into the higher mountains. They have, however, been recorded on the chaparral-covered western slopes of Walker Pass up to about 5000 feet in the extreme southern Sierra.

Their protracted nesting season may extend from December until August, and mated pairs often raise two broods of young per year. Deep within dense foliage of bushes or small trees both parents build a nest coarser than that of the Northern Mockingbird.

Where Found:
Yosemite: West of the park in the Merced River canyon up to El Portal; Tuolumne River drainage near Don Pedro Reservoir and upstream beyond Wards Ferry Bridge; Old Priest Grade, New Priest Grade (Highway 120) and Big Oak Flat. In the park recorded on the Alder Creek Trail near Wawona.
Sequoia-Kings Canyon: Three Rivers, Ash Mountain, Shepherd Saddle Road, Elk Creek, Marble Falls Trail.

PIPITS *(Family Motacillidae)*

Water Pipit *(Anthus spinoletta)* Plate 20

Loose, straggly flocks of Water Pipits rove about the Central Valley and Sierra foothills in winter, gleaning insects from bare ground or low shrubs while wagging and bobbing their tails incessantly. Feeding groups usually spread out and individuals appear to pay little attention to each other. Some birds may fly on to other fields while others linger on posts, fence lines or on the ground.

Water Pipits are common winter visitors to the short-grassed prairies of the Sierra foothills. Some few move to higher elevations during late summer and fall, visiting pond edges, mountain meadows, alpine fell fields and other open terrain. They nest primarily in treeless alpine and tundra habitats to the north and east of California. The State's first nest was discovered in 1974 at the Hall Natural Area, directly east of Yosemite. In 1975, more nesting birds were discovered at Lower Hitchcock Lake near Mt. Whitney in Sequoia National Park. Other recent nesting observations suggest that Water Pipits breed fairly commonly along the Sierra crest north at least to the Yosemite region. They build their nests of dried plant stems and mosses and hide them on the ground near grass tussocks or rocks. Nesting takes place between late June and early September, and females incubate the eggs alone.

The streaky, brownish plumage of Water Pipits pales next to the bold blacks and golds of Horned Larks, which often share the same habitats. Both species walk and run, but do not hop, and both call in flight. The pipits give musical notes that sound somewhat like "sip-sip" or "pip-it." Several grassland birds, including pipits, larks, Western Meadowlarks and Vesper Sparrows, have white-edged tails that stand out when they flush from the ground, suggesting they may serve as a generalized alarm signal. The central feathers of Water Pipits' tails are brown rather than black as in Horned Larks'.

Where Found:
Yosemite: Breeding—Hall Natural Area (Inyo National Forest). Nonbreeding—probably in lower foothill grasslands along Highways 120 and 140; recorded in Yosemite Valley.
Sequoia-Kings Canyon: Breeding—Center Basin, Tyndall Creek, Lower Hitchcock Lake, Mitre Basin. Nonbreeding—probably in foothill grasslands adjacent to Highways 180 and 198. Occasionally seen at the Three Rivers airport and Ash Mountain corrals in winter and spring.

WAXWINGS (Family Bombycillidae)

Cedar Waxwing (Bombycilla cedrorum)   Plate 30
Compact flocks of Cedar Waxwings perched in the tops of leafless trees fill the air with excited, high-pitched calls. A whistled "zee-zee-zee" is their only vocalization, as they have no song. They continue to call as they burst forth in unison in strong, graceful flight. In their tailored, fawn-colored plumages, males and females look identical, but the immatures are streaky through their first autumn. At close range most adults reveal inner wing feathers tipped with waxy, scarlet droplets from which the name derives. The exact function of these wing ornaments is unknown, and a few adults lack them.

Waxwings feed in flocks ranging in size from a dozen up to several hundred birds. They rove about looking for abundant growths of wild berries, fruits, flowers and buds, often gorging themselves on such delicacies. Pairs or even groups sometimes pass ripe fruits from bill to bill, perhaps to strengthen social bonds.

These gregarious birds travel nomadically through the Sierra foothills, and their numbers and locations vary greatly from year to year. Although they might be seen in any month (rarely in July), waxwings appear primarily during fall, winter and spring. Their fondness for fruits and open wooded habitats draws them to suburban parks, gardens, rural farms and orchards. Waxwings mostly keep to the foothills, but also visit ponderosa pine forests to feast on berries of mistletoe and madrone. They breed north of the Sierra, but flocks may linger late into May or June before departing—much later than most wintering songbirds. Some adults with dependent young begin returning by early August. A nesting pair was found at Buck's Lake (5153 feet), Butte County, and future breeding is most likely in the northern Sierra.

The larger Bohemian Waxwing, an extremely rare visitor in some winters, has red, yellow and white on the wings and bright cinnamon feathering under the tail.

Where Found:
Yosemite: Yosemite Valley, El Portal; west of the park at Mariposa, Big Oak Flat, Groveland and Hardin Flat.
Sequoia-Kings Canyon: Three Rivers, Ash Mountain; has been recorded in Giant Forest.

SILKY FLYCATCHERS *(Family Ptilogonatidae)*

Phainopepla *(Phainopepla nitens)* Plate 30

Phainopepla in Greek means "shining robe," a reference to the adult male's glossy black plumage. The females and immature birds, with their mouse-gray coloration and faded wing patches, look like dimmer versions of the males. Phainopeplas fly with slow, unsteady wingbeats and often sing in the air, making soft, low whistles and wheezy warbles. Expert flycatchers, they dart from a perch and hover, snatching insects one after another before alighting. They also seek out mistletoe berries and elderberries, sometimes plucking fruits from outer clusters while fluttering in midair.

Primarily arid-country birds, Phainopeplas concentrate during winter in deserts of the southwest. They are uncommon in the Sierra Nevada, especially in the north, and have not been recorded above about 4000 feet on the western slope. Irregular and unpredictable in their distribution, Phainopeplas breed as a rule in riparian groves along lower stream courses.

They also appear occasionally in foothill chaparral and oak woodlands, especially those with heavy growths of mistletoe. In southern portions of their range, Phainopeplas nest in the relatively cool months of February and March. After breeding, most of the population then moves north and westward along the coast of southern California to join the small numbers of resident birds. A few of these migrants from the south spend the spring and summer in the Sierra foothills and may breed a second time. They weave small bits of vegetation and cobwebs into shallow cup nests and lodge them in crotches of small, scattered trees. The males do most of the nest building, and probably more than half the incubating and feeding of young.

Where Found:
Yosemite: West of the park in drainages of the Merced and Tuolumne Rivers; near the confluence of the Tuolumne and the North Fork Tuolumne (nesting); recorded along Highway 140 near Catheys Valley.
Sequoia-Kings Canyon: Rarely observed at Ash Mountain and Potwisha (recent nesting) and along the lower section of the Mineral King Road. West of the parks, noted around Lake Kaweah, along Dry Creek and in the Tule River Canyon near Coffee Camp (Sequoia National Forest).

SHRIKES *(Family Laniidae)*

Loggerhead Shrike *(Lanius ludovicianus)*   Plate 20
These solitary hunters of open grasslands are among the few North American "songbirds" that regularly kill vertebrate prey. Equipped with remarkable eyesight, they sit patiently on fenceposts, telephone wires or exposed branches and watch for movement. When small birds or mice emerge from hiding, shrikes attack them fiercely with sharp claws and hooked beaks. They kill by severing the neck vertebrae with several quick bites. When their prey have been subdued, they fly with labored wingbeats to favorite perches to eat. They frequently impale their victims on barbed wire, thorns or sharp twigs for later meals. A typical shrike's larder might contain the mummified remains of Water Pipits, Savannah Sparrows, deer mice, lizards, crickets and moths. Despite their small size, shrikes rank as major predators of songbirds, especially nestlings, and have been known to reduce nesting success to zero within their territories. In many areas, however, they subsist mainly on insects. Although they usually pounce on prey from above, shrikes also hawk flying insects in the air. Like hawks, owls and other birds of prey, they cough up pellets of undigested fur, feathers and bone.
    Like American Kestrels, Loggerhead Shrikes often perch along country

roads of the Central Valley and Sierra foothills. Although they are fairly common all year, there is a marked influx to California's lowlands in winter. Shrikes require exposed lookout posts and often space themselves at regular intervals along powerlines or in the tops of blue oaks. They maintain feeding territories in open grasslands and woodlands all year, requiring a few dense-foliaged trees or shrubs for cover and nest placement. Nests are large structures built of thick twigs, roots and grasses on sturdy forked branches. In the foothills, breeding occurs from late February until early June. Shrikes stick largely to the lowlands in spring and summer, but in September and October they turn up occasionally in large, open meadows as high as the red fir zone.

With their grayish plumage and white wing patches, Loggerheads may be confused with Northern Mockingbirds, but shrikes are stouter with larger heads and black face masks. Their songs contain low warblings, buzzes and squeaks, rather than the elaborate mimicry of Mockers. In flight, shrikes beat their wings rapidly a few times and then glide, making deep undulations through the air.

Where Found:
Yosemite: Probably in lower foothill grasslands along Highways 120 and 140; has ranged upslope to Yosemite Valley and higher meadows in fall.
Sequoia-Kings Canyon: Probably in lower foothills along Highway 180, rarely up to Three Rivers and Ash Mountain. Recorded as high as 60 Lakes Basin (10,000 feet) in late summer.

STARLINGS *(Family Sturnidae)*

European Starling *(Sturnus vulgaris)* Plate 38
Starlings have plagued North America since their introduction from Europe almost 100 years ago by a group of misguided but well-intentioned Shakespeare enthusiasts. Their goal was to introduce every bird mentioned in Shakespeare's writing into North America. The first successful colony was established in New York in 1890, and by 1942 starlings had spread with phenomenal speed across the continent to California. They are probably still increasing in numbers today.

Farmers, cattle ranchers and city managers generally regard starlings with contempt. Vast flocks annually consume enormous quantities of grain and fruit and soil city streets with droppings. Perhaps one reason starlings have flourished so in North America is their varied diet. They usually feed on the ground and readily devour many types of insects, fruits, cultivated grains and weed seeds. They forage in trees, too, but prefer open grasslands and grazed pastures. In the eyes of many, the starling's worst habit is its way of usurping the homes of native cavity-nesting birds. Acorn Woodpeckers, Ash-throated Flycatchers, Western Bluebirds and other Sierran hole-nesters may suffer declines as these European invaders proliferate. They nest in riparian forests and oak woodlands, especially in the vicinity of towns, farms and livestock feeding areas. Starlings often produce two broods each breeding season. Abundant in the lowlands of California, they are uncommon in the Sierra foothills and rarely penetrate above the ponderosa pine zone.

Were they not such pests, starlings might be considered attractive, with their spangled breasts in fall and iridescent glossy sheen in spring and summer. When breeding, their bills also turn bright yellow. Starlings are easily confused with blackbirds but are stockier, with shorter tails.

Where Found:
Yosemite: Coulterville, Mariposa, adjacent farmlands and El Portal; occurs rarely in Yosemite Valley; noted in winter and spring up to Hardin Flat and Ackerson Meadow (Stanislaus National Forest).
Sequoia-Kings Canyon: Low foothills up to Three Rivers, Ash Mountain and Potwisha.

VIREOS *(Family Vireonidae)*

Like wood warblers, Sierran vireos search for insects in the foliage of trees and shrubs, but vireos are slower, more deliberate and less colorful. They have small, stocky bodies and relatively stout bills that are slightly hooked at the tip, and males and females of Sierran species look identical. Vireos' deep, cup-shaped nests generally hang by the rim from horizontal forks in branches.

Bell's Vireo *(Vireo bellii)*

Now extirpated as a breeding species in the Sierra and all of northern California, Bell's Vireo deserves mention here because of its tragic decline since the 1930's. Formerly abundant in many parts of the Central Valley, it also ranged into the lower Sierran foothills and nested fairly commonly in low, dense thickets along the Merced, Tuolumne and other rivers. The Least Bell's Vireo (*V. b. pusillus*), the race that occurred in the Sierra, still breeds in southern California but in such reduced numbers that it was recently listed as endangered by the State of California.

Its decline has been attributed partially to destruction of riparian habitat. Perhaps more damage has been done, however, by Brown-headed Cowbirds, which have increased dramatically in its range and frequently parasitize its broods (see p. 197).

Bell's Vireos still turn up extremely rarely in northern California and should be watched for in low-elevation riparian habitats. These birds, probably vagrants from the eastern United States rather than southern California, are reported less than once a year. They resemble Warbling Vireos, but have pale wing bars and narrow whitish eye rings and lack conspicuous eyebrow lines.

Where Found:
Yosemite: Formerly nested along the lower Tuolumne River near La Grange and along the lower Merced River near Snelling; possibly nested in Pleasant Valley (now inundated by Lake McClure).
Sequoia-Kings Canyon: No records located near the parks; apparently nested formerly in the South Fork Kern River Valley (Kern Co.), and migrants still occur there rarely.

Solitary Vireo *(Vireo solitarius)* Plate 26

Although "Solitary" is an accurate name for this vireo, it is not particularly informative, as most North American vireos are rather solitary. Pairs of vireos aggressively defend their breeding territories against intruders, and even after nesting do not gather into flocks.

Solitary Vireos announce their territories with a pleasing series of short, well-spaced phrases, alternating between higher and lower pitches. Although they often sing from high perches, and feed from understory shrubs to treetops, most nests are below 20 feet. They build deep cups on horizontal branches where foliage shades the eggs.

Brown-headed Cowbirds commonly parasitize this species' nests in the Sierra and may pose a grave threat to them in some areas. In Yosemite Valley, Solitary Vireos have declined dramatically since the 1930's, when cowbirds first appeared.

Solitary Vireos are fairly common summer residents of Sierran ponderosa pine and mixed-conifer forests, especially in open stands with abundant shrubs and oaks. They also inhabit moist, streamside forests of conifers and hardwoods and, after nesting, occasionally wander as high as the subalpine zone. By October all have departed to the south, not to return until April, when spring migrants pass through foothill woodlands as well as conifer forests. In the foothills they could be confused with Hutton's Vireos, as both are yellowish green and have a spectacled face. Solitary Vireos have larger bodies and distinctly gray heads that contrast sharply with their white throats and olive backs, and their spectacle marks, more prominent than on Hutton's, are unbroken above the eye.

Where Found:
Yosemite: Yosemite Valley, Peregoy Meadow, Foresta, Hodgdon Meadow, Tuolumne Grove, Crane Flat.

165

Sequoia-Kings Canyon: Redwood Canyon, Colony Mill Road, Eleven Range Overlook, Paradise Creek, Potwisha, Elk Creek, Mineral King Road, Clough Cave.

Hutton's Vireo *(Vireo huttoni)* Plate 26

No other bird is so closely tied to live oaks as this small, spectacled vireo. Because these are evergreen trees, Hutton's Vireos can search for insects in their foliage throughout the year. To a lesser extent they feed in willows, blue oaks and other trees in the vicinity. They nest in almost any kind of tree, or even a large shrub, and usually build near the ends of branches.

Hutton's Vireos breed fairly commonly in the Sierra foothills but only rarely in the ponderosa pine zone, mainly in stands of live oaks. Apparently most do not migrate, but some move upslope in fall and winter, increasing their numbers in the ponderosa pine zone.

The drably attired males produce an impressive array of calls. Each of their various territorial songs consists of a two-note phrase repeated many times in succession.

Although Hutton's Vireos could be confused with Solitary Vireos, the real challenge is distinguishing them from Ruby-crowned Kinglets, whose red crowns are absent among females and usually concealed by males. Hutton's Vireos have bigger heads and heavier bills, move slower and more deliberately and flit their wings less often than kinglets. They also lack the black wing bar found behind the kinglets' white wing bars, and their eye rings, unlike kinglets', connect to the bill by white lines, forming "spectacles." The eye rings of both species, unlike Solitary Vireos', are broken above the eye.

Where Found:
Yosemite: Below Foresta, near El Portal, near Wards Ferry (lower Tuolumne River) and elsewhere in foothills; rare in Yosemite Valley (breeding uncertain).
Sequoia-Kings Canyon: Potwisha Campground, Ash Mountain and scattered localities along the Middle Fork Kaweah River Canyon at low elevations.

Warbling Vireo *(Vireo gilvus)* Plate 26

This vireo's name was well chosen, for the male sings prolifically in a beautiful, warbling voice, even from the nest! Plain colored and snuggled down in the deep, woven cup with only his bill and tail protruding, he is difficult to see, but singing must surely make it easier for predators to find him. How this behavior has survived natural selection is a mystery.

Recent and alarming evidence suggests that Warbling Vireos are declining in some parts of the Sierra due to frequent brood parasitism by Brown-headed Cowbirds (see p. 197). Once common in Yosemite Valley, for example, they have become scarcer since cowbirds invaded the area in the 1930's.

Warbling Vireos thrive amid deciduous trees such as cottonwoods, alders and willows, especially beside streams or moist meadows. More common than other Sierran vireos, they nest from the foothills to the mixed-conifer forests and, sparsely, up into the red firs. Even in conifer forests they spend less time in conifers than in associated hardwoods such as aspen and black oak. In California, they usually nest in deciduous trees at heights of 30 feet or less, considerably lower than is typical in the eastern U.S. They only rarely move upslope after breeding, and most depart for warmer latitudes by mid-August.

Warbling Vireos are best recognized by their extreme plainness. No other Sierran bird is a uniform light gray above and white below, with a pale eyebrow line. The similar but extremely rare Bell's Vireo has wing bars and a narrow, pale eye ring.

Where Found:
Yosemite: Yosemite Valley, Peregoy Meadow, Wawona, Hodgdon Meadow, Tuolumne Grove, Crane Flat, Gin Flat.
Sequoia-Kings Canyon: Zumwalt Meadows, Tokopah Valley, Wolverton, Giant Forest, Mineral King, and Lloyd Meadows Basin (Sequoia National Forest).

EMBERIZIDS *(Family Emberizidae)*

This recently redefined family lumps together a diverse group of New World species ranging from thin-billed insectivores like warblers to seed-eaters such as sparrows. This group includes several large, distinctive sub-families (formerly families), which are described separately below.

WOOD WARBLERS *(Subfamily Parulinae)*

The small, slender-billed wood warblers enliven the Sierra with bright colors and cheery songs. At least some yellow is visible in the plumages of most Sierran species as they flit nervously through the foliage. Wood warblers live mainly on insects gleaned from branches and leaves or captured in midair. They occupy a wide range of habitats including dry chaparral, lush streamside thickets and the lofty boughs of the tallest conifers. Their complex songs may be heard throughout the nesting season but less frequently by midsummer. During the fall many low-elevation nesters and migrants from the north appear in the higher mountains. They often travel in large mixed-species flocks and congregate at meadow edges or in moist patches of willow, alder and shrubs beside Sierran streams. Most western species of wood warblers winter in montane pine and oak forests of Mexico and Central America.

Orange-crowned Warbler *(Vermivora celata)*   Plate 31

Among the first signs of spring in the Sierra foothills are the rapid, musical trills of Orange-crowned Warblers, which breed commonly on the western slope below the ponderosa pine zone. They arrive in March from their wintering grounds and establish nesting territories in open habitats dominated by shrubs. Oak woodlands, riparian thickets and steep canyons clothed in chaparral draw them especially. They dine largely on insects and spiders captured within the protective cover of tree crowns or dense brush. Orange-crowns sing from the highest branches of oaks, cottonwoods and sycamores, but build their nests on dry ground under the shelter of shrubs or other foliage.

As early as late May, some Orange-crowns finish nesting and move upslope to the ponderosa pine and mixed-conifer zones. Some seek out coniferous forests, but most frequent meadow edges or patches of shrubs within meadows and along streams. By July and August, small flocks move up into red fir and subalpine forests as well as brushy portions of alpine meadows. These visitors to high elevations may include both foot-hill nesters that have drifted upslope and migrants from farther north. By October most Orange-crowns depart to the south, but a few remain through the winter in the Sierra foothills and other lowlands of California.

The name of this warbler is misleading, as the orange crown rarely shows, even on breeding males. Both sexes have faintly streaked under-parts and lack the wing bars or eye rings of many other warblers. Compared to most other warblers, Orange-crowns move slowly and deliberately.

Where Found:
Yosemite: Breeding—west of the park in canyons of Merced and Tuolumne Rivers up at least to El Portal and Old Priest Grade (Highway 120). Post-breeding—Yosemite Valley, Wawona Meadow, Hodgdon Meadow, Crane Flat, White Wolf, Tuolumne Meadows.
Sequoia-Kings Canyon: Breeding—Three Rivers, Ash Mountain. Post-breeding—Zumwalt Meadows, Wolverton Meadow, Emerald Lake, Giant Forest, Kern Canyon, Mineral King.

Nashville Warbler *(Vermivora ruficapilla)*   Plate 31

Energetic songs proclaim the presence of Nashville Warblers, birds difficult to spot as they flit through dense foliage on their way to new singing perches. They arrive from their wintering grounds in April to establish nesting territories in open, brushy stands of black oaks, firs, pines and cedars of the ponderosa pine and mixed-conifer zones. Nashvilles search for adult insects and caterpillars in all kinds of vegetation, but seldom stray far from broadleaved trees, such as black oaks, or dense brush cover. Despite their fondness for trees and shrubs as feeding areas and song posts, they hide their nests on the ground beneath stumps or in rocky crevices, usually sheltered by overhanging grasses or foliage. After completing nesting in July, Nashvilles disperse to higher-elevation red fir and subalpine forests, and a few individuals have been observed above tree line. They tend to migrate relatively early; most depart the Sierra by mid-September.

The pioneer ornithologist Alexander Wilson first discovered these birds in migration near Nashville, Tennessee. Their bright yellow throats and complete white eye rings distinguish them from the similar, but gray-hooded, MacGillivray's Warblers.

Where Found:
Yosemite: Breeding—Yosemite Valley, Chinquapin, Big Meadow, Hodgdon Meadow, Crane Flat. Post-breeding—Bridalveil Meadow, Pere-goy Meadow, White Wolf, Porcupine Flat, Tuolumne Meadows.
Sequoia-Kings Canyon: Breeding—Cedar Grove, Zumwalt Meadows, Redwood Meadow, Giant Forest, Colony Mill Road, Paradise Creek, Elk Creek, Mineral King. Post-breeding—up to the High Sierra Trail.

Yellow Warbler (Dendroica petechia)   Plate 32

Like golden flecks of sunlight, Yellow Warblers flit among the lush green foliage of Sierran riparian forests. Once a common sight, they have declined in recent years on the western slope. Dam construction, water diversions and logging have removed much of their streamside habitat, and nest parasitism by Brown-headed Cowbirds (see p. 197) has diminished their numbers even further.

During spring migration their rapid, melodious "sweet-sweet-I'm-so-sweet" songs issue from a variety of habitats, but while nesting, most pairs prefer deciduous streamside forests of alders, willows or cottonwoods with thick understories of tangled shrubs. Some Yellow Warblers in the Sierra, however, breed in wet shrubby meadows, dry montane chaparral with scattered trees and, rarely, open conifer woods. They breed from the foothill woodlands up to the mixed-conifer zone and build nests between the forking stems of low shrubs. Post-nesting birds travel widely through mid-elevation forests where they usually forage in broadleaved trees. They migrate relatively early, departing by early September for their winter homes.

Most western wood warblers have bright yellow patches somewhere in their plumage, but none can match the uniformly brilliant hues of the Yellow Warbler. At a distance the male appears a solid bright yellow above and below, but his breast is actually streaked with chestnut.

Where Found:
Yosemite: Breeding—Yosemite Valley, Wawona Meadow, Hodgdon Meadow, near Crane Flat, and just south of O'Shaugnessy Dam at Hetch Hetchy. Post-breeding—White Wolf, Siesta Lake, Harden Lake.
Sequoia-Kings Canyon: Cedar Grove, Hume Lake, Grant Grove, Sugarloaf Valley, Crescent Meadow, Crystal Cave Trail, Paradise Creek, Hospital Rock.

Yellow-rumped Warbler[1] *(Dendroica coronata)* Plate 32, Figure 15

Somewhat larger and hardier than most of their relatives, Yellow-rumps are the only warblers that commonly reside year-round in the Sierra. In fall and winter they are common in open oak savannahs, foothill woodlands and riparian forests of the lowlands and occasionally range into ponderosa pine forests higher up. Yellow-rumps mostly glean insects from foliage, but often flutter out from tree crowns to snap up prey in midair. Occasionally during the colder months they also take seeds, berries or wild grapes, showing a flexibility of diet that allows them to thrive after other warblers have headed south.

In March and April, populations wintering in California's lowlands head for northern breeding grounds. At about the same time, nesting birds arrive from further south to take up summer residence in the Sierra Nevada. With snow drifts still blanketing the ground, they sing exuberant songs that signal the beginnings of spring. They inhabit all types of coniferous forest from the lowest ponderosa pines up to tree line, but nest most commonly from the mixed-conifer up to the subalpine zone. No other warbler occurs across such a wide range of elevations while breeding, and only the Wilson's shares their nesting haunts above the red fir zone. Yellow-rumps tolerate a wide range of forest conditions, but prefer open stands, forest-meadow edges, lakesides and other habitats providing ample air space for hawking insects. They nest low in shrubs or high in tall trees, hidden by thick sprays of conifer foliage. Post-breeding Yellow-rumps, or migrants from the north, remain in mid- and high-elevation forests through October. During the fall the birds often gather into flocks of twenty or more and flit through tree canopies, flashing white tail spots and uttering their characteristic "chip" notes. These flocks, which may include Orange-crowned, Hermit and Townsend's Warblers, Mountain Chickadees, Red-breasted Nuthatches and Golden-crowned Kinglets, move over

[1]*Formerly, Audubon's and Myrtle Warblers.*

great distances in search of productive feeding grounds.

Yellow-rumps sport a variety of plumages. Nesting males display striking blacks, yellows and grays, but females, immatures and wintering males are brownish and often extensively streaked. In all plumages, except juvenal, the bright yellow rump patch serves as a sure field mark. Males sing complex songs similar to those of the Hermit Warbler, and the two species share many of the same nesting habitats. These vocalizations may be confused, but the Yellow-rump's song sounds bolder and less buzzy.

Recently ornithologists merged the "Audubon's" and "Myrtle" Warblers into one species, the Yellow-rumped, because the two commonly interbreed where their ranges overlap. All of the nesting and most of the wintering Yellow-rumps in the Sierra belong to the Audubon's type (see Fig. 15). The white-throated Myrtles also winter in the Sierra foothills

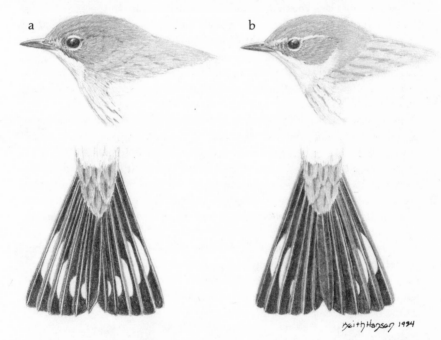

Figure 15. The Audubon's (a) and Myrtle (b) subspecies of the Yellow-rumped Warbler were classified as separate species until recently and can easily be distinguished in the field — even in winter. The Myrtle has a white throat patch and eyebrow that outline a dark cheek. The yellow throat patch of the Audubon's fades to pale yellow or whitish in winter, but does not curve up behind the ear like the Myrtle's. Audubon's, more common in the Sierra, has five pairs of white spots on the underside of its tail, giving a brighter flash than the Myrtle's, which has only three or four.

171

where they usually flock with Audubon's.

Where Found:
Yosemite: Breeding—Yosemite Valley, Big Meadow, Crane Flat, Gin Flat, White Wolf, Tenaya Lake, Tuolumne Meadows, Vogelsang Lake, Glen Aulin. Winter—west of the park at El Portal, Big Oak Flat and lower drainages of the Merced and Tuolumne Rivers.
Sequoia-Kings Canyon: Breeding—Cedar Grove, Grant Grove, Rowell Meadow, Emerald Lake, Giant Forest. Winter—Three Rivers, Ash Mountain.

Black-throated Gray Warbler *(Dendroica nigrescens)*   Plate 32

Aside from a small yellow patch in front of each eye, Black-throated Gray Warblers lack the bright golden hues of their Sierran relatives. They have instead a strikingly beautiful pattern of black, white and gray. At first glance they might be taken for the much more common Mountain Chickadees, which are smaller and have all white cheeks. The wheezy songs of Black-throated Grays may be confused with those of Hermit Warblers, which also nest in the Sierra, and with those of migrant Townsend's Warblers.

From April through mid-July, Black-throated Gray Warblers nest fairly commonly in the foothill woodlands and range sparingly up to the mixed-conifer zone. More than any other Sierran warblers they specialize in oaks, preferring dry, open forests with thick shrub cover. At low elevations they seek extensive stands of canyon live oaks, and in the higher forests they usually frequent black oaks. They build nests in low brush, or occasionally in broadleaved trees near streams. They dine mostly on insects, especially oak caterpillars.

After nesting, in August and September, they sometimes move to higher-elevation red fir and subalpine forests, but not so much as Orange-crowns and Nashvilles. The vast majority leave the Sierra for warmer climates by October, but a few have been recorded in the foothill woodlands of the Sierra during winter.

Where Found:
Yosemite: El Portal, Yosemite Valley, Big Meadow, Hodgdon Meadow; noted up to Wawona Meadow, White Wolf and Tuolumne Meadows in late summer.
Sequoia-Kings Canyon: Oak belt along the Generals Highway, Buckeye Flat, Mineral King Road, Kern Canyon, Sugarloaf Valley; in late summer recorded up to the High Sierra Trail, Colony Mill Road and Middle Sphinx Lake. Once noted at Ash Mountain in December.

Townsend's Warbler *(Dendroica townsendi)*   Plate 32

The Townsend's Warbler is a yellow counterpart of the Black-throated Gray. The two species closely resemble each other in pattern and coloration, save the Townsend's substitution of brilliant yellow for white on its face, breast and flanks. Such similarities of plumage suggest that these warblers share a recent common ancestry. In spring their wheezy songs also resemble each other. The Townsend's has never been recorded nesting in California; instead it moves farther north to the towering spruces and Douglas-firs of the Pacific Northwest.

In spring Townsend's Warblers migrate uncommonly through low elevation oak woodlands and chaparral. By early August, they begin to reappear in the Sierra on their way south. In late August and September their numbers increase as small flocks move through forests from the mixed-conifer to the subalpine zones. More common than in spring, they frequent conifer forests, meadow edges and riparian thickets, often associating with Hermit or Yellow-rumped Warblers. Townsend's Warblers are fairly common winter visitors to coastal California but are extremely rare in the Sierra foothills during the same period.

Where Found:
Yosemite: Yosemite Valley, Chinquapin, Hodgdon Meadow, Tuolumne Grove, Crane Flat, Gin Flat, Porcupine Creek, Tuolumne Meadows. Recorded during spring in the Tuolumne River canyon near the North Fork confluence, west of the park.
Sequoia-Kings Canyon: Noted in late summer or fall at Cedar Grove, Sphinx Lake, Grant Grove, Horse Corral Meadow, Giant Forest, High Sierra Trail, along the Middle Fork Kaweah River and at Mineral King; recorded in winter at Ash Mountain.

Hermit Warbler *(Dendroica occidentalis)*   Plate 32

As its name suggests, the Hermit Warbler was considered solitary and reclusive by early ornithologists. When it was named, few birdwatchers lived in the western half of the continent and its real status had not been discovered. In truth, the Hermit is probably the most common of the Sierran warblers in mid-elevation coniferous forests.

Hermit Warblers migrate in small numbers through the foothill woodlands in spring, but they confine nesting to the ponderosa pine and mixed-conifer zones. They forage and sing in the tallest pines, firs and other conifers and often hawk flying insects from treetop perches, like Yellow-rumps. Occasionally they descend to hunt for prey near the ground in patches of low shrubs or conifer seedlings. Their rapid, energetic songs are highly variable and may easily be confused with those of the closely related Black-throated Gray and Yellow-rumped Warblers. Their breeding distribution overlaps extensively with both species.

The breeding behavior of Hermit Warblers remains little known, despite their abundance. The few nests discovered in the Sierra have been hidden in the boughs of conifers, making them difficult to study. Hermit Warblers arrive in the Sierra in April and finish nesting by July, after which some move upslope to red fir and subalpine forests. Their southward migration begins in early August and most birds have left the Sierra by mid-September.

Where Found:
Yosemite: Yosemite Valley, Mariposa Grove, Hodgdon Meadow, Tuolumne Grove, Crane Flat, Gin Flat.
Sequoia-Kings Canyon: Grant Grove, Little Baldy Trail, Wolverton, Giant Forest, Crescent Meadow, Colony Mill Road, Paradise Creek, Mineral King.

MacGillivray's Warbler *(Oporornis tolmiei)*   Plate 31

A loud, metallic "chip," much like a junco's, is often the first clue that a MacGillivray's Warbler is near. Typically it utters such notes while skulking through dense shrubbery, a cover that offers only brief glimpses to an observer. During the nesting season, however, male MacGillivray's Warblers often ascend the tallest bushes and break into full song.

In the western Sierra, MacGillivray's breed from April through early July and unlike many other warblers keep to low vegetation. They nest fairly commonly from the ponderosa pine to the red fir zone where they seek out moist, low tangles of vines, dogwoods, willows and alders along streams, or shrubs, tall grasses and wildflowers in wet meadows. Apparently shrubs are more important than moisture to them, as they also nest in dry, open forests and on rocky hillsides with dense growths of huckleberry oak, snow brush or manzanita, a habitat they share with Green-tailed Towhees and Fox Sparrows. MacGillivray's Warblers attach their nests to forked branches of low shrubs. They also feed near the ground by gleaning from foliage and probing in leaf litter for insects. After nesting small numbers move through meadow edges and riparian corridors up to the alpine zone. The departure of MacGillivray's Warblers from the Sierra occurs in August, but a few birds may linger into September.

MacGillivray's might be confused with Nashville Warblers, but their gray hoods, broken eye rings and lack of bright yellow throats distinguish them.

Where Found:
Yosemite: Yosemite Valley, Chinquapin, Wawona Meadow, Mariposa Grove, Bridalveil Creek, Merced Grove, Hodgdon Meadow, Tuolumne

Grove, Crane Flat, Yosemite Creek, Indian Creek Canyon, Porcupine Creek.
Sequoia-Kings Canyon: Cedar Grove, Zumwalt Meadows, Grant Grove, Giant Forest, High Sierra Trail; also south of the parks at Lloyd Meadows and Redwood Meadow (Sequoia National Forest).

Common Yellowthroat *(Geothlypis trichas)*   Plate 31
These denizens of lowland marshes, lake shores and meandering streams rarely stray from wetlands. Aquatic habitats need not be extensive, however; damp, brushy margins of sloughs and drainage ditches, patches of tules and cattails around farm ponds, or small stands of willows near streams often support a nesting pair. Yellowthroats hide from view, like Marsh Wrens, in thick vegetation and only their frequent, deep "chalk" calls reveal their presence. Sometimes they ascend the tallest reeds and burst into loud, energetic "wichety-wichety-wichety" songs. Yellowthroats pick dragonflies, grasshoppers, adult butterflies and caterpillars off marshland plants.

Surrender of natural wetlands to urbanization and agriculture has greatly reduced yellowthroat populations. Where suitable habitats remain in the Central Valley and Sierra foothills, however, they can still be found. In the spring and summer yellowthroats build large, bulky nests and secure them to low plants near water. While breeding they keep primarily to the lower foothills, but rare migrants have been seen in wet meadows and streamside thickets up to the mixed-conifer zone. Most high-elevation records in the Sierra have fallen between late July and mid-October.

Where Found:
Yosemite: Probably breeds west of the park in moist habitats along Highways 120 and 140. Most migrants in the park have been recorded in Yosemite Valley; also noted at Crane Flat and Peregoy Meadow (possible nesting).
Sequoia-Kings Canyon: Below Terminus Dam (Lake Kaweah); recorded on the north side of Tokopah Falls.

Wilson's Warbler *(Wilsonia pusilla)*   Plate 31
Signalling the arrival of spring in the high country, Wilson's Warblers adorn the naked, snow-laden branches of willows and alders like animated golden ornaments. They arrive in the Sierra during mid-April and nest fairly commonly along shrub-bordered streams, lakes and wet meadows from the mixed-conifer zone to above tree line. At mid-elevations on the western slope they sometimes share nesting haunts with MacGillivray's Warblers, but Yellow-rumps are the only other warblers to breed in or above the subalpine zone. Selecting moist glades with luxuriant growths of

ferns, dogwoods, chokecherries and other low vegetation, Wilson's Warblers hide their nests under shrubs, roots or logs. Many of these highest-elevation populations do not finish nesting until August due to delayed snowmelt in alpine meadows. In contrast to most songbirds, male Wilson's Warblers in the Sierra sometimes secure several mates.

Although restricted to moist, shrubby habitats while breeding, Wilson's Warblers venture into arid terrain during migration. In spring many appear in foothill woodlands and chaparral, and in fall some travel through coniferous forests. Wilson's do some flycatching, but usually forage for insects and sing their chattery songs within the protective cover of low foliage.

Where Found:
Yosemite: Recorded breeding near the Yosemite Creek Trail, Porcupine Creek, Snow Creek, Tuolumne Meadows and Tioga Pass. In migration observed in El Portal and Yosemite Valley.
Sequoia-Kings Canyon: Recorded at Cedar Grove, Zumwalt Meadows, Grant Grove, Wolverton, Giant Forest, Crescent Meadow, High Sierra Trail, Colony Mill Road.

Yellow-breasted Chat *(Icteria virens)*

Grouped with the wood warblers by taxonomists, the Yellow-breasted Chat looks very different from most of its relatives. Far larger than the "typical" warblers, it has a thick, heavy bill and a dazzling array of musical whistles and harsh chattery songs. Something like a mockingbird, the chat imitates the calls of other species such as robins, jays and even woodpeckers.

Yellow-breasted Chats in the Sierra keep to broad stands of moist riparian forest where they dwell in the jungle-like tangles of willows, wild grape, berries and other vines that blanket the banks of lowland streams. While foraging, they usually stay low in vegetation, searching for insect swarms and occasionally fruits and seeds. They hide their nests in low growths near water. Chats once were fairly common and widespread in the Central Valley and along lower foothill streams of the western Sierra, but dams, water diversions and logging have eliminated most riparian habitats and they are now rare and restricted to a few remnant stands. Chats nest near Folsom Lake and up to about 2000 feet in Shasta, Tehama and Butte Counties in the northern Sierra. Farther south, they have been noted up as high as Yosemite Valley in late summer and fall. They are one of the latest-arriving warblers in spring and depart the Sierra in August or early September.

Where Found:
Yosemite: Regular through the summer at Turlock Lake State Recreation Area, along the lower Tuolumne River; found singing in early June along Redhill Road, a few miles south of Chinese Camp. A few sightings up to Yosemite Valley.
Sequoia-Kings Canyon: Riparian areas west of Terminus Dam (Lake Kaweah). Nests south of the parks along the South Fork Kern River (Kern Co.).

TANAGERS *(Subfamily Thraupinae)*

Western Tanager *(Piranga ludoviciana)* Plate 33, Cover

Western Tanager is too drab a name for these bursts of sunshine from the tropics. Males in their crimson, gold and black raiment adorn Sierran forests during spring and summer. They are the only Sierran representatives of a largely tropical subfamily that includes some of the world's most brilliantly colored birds.

From their wintering grounds in southern Mexico and Central America, Western Tanagers filter into lowland riparian forests, foothill woodlands and chaparral of the Sierra by early May. Five or more often flock together during spring migration, occasionally mingling with other long-distance migrants such as flycatchers, vireos and warblers. By late May, Western Tanagers move upslope into coniferous forests and begin nesting. They are fairly common in the ponderosa pine and mixed-conifer zones and occur sparingly up into the red fir forests. Tanagers prefer mature, open stands or the edges of denser forests, but they also inhabit deciduous trees along streams and lake shores, as well as clumps of black oak growing with conifers. Tall trees and open forests provide lofty song perches and airspace for hawking flying insects. Tanagers also search for insects by moving slowly and deliberately along sprays of leaves. They usually keep to high, dense foliage, perhaps to hide from *Accipiter* hawks and other predators that might spot them by their gaudy plumages. Later in the summer, they glean fruits and berries from ripening shrubs.

Tanagers build cup-nests on horizontal branches from 5 to 50 feet above the ground. Males sing during most of the nesting season. Their songs are often confused with those of American Robins and Black-headed Grosbeaks, but the tanagers are noticeably hoarser and less varied than either. Their "pit-a-dik" call notes are easier to learn. After the nesting season in August and September, the males begin to lose their bright red head feathers, but their wings remain black. Females look a bit like Northern Orioles, but have thicker, paler bills, all yellow underparts and darker greenish backs. Tanagers remain in Sierran forests until mid-September, when some of them wander up to the subalpine zone. By October these glorious birds have departed for warmer tropical latitudes and their golden hues are replaced by the fall colors of black oaks, aspens and cottonwoods.

The closely related Summer Tanagers nest rarely in mature groves of cottonwoods along the South Fork Kern River near Lake Isabella (Kern Co.). These rosy red tanagers are common in similar habitats of the southwestern and eastern U.S., but their range in southern California is shrinking dramatically due to destruction of riparian forests along the Colorado, Mojave, Kern and other western rivers.

Where Found:
Yosemite: Yosemite Valley, Chinquapin, Wawona, Mariposa Grove, Hodgdon Meadow, Tuolumne Grove, Crane Flat, Gin Flat, White Wolf, Porcupine Flat.
Sequoia-Kings Canyon: Cedar Grove, Grant Grove, Redwood Mountain, Wolverton, Giant Forest and Colony Mill Road; during spring migration, at low elevations in the Middle Fork Kaweah River Canyon.

BUNTINGS AND GROSBEAKS *(Subfamily Cardinalinae)*
Much like tanagers and warblers, the brightly colored Cardinalinae winter primarily south of the Sierra. Males typically wear vivid plumages compared with the drab females. Their heavy, conical bills help to crack the hard coats of seeds and nuts. Adults also eat fruits and buds, and insects provide an important source of protein for growing nestlings.

The name grosbeak means "large beak," and has no special taxonomic significance. Black-headed and Blue Grosbeaks of the subfamily Cardinalinae are only distantly related to Pine and Evening Grosbeaks of the family Fringillidae.

Black-headed Grosbeak *(Pheucticus melanocephalus)*   Plate 33
Among the first sounds of spring mornings in the Sierra are the loud, complex warblings of Black-headed Grosbeaks. These rapid songs resemble those of the American Robin but have a richer and more varied quality, full of clear trills and chirps. Male grosbeaks often burst into song while fluttering out from high perches, displaying their vivid plumage and stunning lemon underwings.

Black-headed Grosbeaks return to oak and riparian forests of the western Sierra in mid-April. Males arrive before the females to establish their nesting territories. These conspicuous singers favor broadleaved trees such as oaks, cottonwoods and willows, especially near water, but also live in dry, open conifer forests with shrubby undergrowth. From early May until late July they nest in foothill woodlands and up to the firs, pines and black oaks of the mixed-conifer zone. These grosbeaks thrive near human habitations and commonly forage in orchards and campgrounds where they snatch crumbs from picnic areas along with other scavengers such as Steller's Jays. Grosbeaks also relish fruits, berries, buds, insects and seeds, which they easily crack with their massive bills.

Black-headed Grosbeaks nest in flattened platforms thinly woven from weeds, twigs and rootlets. These they construct in bushes near the ground or at low levels in trees, usually near streams. When not engaged in territorial defense, males, unlike most songbirds, help their mates incubate the eggs. Males usually sing within 100 feet of their nests, and occasionally even while sitting on the eggs. By the end of July, their songs have largely ceased and nesting activities drawn to a close. In the Sierra, grosbeaks rarely venture upslope above their normal nesting range, and by mid-September they have departed for tropical wintering grounds.

Where Found:
Yosemite: El Portal, Yosemite Valley, Chinquapin, Wawona, Big Meadow, Merced Grove, Hodgdon Meadow, Tuolumne Grove, Crane Flat.
Sequoia-Kings Canyon: Cedar Grove, Grant Grove, Ash Mountain, Potwisha, Buckeye Flat Campground, Hospital Rock and lower section of the Mineral King Road.

Blue Grosbeak *(Guiraca caerulea)*

Luxuriant tangles of vines, shrubs and small trees along lowland streams and backwaters are the favored, but dwindling, haunts of Blue Grosbeaks. Most riparian habitats in California were destroyed long ago by clearing for agriculture, logging and bank "improvement," and Blue Grosbeaks and many other birds declined dramatically as a result.

Today Blue Grosbeaks are uncommon spring and summer residents of the Central Valley and rare in the lower Sierra foothills. Preferring open habitats, they frequent woodland borders, willow thickets and tufts of weeds along sloughs and irrigation ditches. Their nests are flimsy constructions of grass and weeds in low foliage. They forage for insects, spiders, seeds and wild fruits in low brambles and trees but also feed on the open ground. Blue Grosbeaks arrive on their breeding territories in early May and begin fall migration by the end of August. They rarely travel above the foothill woodlands.

Males are a deep blue with chestnut wing bars, but in poor lighting might be confused with the similarly dark and thick billed Brown-headed Cowbird. Female and immature Blue Grosbeaks are almost entirely brown, also with dark chestnut wing bars.

Yosemite: Recorded historically in Yosemite Valley; west of the park observed at Snelling (Merced Co.) and Indian Flat (Mariposa Co.).
Sequoia-Kings Canyon: Regular south of the parks along the South Fork Kern River, east of Lake Isabella (Kern Co.).

Lazuli Bunting *(Passerina amoena)* Plate 27

The exquisite turquoise plumage of the male Lazuli Bunting equals in splendor the semiprecious stone, lapis lazuli. The bunting sings his intricate songs persistently throughout the day from the tops of trees. His dull, brownish mate skulks more secretively amid the tangled undergrowth below. In habitats especially rich in insects or seeds, males holding choice territories may attract several mates. Nests are built in low brush, grasses or vines above dry ground, but usually near water. Unsuccessful males, often first-year birds, lurk in less productive peripheral areas.

Lazuli Buntings occur fairly commonly in the western Sierra in shrubby riparian growths, usually with at least a few taller cottonwoods, sycamores or oaks to serve as song posts. Extremely arid conditions such as foothill chaparral may be tolerated as long as some source of moisture is available. Most numerous at low elevations in the Sierra, buntings also nest in small numbers in shrublands, second-growth forests and meadow edges up to the mixed-conifer zone. They arrive in the Sierra foothills in April, but do not invade the higher mountains until mid-May. Rarely a few move upslope above their normal breeding grounds after nesting. Even in the high country they frequent low, dense riparian shrubs such as alders and willows. Lazuli Buntings make their fall departure from the Sierra by mid-September.

Indigo Buntings, the Lazuli's all-blue cousins, breed in the South Fork Kern River Valley, and hybrids between the two closely-related species have been observed there. Because such hybrids are rare, the two still qualify as separate species. The Indigo, largely an eastern species, has been pushing westward through the Southwest in recent years, but so far this is its only outpost in the Sierra.

Where Found:
Yosemite: El Portal, Yosemite Valley, Wawona Meadow, Big Meadow, Hodgdon Meadow, Crane Flat.
Sequoia-Kings Canyon: On slopes of Kings Canyon and at Wolverton, Hospital Rock, Marble Falls Trail, Ash Mountain, Shepherd Saddle Road and along Generals Highway below Giant Forest.

TOWHEES, SPARROWS AND JUNCOS
(Subfamily Emberizinae)

Although superficially similar to the finches (Fringillidae) and once included in that family, the towhees, juncos and sparrows are now considered more closely related to the warblers, tanagers, blackbirds and orioles. Unlike those colorful groups, the Emberizinae usually come in conservative shades of brown, gray, black and white, and most females resemble the males. The cutting edges of their short, thick bills are angled at the base, an adaptation for cracking seeds, their main food in fall and winter. During the breeding season most species prey heavily on insects as well as seeds and feed them to their young as a vital source of protein. They build open, bowl-shaped nests on the ground or in shrubs or trees.

Green-tailed Towhee *(Pipilo chlorurus)* — Plate 34

This colorful towhee features olive-green upperparts and bright yellow underwings, but its most striking marks are its reddish cap and clean white throat. Like the other two Sierran towhees, the Green-tailed is larger and longer-tailed than most sparrows and lives in brushy habitats. This is the towhee of higher elevations, occurring primarily from the mixed-conifer to the red fir zone. On the west slope it favors dense patches of low shrubs, particularly mixed stands of snow brush, manzanita and huckleberry oak interspersed with small openings. It avoids areas with more than a scattering of trees.

Such areas also attract the Fox Sparrow, a species remarkably similar in body size, nest-site, feeding behavior and song. Both nest on or near the ground under a dense shrub canopy and scratch for seeds and insects in leaf litter, under shrubs or nearby. Some of their songs sound nearly identical in pattern, but the towhee's has a weaker, wheezy quality unlike the clear, forceful tones of the Fox Sparrow. The towhee also makes a distinctive cat-like mewing call.

The Fox Sparrow is much more abundant in the western Sierra, while the Green-tailed Towhee is more numerous east of the crest, particularly in mixed stands of sagebrush, bitterbrush and other shrubs. The towhee is rather rare in northern and central portions of the west slope but fairly common locally in the southern Sierra. In May, August and September, migrating Green-tailed Towhees sometimes show up in brushy areas below and above their breeding range. With rare exceptions, they winter south of California.

Where Found:
Yosemite: Chinquapin, Gin Flat, Tamarack Flat, Yosemite Creek, Indian Canyon Creek.
Sequoia-Kings Canyon: Slopes above Cedar Grove and at Grant Grove,

Rufous-sided Towhee *(Pipilo erythrophthalmus)*   Plate 34

In the foothill chaparral a noisy but hidden scratching in dead leaves often turns out to be a Rufous-sided Towhee at work. Like the Fox Sparrow, which shares its habitat in winter, this striking towhee uncovers insects and seeds with a short forward hop and a vigorous backward kick. Because it likes to forage in deep accumulations of leaf litter, it often frequents stands of dead or dying shrubs. It is common in brushy habitats up to the ponderosa pine zone and occurs sparingly even higher. More tolerant of trees than the Green-tailed Towhee, it sometimes nests in open forests with shrubby understories.

Rufous-sided Towhees are as conspicuous to the ear as to the eye, thanks to their varied and frequent songs and calls. Males often mount a prominent perch to deliver their rapid, high-pitched trill, more musical than a Chipping Sparrow's, more rapid than a junco's, and more forceful and explosive than either. The paler female builds her nest in dense shrubs or vine tangles, on or near the ground.

In September and October, Rufous-sided Towhees may be seen at higher elevations but rarely above the mixed-conifer zone. Winter snows drive them down to the foothills, where many take up sites around homes with overgrown gardens or well-stocked feeders.

Where Found:
Yosemite: Yosemite Valley, Wawona Meadow, Henness Ridge, Foresta, Merced Grove trail, Hodgdon Meadow and near Tuolumne Grove.
Sequoia-Kings Canyon: Three Rivers, Ash Mountain, Elk Creek, Potwisha, Hospital Rock, High Sierra Trail, Cedar Grove area.

Brown Towhee *(Pipilo fuscus)*   Plate 34

Despite their plain plumage and unspectacular song, Brown Towhees are familiar and well-loved dooryard birds throughout much of California. In the Sierra they live in foothill habitats where dense shrubs border open ground. They also thrive in gardens, vacant lots, edges of fields and other disturbed areas that resemble their native habitats. They feed in openings but sing, nest and hide in shrubs; they tolerate trees only in small numbers. Extremely sedentary, they rarely wander beyond their nesting range.

Brown Towhees nest in dense shrubs and occasionally on the ground or up to 20 feet in trees. They search for insects and seeds on the ground like other towhees but scratch less vigorously and less frequently. While feeding they often utter a sharp, high "pink." Brown Towhees do not sing as often as Rufous-sided Towhees, but nevertheless are strongly territorial. The male's territorial song consists simply of a rapid series of "pink" notes.

Less often heard is a sound that males make when seeking mates, consisting of three or four "pinks" followed by a trill—somewhat like a Wrentit's call.

Where Found:
Yosemite: West of the park at Mariposa, El Portal, Big Oak Flat, New Priest Grade (Highway 120) and Redhill Road (south of Chinese Camp).
Sequoia-Kings Canyon: Three Rivers, Ash Mountain, Potwisha, Hospital Rock, Generals Highway below Giant Forest, and along the Mineral King Road.

Rufous-crowned Sparrow *(Aimophila ruficeps)* Plate 35

Pleasant, twittery songs, seldom heard in the Sierra, pour forth in spring from certain open, arid slopes in the foothills. Experienced observers may be reminded of House Wrens, but the sparrow-like tone identifies the songsters as Rufous-crowned Sparrows. Although their reddish caps suggest a Chipping Sparrow's, they can be recognized by their black "whisker" marks, less contrasty eye-stripes and dusky-gray rather than white underparts.

These year-round residents of the foothills avoid tall shrubs, dense chaparral and oak woodlands. Instead they favor dry, grassy hillsides with scattered low shrubs to use as singing posts and lookouts. Small rock outcrops are used in the same way and sometimes compensate for a lack of shrubs. These habitat specialists are rather uncommon in the Sierra, apparently because their required habitat is scarce. There is a resident population in Bidwell Park, in Chico, as well as at the locations listed below. Occurrence above the foothills is extremely rare.

Rufous-crowns nest on the ground and usually feed there, but sometimes glean insects from the foliage of shrubs and trees. They sink their nests level with the ground surface and conceal them beneath shrubs or low plants.

Where Found:
Yosemite: West of the park at El Portal and on slopes north of Wards Ferry and near Early Intake on the lower Tuolumne River.
Sequoia-Kings Canyon: Base of Terminus Dam (Lake Kaweah), Yucca Point (Ash Mountain Headquarters), Potwisha area and around rocky shores of Lake Success (Tulare Co.).

Chipping Sparrow *(Spizella passerina)* Plate 35

Although distinctive in plumage, Chipping Sparrows resemble Dark-eyed Juncos remarkably in their habits and ecology. Even their songs can be extremely difficult to tell apart, although the trill of the "Chippy" is less musical and faster than most junco songs. Both species prefer forest clearings and edges and also forage out into open meadows. Chipping Sparrows, however, frequent dry habitats where the ground cover is sparse, and avoid lush, grassy areas.

Chipping Sparrows forage on the ground for small seeds and insects but take more of the latter during spring and early summer. They nest in trees, usually conifers, near the outer ends of branches. They breed across a remarkable range of altitudes, from the Central Valley (at least formerly) and the foothills up to tree line. After nesting they feed in flocks, often mixed in with juncos, White-crowned Sparrows and other seed-eaters. They linger until late September but desert the Sierra to winter farther south and, rarely, in the San Joaquin Valley.

The Brewer's Sparrow, a rare visitor from east of the crest, closely resembles the immature Chipping, which lacks the reddish cap of the breeding adult. The Chipping can be told by its dark lores (between the bill and the eye) and distinctly gray rump; the Brewer's rump is brownish-gray. Juvenile Chipping Sparrows, which do not molt into immature plumage until late October or early November, also have brown rumps, but are finely streaked below. They look much like juvenile Brewer's, but the Brewer's has pale lores and it molts into immature plumage (much like the adult's) before leaving its breeding grounds.

Where Found:
Yosemite: Yosemite Valley, Wawona Meadow, Peregoy Meadow, Hodgdon Meadow, Crane Flat, White Wolf, Tuolumne Meadows.
Sequoia-Kings Canyon: Cedar Grove, Grant Grove, Wolverton, Giant Forest, Colony Mill Road.

Black-chinned Sparrow *(Spizella atrogularis)*   Plate 27

To find this handsome but elusive chaparral sparrow it is best to learn its song, which is similar in pattern to that of its frequent neighbor, the Wrentit, but sweeter and less forceful. Timing is critical, for the Black-chinned does not arrive until mid-April and becomes rather quiet after May. It sings mostly around dawn.

The Black-chinned Sparrow nests only at scattered locations in the Sierra foothills, usually in fairly dense, arid chaparral of mixed species, typically chamise, sagebrush and ceanothus. Recently burned areas where the shrubs have regrown are excellent habitat. Black-chinned Sparrows feed in and under shrubs and conceal their nests among low branches, off the ground. By early September they depart for their wintering grounds south of California.

Where Found:
Yosemite: Foresta Road, below Foresta Falls; New Priest Grade, below

Groveland; above Cherry Creek, near Tuolumne River; also found singing near Hetch Hetchy Reservoir and near Black's Creek, west of Coulterville. **Sequoia-Kings Canyon:** One record above Barton's Flat Store in Kings Canyon and another record of an immature bird at Potwisha.

Vesper Sparrow *(Pooecetes gramineus)* Plate 36

In foothill grasslands, mostly in the southern half of the Sierra, winter groups of Savannah and Lark Sparrows sometimes include a few of the rarer Vespers. These streak-breasted sparrows occur in the foothills of the northern Sierra as rare migrants in spring and fall, and very rarely show up at high elevations. They resemble Savannah Sparrows, which lack the Vesper's white outer tail feathers, and Water Pipits, which have slender bills and walk rather than hop.

Vesper Sparrows prefer short, sparse grasslands scattered with shrubs for cover and few if any trees; most inhabit rather dry, level plains or gradual slopes. They nest on the ground under the cover of low plants. Vesper Sparrows breed all along the eastern base of the Sierra and, on the west slope, in high mountain meadows of the upper Kern River drainage.

Where Found:
Yosemite: Recorded at Yosemite Valley, White Wolf, Tuolumne Meadows and west of the park at La Grange and east of Coulterville.
Sequoia-Kings Canyon: Apparently breeds at Whitney, Monache and Troy Meadows in the upper Kern River drainage just south of Sequoia National Park. Winters in foothills west of the parks.

Lark Sparrow *(Chondestes grammacus)* Plate 35

With their bold facial markings and wonderfully varied songs, Lark Sparrows rank as favorites among many birdlovers. Permanent residents of the foothill woodlands, they may often be seen perched on fences or flying away, flashing the white outer margins of their tails.

Like Western Bluebirds and other "edge" species (see p. 150), they require open areas bordered by shrubs or trees, where they sing, rest, and take cover. Lark Sparrows forage on the ground in openings, looking for grasshoppers in particular, as well as other insects and seeds. They nest in small depressions on the ground that are shaded and concealed by small plants, or up to 20 feet in trees and shrubs. In mid-spring and late summer they occasionally visit meadows and grassy forest openings above the foothills.

Where Found:
Yosemite: El Portal, Moccasin, Groveland, Hardin Flat. Very rare migrant in the park, recorded from Yosemite Valley up to Tuolumne Meadows.

185

Sequoia-Kings Canyon: North Fork Drive, Three Rivers, Shepherd Saddle Road, Ash Mountain, Potwisha, Mineral King Road.

Sage Sparrow *(Amphispiza belli)* Plate 35

Although Sage Sparrows are much more widespread in the sagebrush scrub east of the Sierra, two races breed on the west slope. The southern race, true to its name, lives in relatively dense sagebrush and other arid shrublands. When frightened, rather than flying like most sparrows, it runs from bush to bush. A rather uncommon nesting bird in Tulare and Kern Counties (up to 8000 feet), it leaves the Sierra to winter in the San Joaquin Valley and southern deserts.

A noticeably darker race, once considered a separate species (Bell's Sparrow), lives year-round in scattered locations from El Dorado to Mariposa County. It shows a strong preference for foothill chaparral dominated by chamise, usually fairly dense and two to five feet high. It could be more common than the scattered records suggest, as it spends most of its life beneath a concealing canopy of shrubs. In spring, however, the males perch conspicuously on bushtops to produce their short, tinkly songs.

Both races build nests low in shrubs or beneath them on the ground. Feeding mainly on the ground and in shrubs, they eat seeds primarily, along with some insects and succulent vegetation.

Where Found:
Yosemite: Near El Portal; at Black's Creek, west of Coulterville; and along Highway 49 two miles north of Coulterville.
Sequoia-Kings Canyon: In upper Kern River drainage near Junction Meadow, Kern Hot Springs and Kern Canyon Ranger Station; also recorded at Ash Mountain, Shepherd Saddle Road, Elk Creek, Potwisha and Mineral King.

Savannah Sparrow *(Passerculus sandwichensis)* Plate 36

Although often seen with others of their kind, Savannah Sparrows do not as a rule flock together, even in winter. Retiring and rather quiet, they are difficult to observe, as much of their life is spent beneath a concealing canopy of grass or sedge. Sometimes they perch on low shrubs or fence lines, but when disturbed they disappear quickly into their grassy realm.

Savannah Sparrows nest all along the eastern base of the Sierra, but apparently only at the extreme southern end of the west slope, in the foothills of the South Fork Kern River Valley. A nesting record on the west slope of Mt. Lassen suggests they may also breed at the northern end of the western Sierra. They nest on the ground, well hidden beneath low plants, usually in moist grasslands. In fall and winter, migrants invade the west slope, frequenting open, grassy fields throughout the foothills. Although they feed mainly on small seeds, they also eat insects during the nesting season. In late summer and fall they appear rarely in meadows and open habitats up to the red fir zone and occasionally higher.

Where Found:
Yosemite: Winters at Snelling, La Grange, and elsewhere in the lower foothills. Late summer and fall migrants recorded at Yosemite Valley, Peregoy Meadow, Miguel Meadow and Harden Lake.
Sequoia-Kings Canyon: Winters in foothills below Lake Kaweah. Late summer and fall migrants recorded at Ash Mountain, Potwisha, Giant Forest and Bullfrog Lake (Kings Canyon N.P.).

Grasshopper Sparrow *(Ammodramus savannarum)* Plate 36

This plain sparrow of open grasslands was aptly named. Not only does it prefer grasshoppers over other foods, but it also sings a grasshopper-like song, ending in a weak, high-pitched, buzzy trill. Its song sounds much like that of the Savannah Sparrow, which nests very locally in Sierran foothill grasslands. The trills of the Savannah, however, lack the buzzy quality of the Grasshopper's and are interspersed with high-pitched "chips." When the furtive Grasshopper emerges from its grassy hideaways to sing or perch on a tall weed stalk, it can easily be told from Savannah and Vesper Sparrows because its breast is unstreaked and its tail short and pointed.

Only a few nesting pairs of Grasshopper Sparrows have been reported on the west slopes of the Sierra and Mt. Lassen, in mountain meadows of the ponderosa pine zone. Due to their secretive behavior and quiet songs, however, they could easily escape notice. A careful search of suitable meadows and foothill grasslands could reveal additional breeding localities as have recent studies in Marin County. The reasons for these sparrows' patchy distribution in California have not been fully explained, but many California grasslands are probably too sparse for their liking. They seem to prefer well-drained areas with few shrubs or trees and a diversity of herbaceous plants dense and tall enough to conceal their nesting and feeding activities. Besides grasshoppers, they eat many other insects and small seeds.

Grasshopper Sparrows occur in the Sierra from May through September and migrate south for the winter.

Where Found:
Yosemite: Several probable breeding records from Smith Creek, east of Coulterville; several singing males observed recently at Ackerson Meadow, just west of the park.
Sequoia-Kings Canyon: No records.

Fox Sparrow *(Passerella iliaca)*   Plate 36

The Fox Sparrow exhibits remarkably different colorations among its many races, but all have reddish-brown tails and heavily streaked underparts. Those that winter in the eastern U.S. have bright rusty upperparts like a red fox, thus inspiring the name. Races nesting in the Sierra, however, display duller rusty-brown wings and tails that contrast with their grayish heads and backs. These breeding birds mostly leave the Sierra by late summer and are replaced by visitors from Canada and Alaska, with uniformly dark-brown heads and backs. Gray-headed birds, from the Sierra and elsewhere, are a distinct minority through the winter.

In many areas of Sierran montane chaparral, Fox Sparrows are the most common breeding species. Their brilliant, clear-toned songs resemble those of Green-tailed Towhees, which often share their haunts. Fox Sparrows typically summer in dense stands of ceanothus, manzanita and chinquapin, from the mixed-conifer to the subalpine zone. Even a relatively small patch of shrubs often provides sufficient cover for a nesting pair; nests are built in thick foliage or occasionally beneath it on the ground. Fox Sparrows tolerate trees in moderate density, but do not need them.

These ground-feeders uncover seeds and insects in humus and leaf litter by kicking vigorously backward with both feet, much like Rufous-sided Towhees. One study suggested that the great success of Fox Sparrows in the Sierra is due to their large, strong bills, which, unlike those of Green-tailed Towhees and other birds in their habitat, are capable of cracking the hard coats of ceanothus seeds.

Fox Sparrows from the north often linger in the mountains well into fall, sometimes venturing up to tree line, but heavy snows force them down to foothill chaparral for the winter. Rather solitary, they do not feed in flocks like many seed-eaters.

Where Found:
Yosemite: In summer, at Chinquapin, Ostrander Rocks, Panorama Trail, Crane Flat Lookout, Gin Flat, Tamarack Flat and Siesta Lake.
Sequoia-Kings Canyon: In summer, on the slopes above Cedar Grove and at Park Ridge, Little Baldy Trail, High Sierra Trail and Giant Forest.

Song Sparrow *(Melospiza melodia)*   Plate 36

The beautiful, ringing voice of the Song Sparrow is a familiar and welcome sound in parks, gardens and moist natural habitats throughout much of North America. In the Sierra foothills, these sparrows inhabit dense, low vegetation along streams, lakes, meadows, marshes and irrigation ditches. They conceal their nests in low cover like willow thickets, nettle patches or cattails, or on the ground beneath. Present up to the ponderosa pine zone or rarely higher while nesting, Song Sparrows descend to the foothills for the winter. Like Fox Sparrows, they do not form flocks.

Although they sing from exposed perches, Song Sparrows prefer to feed in dense undergrowth, scratching quietly in moist litter for small seeds and invertebrates. Insects, taken from low-lying plants, make up almost half of their diet in spring and summer.

Before 1940 Song Sparrows rarely nested above 200 feet in the central Sierra; now they nest commonly up to 4000 feet, and sometimes higher. Their population in the southern Sierra has apparently grown as well. Increases at low elevations may be attributed to a proliferation of irrigation ditches, but those at higher elevations remain unexplained. It is surprising that Song Sparrows have not declined in numbers, as they are particularly susceptible to nest parasitism by Brown-headed Cowbirds, which have recently invaded the west slope and seem implicated in the decline of other local songbirds (see p. 197). Song Sparrows, however, like other birds their size and larger, can often raise both cowbirds and their own young successfully.

Where Found:
Yosemite: In summer, at Yosemite Valley, Wawona Meadow, Peregoy Meadow and Hodgdon Meadow. In winter, at La Grange, Snelling, El Portal and, very rarely, as high as Yosemite Valley.
Sequoia-Kings Canyon: In summer, at Cedar Grove, Zumwalt Meadow, Bubbs Creek, Crescent Meadow and Mineral King. In winter, at Ash Mountain, below Terminus Dam (Lake Kaweah), along the South Fork Kaweah River and at Three Rivers.

Lincoln's Sparrow *(Melospiza lincolnii)* Plate 36

Like some of the chaparral sparrows, Lincoln's may be overlooked by those unfamiliar with their calls or habitat preference. They commonly forage beneath dense ground cover, and when flushed, disappear into thickets of willows or tall meadow plants. They may even sing from concealed perches. Only on occasion do singing males or alarmed parents near their nest provide the observer with a clear view. Unlike Song Sparrows, they sing for only a short period during the breeding season.

In the Sierra, Lincoln's Sparrows typically spend the summer in the mixed-conifer and red fir zones in lush, moist meadows with willow thickets, but some live in brushy areas along the borders of streams and lakes. They hide their nests on the ground at the base of willows or herbaceous plants. These Sierran breeders depart by August or September and are replaced by migrants from Alaska. Few of these northerners linger past September in the conifer forest zones; they winter in the lower foothills, in dense grasslands and streamside and lakeside thickets. Like many other sparrows, Lincoln's feed principally on small seeds, heavily supplemented by insects during the nesting season. Sometimes they hawk for insects in midair, a rather unsparrow-like approach to feeding.

The Lincoln's resembles Song or Savannah Sparrows, but it has finer breast streakings against a buffy background. Breast markings of immature Song Sparrows are similar, but those of the Lincoln's end in a more abrupt line across the breast, and the Lincoln's shows more distinct crown-stripes.

Where Found:
Yosemite: In summer at Peregoy Meadow, Crane Flat, White Wolf, Tuolumne Meadows. In winter at Snelling and La Grange, in the lower foothills.
Sequoia-Kings Canyon: In summer, at Crescent Meadow, Log Meadow, Round Meadow, Wolverton and Grant Grove Meadow. In winter, at Three Rivers.

Golden-crowned Sparrow *(Zonotrichia atricapilla)*   Plate 37

Golden-crowned Sparrows commonly sing in the Sierra foothills in the spring, voicing three plaintive, whistled notes, but none remain to breed. Rather, they depart by early May for northern nesting grounds and do not return until late September to spend the winter in the foothills and lowlands. In early fall, a few migrants wander regularly as high as the subalpine zone.

These common winter birds feed in flocks, often with White-crowned Sparrows and juncos, searching for small seeds and green shoots on the ground. They also take buds and flowers, including those of oaks and other trees. Golden-crowneds feed on open ground near shrubs or thickets and when alarmed fly up into this protective vegetation. Compared with White-crowneds, they prefer areas with more brush cover and less open ground.

Where Found:
Yosemite: Fall visitor from Yosemite Valley up to Tuolumne Meadows and occasionally higher. Winters in foothills near Early Intake (Tuolumne River) and at Moccasin, Groveland, El Portal and Snelling.
Sequoia-Kings Canyon: Winters at Three Rivers, Ash Mountain and Mineral King Road (low section).

White-crowned Sparrow *(Zonotrichia leucophrys)*

Plate 37, Figure 16

Except for game birds and endangered species, the White-crowned Sparrow is one of the most thoroughly studied birds in North America. It makes an ideal subject for casual nature study as well as scientific research because it is common and occupies open habitats where it can be readily observed.

The race that breeds in the Sierra (*Z. l. oriantha*) may be recognized by its black lores, the small areas between each eye and the upper edge of the bill (see Fig. 16). These birds live in high mountain meadows and in moist, grassy areas beside lakes and streams. There must be thickets of willows, young lodgepole pines, or shrubs for hiding places and nest-sites. They nest underneath such plants or on low branches. White-crowned Sparrows mainly scratch for small seeds on the ground, but also eat green shoots and berries and, during the nesting season, large numbers of insects. The male's clear, sweet song comes in many variations. Ornithologists have discovered local *oriantha* "dialects" that vary noticeably from one river drainage to the next!

White-crowned Sparrows nest from the red fir to the alpine zone. By late summer the *oriantha* have migrated south, and a white-lored race, *Z. l. gambelii*, appears. Flocks of *gambelii*, often mixing with other seed-eaters, range up to the subalpine zone on both slopes, feeding in open habitats where scattered shrubs or thickets provide refuge from predators. By winter they have moved down to the foothills and Central Valley, where

Figure 16. Heads of breeding (a — *oriantha*) and wintering (b — *gambelii*) subspecies of White-crowned Sparrows in the Sierra. *Oriantha* can be told by its entirely black lores that make the white eyeline appear to start from the eye rather than from the bill as in *gambelii*.

they often mingle with juncos and Golden-crowned Sparrows. Males sing on sunny days throughout the winter.

Where Found:
Yosemite: In summer, at White Wolf, Porcupine Flat, Tuolumne Meadows, Gaylor Lakes and Mt. Dana. In fall, from Yosemite Valley up to Tuolumne Meadows. Winters west of the park, as at Wards Ferry (lower Tuolumne River), La Grange, El Portal and Snelling.
Sequoia-Kings Canyon: In summer, at Bubbs Creek, Emerald Lake, Guitar Lake, Crabtree Lake and Mineral King. In winter at Three Rivers and Ash Mountain.

Dark-eyed Junco[1] *(Junco hyemalis)*   Plate 37, Figure 17
With their black hoods and flashy white tail-edges, these handsome little birds are among the most familiar in the Sierra, and few if any species are more abundant or widespread. Many people know them from feeders, campgrounds and picnic areas. Juncos spend summer from the ponderosa pine forests up to tree line, typically in meadows or moist, open forests where grasses and herbs provide a good supply of seeds and trees offer shade, singing perches and refuges from predators. They avoid dense brush-fields and do not nest in oak woodlands as they do in the Coast Range.

Often a pair of anxiously chipping parents betrays the presence of a nearby nest, but pinpointing the nest's exact location can be difficult. They hide their nests on the ground under low plants, fallen logs or rocks. At lower elevations, pairs typically raise two broods each summer.

Nesting juncos consume large numbers of insects and feed them to their young, thereby providing protein important for growth. During other seasons they take mainly small seeds on the ground. Although territorial while nesting, they feed in flocks during the rest of the year, often associating with other seed-eating birds. Large flocks visit higher elevations in late summer and fall, but they descend below the heavy snows in winter to permit continued ground-feeding. At this season they occupy almost any habitat that combines open areas for foraging and trees or brush for cover.

The male junco's song, an even series of bell-like notes, may be delivered at different speeds. At its fastest it sounds much like the trill of a Chipping Sparrow but is more musical in tone.

The Slate-colored Junco, a race (or group of races) of Dark-eyed Junco that breeds in Alaska and Canada, occurs rarely in Sierran flocks during

[1]*Includes four types of juncos, formerly considered separate species: Oregon (the common Sierran type), Slate-colored, White-winged and Grayheaded.*

Figure 17. Male Dark-eyed Junco.

migration and winter. This northern visitor lacks any sharp contrast between its head and back; males are uniformly slate gray above, while females are brownish-gray.

Where Found:
Yosemite: Breeds at Yosemite Valley, Glacier Point, Peregoy Meadow, Wawona, Crane Flat, White Wolf, Tuolumne Meadows and Tioga Pass. In winter, mostly west of the park, as at El Portal and in the Tuolumne River drainage at Moccasin, Wards Ferry and Early Intake; sparsely as high as Yosemite Valley.
Sequoia-Kings Canyon: Breeds at Cedar Grove, Grant Grove, Giant Forest and Mineral King. Winters at Three Rivers and Ash Mountain.

BLACKBIRDS, ORIOLES AND MEADOWLARKS
(Subfamily Icterinae)
Members of this New World group generally have long, pointed bills, and males often flaunt bright orange, yellow or iridescent black plumage. Females are typically drab in color. Many species are highly gregarious, forming large flocks after the breeding season and through the winter. Mixed flocks of blackbirds and cowbirds often travel and feed together.

Sierran members of this group are most common in the foothills and rather rare above the middle elevations.

Red-winged Blackbird *(Agelaius phoeniceus)*   **Plate 38**

In marshes choked with tules and cattails, male Red-winged Blackbirds voice their throaty songs. Perched on swaying stems they puff out their glossy black wings, prominently displaying scarlet shoulder patches. These bright "epaulets," and the frequently repeated, gurgly songs signal neighboring Red-wings that nesting territories will be defended vigorously. Adult males arrive first on the nesting grounds and stake out small areas with songs and chases. A few days later when the streaky females arrive, most boundary disputes will have been resolved and the entire marsh divided into individual male territories. Females inspect the displaying males, and the quality of their real estate, before choosing their nest sites. Successful males possessing particularly productive territories may attract harems of up to five females. Females, sometimes assisted by males, construct nests and fasten them to marsh plants, low tufts of grass, dense shrubs or small trees, usually near water and often directly above it.

Marshy habitats along ponds, lakes and streams of the Sierra foothills often harbor Red-winged Blackbirds in abundance. Small colonies breed in meadows and other wetlands up to the subalpine zone but retreat to the lowlands in winter, when huge flocks roam the Central Valley searching for weed seeds, waste grain and insects. They prefer to forage in moist habitats such as flooded fields and marshlands where they probe the soil and glean low vegetation. Often, feeding flocks of Red-wings associate with European Starlings, Brown-headed Cowbirds, Brewer's and Tricolored Blackbirds in winter. One race of Red-wings (*A. p. nevadensis*) has yellow margins to its red epaulets; it breeds at middle and high elevations of the Sierra and out into the Great Basin but winters in the Central Valley. The other Sierran race (*A. p. californicus*) has entirely red shoulder patches and resides all year in the Central Valley and lower foothills.

Where Found:
Yosemite: Occurs year-round west of the park along the lower reaches of the Merced and Tuolumne Rivers and at Don Pedro Reservoir and Hardin Flat. Breeds in Yosemite Valley and at Wawona Meadow, Hodgdon Meadow and Tuolumne Meadows (small colony).
Sequoia-Kings Canyon: Found year-round along lower portions of the Kaweah River up to Three Rivers. Breeds at Grouse Meadow, Zumwalt Meadows and Wolverton Meadow.

Tricolored Blackbird *(Agelaius tricolor)*

These gregarious birds live in flocks all year long, even while breeding.

They nest in compact colonies in dense cattails or tules rather than spreading out like their relatives, the Red-wings. A nesting marsh must be large enough to support the minimum colony size of about 50 pairs; some colonies are immense, numbering tens of thousands. Instead of feeding near their nests, Tricolors search for insects and seeds in open farmlands, flooded fields and along open pond margins, sometimes several miles away.

Common in the Central Valley, Tricolored Blackbirds also inhabit the low foothills of the Sierra. A few small breeding colonies have been found in marshy areas, where they remain all year. Flocks of several hundred birds have been noted in fields west of Folsom Lake in Placer County.

Male Tricolors are black overall, but have blood-red epaulets with striking white margins (buff-colored in fall). Their songs are shorter and less musical than those of the more common Red-wings. Female Tricolors and Red-wings have nearly identical streaky brown plumage.

Where Found:
Yosemite: Historical nesting near the lower Tuolumne River below La Grange.
Sequoia-Kings Canyon: A flock was once reported at Ash Mountain in early spring.

Western Meadowlark *(Sturnella neglecta)* Plate 20

The preeminent voice of California grasslands, the male Western Meadowlark, broadcasts his flute-like songs from tall weeds, fenceposts or treetops during the nesting season. Unlike most female Icterinae, which wear subdued plumages for the sake of nest camouflage, the female Western Meadowlark bears colors as vivid as her mate's. Her bright golden breast disappears when she sits on the nest, however, and her streaked brown back renders her almost invisible. As a further precaution against predators, the female conceals her nest under a dome of dried grasses, and approaches it circuitously through tunnels of weeds. Meadowlarks' coloration also camouflages them when foraging amid dirt clods, tussocks of grass and low shrubs. They pick adult and larval insects and waste grains from the ground.

Through spring and early summer, Western Meadowlarks nest fairly commonly in grasslands and open shrublands of the Sierra foothills. They prefer sites with relatively tall grasses and exposed song and lookout perches. A few individuals may also nest in scattered open habitats up to the ponderosa pine zone. Western Meadowlarks remain in the lowlands all year, but in summer small flocks travel upslope to mountain meadows, exposed ridgetops and alpine fell fields. They typically winter below the snow zone, but one bird was flushed from a juniper tree near the North

Fork American River (6000 feet) following one of the heaviest snow storms on record.

Where Found:
Yosemite: Foothill grasslands west of the park along Highways 120 and 140; in late summer and fall noted regularly up to Yosemite Valley and uncommonly to Tuolumne Meadows.
Sequoia-Kings Canyon: Foothill grasslands up to Ash Mountain; in fall recorded at Sugarloaf Meadow, Zumwalt Meadows and Wolverton Meadow; late spring observation at Lloyd Meadows (Sequoia National Forest).

Brewer's Blackbird *(Euphagus cyanocephalus)* Plate 38

Even non-birdwatching visitors to the Sierra may notice these glossy, bright-eyed birds strutting about, picking crumbs from picnic tables and campsites. Brewer's Blackbirds can make a living without the aid of human leavings, but they tend to concentrate around developed areas and near farms and corrals where livestock are fed. Besides eating waste grain and scraps, they probe in the ground with their sharp bills and turn over rocks looking for insect larvae and seeds.

Brewer's Blackbirds breed in grasslands, open shrublands, marshy areas, and along lakes and rivers, especially where trees are available for nest sites. Although fairly common year-round in the lower foothills, they breed rather sparingly above the ponderosa pine zone. They prefer to nest in dense foliage, particularly in conifers, but unusual nests have been found in rock crevices, on stumps along lake margins and even on the ground. Pairs may breed alone or colonially in large groups; they defend small territories around their nests.

At first glance the male looks rather plain, with only his golden eyes to offset a somber black plumage. In the sun, however, metallic hues of steel-blue to greenish-violet glint off his sleek features. The female remains an unremarkable dark brown. One might mistake her for a female Brown-headed Cowbird except she is larger and has a longer tail and longer, thinner bill.

Where Found:
Yosemite: Breeding—Yosemite Valley, Wawona and west of the park at El Portal and Don Pedro Reservoir. Post-breeding—Tenaya Lake, Tuolumne Meadows, Tioga Pass.
Sequoia-Kings Canyon: Breeding—Cedar Grove, Grant Grove, Lodgepole, Wolverton, Ash Mountain and Mineral King. Post-breeding—Rae Lakes, Sixty Lakes Basin.

Brown-headed Cowbird (*Molothrus ater*) Plate 38

Brown-headed Cowbirds devote not one iota of energy to rearing their own young. Instead, a breeding female cowbird lurks near a nesting pair of songbirds, waits for an opportune moment when both parents are away, then swiftly lays one of her own eggs among the host's clutch and makes a rapid getaway. Cowbirds often remove a host egg and so fool the unsuspecting foster parents. A female cowbird may return to lay more eggs in the same nest; over half the parasitized songbird nests reveal more than one egg. The returning parents may faithfully incubate the alien eggs as if nothing were amiss. Some larger species such as American Robins and Northern Orioles, however, defend against cowbirds by abandoning their parasitized nests, covering a clutch of eggs over with new material, or tossing cowbird eggs from nests altogether. For these reasons, more than half the cowbird eggs laid never hatch. Red-winged Blackbirds regularly drive cowbirds away from their nesting areas, but few other birds do this.

If the host parents cooperate, however, cowbird young usually hatch a day or two ahead of their nestmates. Being larger and noisier, they demand, and often receive, a larger share of the food brought by the foster parents. Some or all of the host's own nestlings may miss so much food that they weaken and die. A single female Brown-headed Cowbird may lay up to 30 eggs per season and be responsible for the loss of countless nests over her lifespan. Cowbirds parasitize virtually all kinds of songbirds except the largest species and the hole-nesters. They prefer hosts that feed insects to their young. In the Sierra Nevada four species in particular have apparently declined due to cowbird increase—Willow Flycatchers, Solitary and Warbling Vireos and Yellow Warblers. Bell's Vireo has died out in the Sierra and Northern California, due probably to cowbirds and to extensive destruction of their preferred lowland riparian habitats.

Although native to North America, Brown-headed Cowbirds visited California only rarely in winter prior to 1900. In their early explorations of the Yosemite region, Grinnell and Storer (see Bibliography) reported them only in the Central Valley and at Mono Lake in 1924. Apparently cowbirds first invaded Yosemite Valley in 1934, and their range in the Sierra has expanded ever since. They are now fairly common at all elevations, frequenting moist meadow edges and riparian thickets during spring and summer and avoiding unbroken tracts of forest. Logging and urbanization of the Sierra have contributed to the cowbird's dramatic range extension by providing cleared, open habitats. As their name suggests, cowbirds often associate with cattle, horses and sheep in order to feed on waste grain and stirred-up insects on the ground and in manure. Perhaps the increase in pack stations and livestock grazing provided food that drew cowbirds into the high country. Luckily, their specific requirements confine them to localized areas and they have not yet reached large portions of the Sierra.

Residents year-round in California, most cowbirds spend the fall and winter in the Central Valley.

Where Found:
Yosemite: El Portal, Yosemite Valley, Wawona, Big Meadow, Hodgdon Meadow, Crane Flat, White Wolf, May Lake, Tenaya Lake, Vogelsang Lake, Tenaya Lake, Tuolumne Meadows, Glen Aulin.
Sequoia-Kings Canyon: McClure Meadow (often seen near corrals), Cedar Grove, Wolverton, Giant Forest, Ash Mountain, Mineral King.

Northern Oriole[1] *(Icterus galbula)* Plate 33

The vibrant oranges and blacks of male Northern Orioles stand out like living embers in the green foliage of Sierran trees. Males arrive in the foothills by early April, voice their loud, melodic songs and utter harsh chatters from the treetops. The yellowish females, plain only by comparison with their flaming mates, filter in a few days later. They select nest sites in tall trees near streams, especially in sycamores, cottonwoods, willows and deciduous oaks. Less commonly they choose live oaks or orchard trees. Females gather plant fibers, horse hair or even fishing line and weave them into intricate hanging pouches for their eggs. It is a pity their clutches are concealed by these bag-like structures, for the eggs are exquisitely colored with purplish scrawls on fields of pale blue-gray.

Northern Orioles are fairly common throughout the spring and summer in the foothill woodlands of the western Sierra. Although widespread in most oak forests, they prefer streamside sites for feeding. Orioles forage in trees and shrubs, looking for caterpillars, ants or bugs. They also eat some ripe fruit in fall. Orioles nest only up to the ponderosa pine zone. Very rarely some may wander higher in late summer and fall, even up to the red fir zone, along riparian corridors or in stands of black oak. Unlike most of their blackbird relatives, they do not flock after breeding. By the end of August, most Northern Orioles have departed for Mexico and Central America.

Female orioles might at first be confused with female Western Tanagers, but orioles are brownish-yellow rather than greenish-yellow, with white (instead of yellowish) wing bars and long, pointed bills.

Where Found:
Yosemite: El Portal, Yosemite Valley, Wawona, Foresta, Hetch Hetchy. After breeding, up to Chinquapin and Crane Flat.
Sequoia-Kings Canyon: Three Rivers, Ash Mountain, Potwisha, Colony

---

[1]*The Bullock's Oriole of the western U.S. and the Baltimore Oriole of the East have been combined into this single species.*

Mill Road, Giant Forest, Cedar Grove.

FINCHES *(Family Fringillidae)*

Until recently the family Fringillidae included many species of birds with stout, conical bills such as buntings, grosbeaks and sparrows. Bird taxonomists recently placed many of these into another large and diverse family, the Emberizidae. Most birds in the newly defined Fringillidae reside in Europe and Asia, but some, such as Red Crossbills and Pine Grosbeaks, live in boreal forests throughout the Northern Hemisphere, and a few are confined to the New World.

Heavy seed-cracking bills characterize most Sierran fringillids, and breeding males are usually boldly colored in reds or golds. Their natural diets help maintain these bright plumages; captive birds fed unnatural foods often molt into drab browns or grays like the females and immatures. Finches flock and often sing in flight. Unpredictable, they can be abundant in an area one year and rare or absent there the next. Many species rove widely in search of bountiful crops of cones, buds, berries or seeds, and some also eat insects while nesting. Only the Lawrence's Goldfinch leaves the Sierra entirely in winter.

Rosy Finch[1] *(Leucosticte arctoa)* Plate 39

Inhospitable and windswept, snow-laden peaks are home to Rosy Finches. No other Sierran bird ventures to such lofty heights with the apparent ease of these alpine specialists. The chilling winds of fall force most other alpine birds to warmer regions and leave Rosy Finches to brave winter alone. The understandable scarcity of winter bird records from the high Sierra means ornithologists do not know for certain where Rosy Finches go during the coldest months. Probably many stay in their alpine habitats, but some wander down the west slope during severe storms to the relatively protected subalpine forests. Large flocks of Rosy Finches also winter regularly in canyons and mountain ranges east of the Sierra crest.

Rosy Finches are fairly common above tree line in the central and southern Sierra, mostly above 10,000 feet. In the northern portion of the range few peaks exceed 9,000 feet, and Rosy Finches are rare. Isolated populations occur on some of the higher summits, such as the Sierra Buttes in Sierra County, and on Mt. Lassen, just north of the Sierra. They feed actively on snowbanks or in lush patches of mosses or heather. In addition to seeds, they exploit a unique food resource—insect larvae and adults

[1]*Includes Gray-crowned, Brown-capped and Black Rosy Finches, formerly considered separate species but now regarded as races of a single species. The Gray-crowned race occurs in the Sierra Nevada.*

entombed within melting ice or frozen on the surface of snowfields. Most of these insects are blown upslope from more productive habitats below. Rosy Finches can be quite tame and easily approached, but may move nervously and take flight for no apparent reason.

Female Rosy Finches secure their sturdy nests of woven grasses and moss beneath boulders or in crevices on rock walls, out of the reach of predators. They incubate clutches of snow-white eggs while their mates return frequently with their squirrel-like cheek pouches filled with food.

Where Found:
Yosemite: Mt. Gaylor, Roosevelt Lake, Mt. Conness, Mt. Hoffmann, Mt. Dana, Mt. Lyell.
Sequoia-Kings Canyon: Muir Pass, Baxter Pass, Center Basin, Milestone Basin, Silliman Crest, Kaweah Basin, Mt. Whitney, Mitre Basin, Farewell Gap.

Pine Grosbeak *(Pinicola enucleator)*   Plate 39

Pine Grosbeak flocks roam widely in their search for conifer cones, tender buds, insects and berries, and their whereabouts from one year to the next can never be predicted. They occur in high-elevation forests, sometimes in dense stands, but more often at meadow edges, in forest clearings or in deciduous trees along mountain streams. In areas where ripe cones abound, they are fairly common at times, yet many experienced birdwatchers have searched such habitats in vain for these elusive birds. Once located, Pine Grosbeaks seem quite tame and allow approach. Sometimes they feed near mountain cabins and may even venture inside to pick crumbs from floors, tables and shelves.

They nest in the Sierra from Plumas to Tulare Counties, generally in red fir and subalpine forests, in bulky structures built well up in conifers. Although they reside in the higher mountains all year, flocks sometimes descend as low as the ponderosa pine zone from October through April.

A flock of Pine Grosbeaks at a distance might be confused with similarly reddish relatives such as Purple Finches, Cassin's Finches and Red Crossbills. Grosbeaks, however, are noticeably larger than any of those species. They also have darker bills and both males and females show strong, white wing bars.

Where Found:
Yosemite: Peregoy Meadow, Siesta Lake, White Wolf, Porcupine Flat, Ten Lakes, May Lake, Tenaya Lake, Tuolumne Meadows, Young Lakes, Tioga Pass.
Sequoia-Kings Canyon: McClure Meadow, Evolution Valley, Sphinx Lake, Twin Lakes, Mineral King near Eagle Lake.

Purple Finch (*Carpodacus purpureus*) Plate 40

The clear, liquid, warbly songs of Purple Finches resonate through moist forest glades of the Sierra during spring and summer. Flocks of bright red males and streaked females and immatures are fairly common year-round in shaded groves, canyon bottoms and meadow edges. From April through July they nest in open woodlands of the foothills and up through the mixed-conifer zone. Purple finches build cup-nests in dense outer foliage of conifers or deciduous trees near a source of water. Even while nesting, these highly social birds tend to feed in flocks, seeking weed seeds, fresh buds of deciduous trees, adult insects and caterpillars. During the winter Purple Finches are unpredictable, but tend to remain below the heavy snows, rarely appearing above the ponderosa pine zone. Some years they visit the foothills and Central Valley fairly commonly where they frequent woodlands, gardens and city parks. Other years they apparently migrate to the south of California.

The Purple Finch's range in the Sierra overlaps with that of the House Finch at low altitudes and with Cassin's Finch in the higher forests. These three species look extremely similar. Purple Finches have thick, slightly rounded bills and deeply notched tails. Males have deep burgundy red (not purple!) on their heads and crowns that extends down to their backs. Females and immature males are brownish with strong eye lines bordering distinct cheek patches. Their breast streaking is broad and messy, ending abruptly before the tails. First-year males often sing and may even breed while in immature, "henny" plumage. The songs of Purple, Cassin's and House Finches sound similar, but the Purple's is the most melodic of the three. The surest vocal clue to identification is the loud, sharp "pik" call given by Purple Finches either perched or in flight.

Where Found:
Yosemite: El Portal, Yosemite Valley, Mariposa Grove, Big Meadow, Merced Grove, Big Meadow, Hodgdon Meadow, Tuolumne Grove, Crane Flat, Gin Flat.
Sequoia-Kings Canyon: Cedar Grove, Grant Grove, Wolverton, Giant Forest, Colony Mill Road.

Cassin's Finch (*Carpodacus cassinii*) Plate 40

Cassin's Finches sing and feast on conifer buds among the highest branches and search for seeds on grassy forest floors, in clearings or along meadow edges. Open lodgepole pine forests attract them most, but they also nest less commonly in mixed-conifer and red fir forests, from May through early August. They often flock, even while breeding. They line their cup-nests with shredded bark or hair and secure them at the ends of flat sprays of conifer foliage, anywhere from 5 to 150 feet above the ground. Fairly common in higher forests, Cassin's Finches like many fringillids fluctuate widely in abundance from one year to the next.

In winter, Cassin's Finches descend to lower elevations on both slopes of the Sierra and some probably migrate south. On the west slope they take to ponderosa pine and mixed-conifer forests, where they sometimes keep company with Purple Finches. Such mixed flocks pose a challenge for birdwatchers trying to distinguish these look-alike species. Male Cassin's Finches have a deep red on the head that ends abruptly where it meets the brown of the neck and back. The head is a brighter red than the pinkish breast and rump. Females and immature males have an indistinct eye line that does not form as noticeable a cheek patch as in the Purple Finch. Their narrow, clean breast streaking, in good lighting, can be seen to extend under the belly to the base of their tails. The bills of both sexes are straight on the upper edges, giving them a slightly slender, pointed appearance. As with Purple Finches, the immature males require more than a year to reach the reddish adult plumages. Thus, "singing females" are actually only first-year males. Songs of the Cassin's resemble those of Purple Finches but are usually longer.

Where Found:
Yosemite: In breeding season, at Peregoy Meadow, White Wolf, Ten Lakes, Tenaya Lake, Tuolumne Meadows, Young Lakes and Roosevelt Lake. In winter, at Yosemite Valley, Big Meadow and Hodgdon Meadow.
Sequoia-Kings Canyon: Evolution Valley, Chagoopa Plateau, Little Five Lakes, Rock Creek, Hockett Meadows, Coyote Pass.

House Finch (*Carpodacus mexicanus*)   Plate 40

In the spring, House Finches sing monotonous warbling phrases throughout the day from the tops of barns, houses and power lines. Although native to western North America, they occupy habitats similar to those favored by House Sparrows (introduced). Both species commonly frequent human habitations, urban parks and farms. In many areas, both are considered agricultural pests. They feed on grains, fruits, berries and seeds of thistles, dandelions and other weeds.

In the western Sierra, House Finches live all year in open low-elevation habitats with a source of water, shrubs and trees for escape cover and high song perches. They are the lowland counterpart of the mountain-dwelling Purple and Cassin's Finches and only rarely venture above the foothill woodlands. Their vegetarian preference may explain why House Finches do not invade the insect-rich higher mountains in late summer and fall as many insectivorous birds do.

The generalist breeding behavior of House Finches probably accounts for their prosperity in association with humans. They nest almost anywhere, in the eaves and rafters of barns and other buildings, in chimneys, cavities in cliffs, or in trees. They quickly occupy nesting sites abandoned by other species and fortify them with horsehair, straw or twine. Even while nesting, from April to July, most of them continue to flock, except when incubating eggs or feeding young.

House Finches look much like their close relatives, the Purple and Cassin's Finches. House Finches, however, are smaller, with shorter, rounded bills, and their tails are less deeply forked. The females and immature males have uniformly brown heads and backs, and their breast streaking is blurry and indistinct. Adult males are reddish with definite brown flank streaking, missing on the Purple and Cassin's Finches. Occasionally male House Finches show orange rather than red, the intensity of their coloration being due to their diet. Captive birds fed unnatural foods often lose their bright colors after the first molt.

Where Found:
Yosemite: Groveland, Big Oak Flat, Mariposa, El Portal; rare in Yosemite Valley.
Sequoia-Kings Canyon: Three Rivers, Ash Mountain, Elk Creek, Potwisha, Hospital Rock, Buckeye Flat.

Red Crossbill *(Loxia curvirostra)* Plate 39, Figure 18

Few other Sierran birds have adapted so closely to a single food source as Red Crossbills. Their crossed bill tips make perfect tools for extracting seeds from unopened lodgepole pine cones. As they pry cone scales apart, they deftly lift out the seeds with their tongues (see Fig. 18). In this manner, they achieve access to a rich food source that is available only to Clark's Nutcrackers, Douglas Tree Squirrels and a few other animals. Like many fringillid finches, Red Crossbills rove widely in search of productive food sources. Consequently, they may be abundant in an area one year and rare or absent the next. In the Sierra, they strongly prefer extensive stands of lodgepole pines in the subalpine zone, but they also wander among Jeffrey and whitebark pines, red firs and mountain hemlocks. In addition to conifer seeds, they feed on fresh buds and insects. Crossbills reside in the higher mountains all year, but a few descend to lower elevations in some winters, particularly in years of poor lodgepole pine cone crops. During these "eruptions" they venture down to the ponderosa pine zone and, rarely, even the foothill woodlands. A very few have been recorded in the Central Valley, usually in planted conifers.

Throughout their range in the Northern Hemisphere, Red Crossbills have been observed breeding at all times of the year. Their nesting usually synchronizes with the availability of pine cones rather than with season. Lodgepole pine cones generally ripen in late summer and fall, but some

Figure 18. Red Crossbill extracting seeds from a lodgepole pine cone. See comments in text.

stay closed for years. In the Sierra, most crossbill nesting records fall between February and June, before the cone scales open and their seeds disperse. Crossbills typically construct nests near the ends of horizontal conifer branches.

Highly gregarious, Red Crossbills often gather in nervous flocks and flit between trees uttering distinctive "pip-pip" calls in flight. Flocks of young and old birds vary greatly in color; adult males are brick red, females are yellow and olive-gray, immature males are intermediate and young fledglings have streaked breasts.

Where Found:
Yosemite: White Wolf, Porcupine Creek, May Lake, Tenaya Lake, Tuolumne Meadows, Young Lakes, Vogelsang Lake. In winter recorded down to Gin Flat, Crane Flat and Big Meadow. Observed west of the park at Groveland and Ackerson Meadow (Stanislaus National Forest).
Sequoia-Kings Canyon: McClure Meadow, Rae Lakes, Wolverton, High Sierra Trail, Chagoopa Creek Meadow, Mt. Guyot, Rock Creek, Hockett Plateau, Siberian Pass. In winter recorded at Rae Lakes, Guyot Creek, Rock Creek, Siberian Pass, Horseshoe Pass and down to Ash Mountain.

Pine Siskin *(Carduelis pinus)* Plate 41

At rest Pine Siskins look drab and undistinguished, but in flight their wings and tails flash bold yellow patches, signalling their close kinship with the brilliant goldfinches. Pine Siskins travel in flocks of a few to more than one hundred birds that often erupt in a chorus of hoarse, wheezy calls.

Widespread in the western Sierra, Pine Siskins usually live in or near conifer forests. They scour all kinds of trees for fresh buds and seeds and pick insects from the foliage. They often concentrate at forest clearings, logged areas, mountain meadows and roadside ditches to look for thistle patches or other sources of seeds. Flocks move nomadically through forests and their presence in an area is highly unpredictable. Like many finches, Pine Siskins visit mineral springs and salt licks to supplement their diet.

Pine Siskins nest from the ponderosa pine to the subalpine zone, but are most common in red fir and lodgepole pine forests. They keep to the high mountains all year and nest from April through July, when food supplies are greatest. Even while breeding they remain in small colonies. They space their nests about 10 yards apart and conceal them within the densest conifer boughs, near the ground or high above it. In winter, some birds descend to the foothill woodlands. In exceptional years, particularly during severe winters, large numbers move down into the Central Valley, where they often visit conifers in urban parks and gardens.

Where Found:
Yosemite: Yosemite Valley, Little Yosemite Valley, Chinquapin, Peregoy Meadow, Crane Flat, Gin Flat, White Wolf, Porcupine Flat, Tuolumne Meadows.
Sequoia-Kings Canyon: Cedar Grove, Grant Grove, Wolverton, Giant Forest, Crescent Meadow.

Lesser Goldfinch *(Carduelis psaltria)*   Plate 41
The plaintive calls of Lesser Goldfinches fill the air as flocks flush from weed patches or fly overhead. Most widespread of the goldfinches in the Sierra, they inhabit oak woodlands, riparian forests, lowland chaparral and grassy hillsides. Flocks of these social birds hunt for seeds, often hanging on weed stalks that bend precariously with their weight. They also eat insects or ripening fruit and, like many other finches, seek out salt licks. Lesser Goldfinches commonly reside in the Sierra foothills, although a few nest as high as the ponderosa pine zone. Some travel up to the subalpine zone in late summer and fall, usually keeping to shrubfields, mountain meadows or other sparsely forested areas.

Lesser Goldfinches nest in a diversity of lowland habitats, from moist riparian forests to arid chaparral. They consume great quantities of water, however, and never stray far from a place to drink. They weave nests between well-shaded terminal branches of oaks, conifers and shrubs. Nesting begins in April and the young fledge by June or July.

As its name suggests, the Lesser is the smallest of the goldfinches. During the nesting season males are easy enough to identify by their large white wing patches, golden underparts (including the belly) and greenish backs and rumps. Females, immatures and wintering birds are rather drab and may be confused with American Goldfinches. The Lesser Goldfinch can be recognized by its dark rump and entirely yellow underparts; the rump and undertail coverts (between the legs and the tail) of the American Goldfinch are whitish in color.

Where Found:
Yosemite: Yosemite Valley, Wawona Meadow and west of the park at Big Oak Flat, Groveland and El Portal.
Sequoia-Kings Canyon: Three Rivers, Ash Mountain, Potwisha, Hospital Rock.

Lawrence's Goldfinch *(Carduelis lawrencei)*   Plate 41
Rarest of the Sierran goldfinches, Lawrence's are also the least predictable. Like many other fringillid finches, their numbers and distribution vary erratically from year to year. They winter out of the Sierra in warm, arid

portions of southern California, other southwestern states and Mexico. In spring and summer, flocks of these gray and gold birds visit the Sierra foothills where they extract seeds from fiddlenecks, thistles and other weeds.

Lawrence's Goldfinches breed near each other in small colonies. Although they may forage on open, rocky hillsides, they nest in thick stands of blue or live oaks. They typically use extremely arid sites near a source of water such as a creek or small lake. They suspend nests woven from grasses and lichens on terminal branches twenty feet or more above the ground. Females incubate their eggs alone, but their attentive mates bring food at frequent intervals. The bright males display golden wings and sing vigorously in defense of their small nesting territories. Lawrence's Goldfinches breed in the foothills, but from June to August flocks may stray up to meadow edges and streamside thickets in the mixed-conifer zone.

Where Found:
Yosemite: Recorded in summer up to Big Meadow and Crane Flat; west of the park near Coulterville, along Moccasin Creek near Don Pedro Reservoir, at Hardin Flat and at Ackerson Meadow (Stanislaus National Forest).
Sequoia-Kings Canyon: Three Rivers, North Fork Drive, Shepherd Saddle Road, Ash Mountain, Potwisha, Mineral King Road.

American Goldfinch (*Carduelis tristis*)   Plate 41

Flocks of American Goldfinches sing cheerfully on spring mornings as they feast on willow catkins, caterpillars or grasshoppers. For no apparent reason, they move from one tree to the next, calling "chup-chup" as they bound through the air in disorganized flocks. Just as suddenly they drop down to feed on thistle heads, dandelions or seeds of annual grasses and flowers (especially those in the sunflower family).

American Goldfinches reside all year in the Sierra foothills. Although they occasionally nest in open grasslands, chaparral, oak woodlands and orchards, ideally they prefer lush streamside groves of willows, cottonwoods and alders. In April and May females construct nests from plant fibers and thistle down and anchor them to forked branches of shrubs and trees. While restricted to the lowlands in the nesting season, American Goldfinches wander rarely through riparian corridors and montane chaparral up to the ponderosa pine zone in fall. They range widely through a great variety of habitats during winter, searching for abundant sources of buds or seeds.

In their golden breeding raiment, male American Goldfinches are unsurpassed in brilliance. As fall approaches, males and females alike shed their summer dress for more subdued shades of yellow-brown. The male loses his black cap but not his contrasting black and white wing markings. In winter, American Goldfinches may be distinguished from Lessers by their dusky white, rather than yellowish, bellies and rumps.

Where Found:
Yosemite: West of the park along the lower Merced and Tuolumne Rivers and at El Portal; recorded in Yosemite Valley.
Sequoia-Kings Canyon: Recorded rarely at Three Rivers and Ash Mountain.

Evening Grosbeak *(Coccothraustes vespertinus)* Plate 33

Evening Grosbeaks' huge pale-green bills and striking white, black and gold plumages make these gaudily dressed birds as striking as any warbler, tanager or other tropical migrant. Evening Grosbeaks, however, remain all year in the Sierra. They seldom travel alone but move in flocks to scour forests for seeds and buds of conifers and hardwoods, as well as insects. Calling constantly to maintain contact, they fly headlong through the air in undulating waves that vividly display their white wing patches.

Evening Grosbeaks breed in mature conifer forests from the ponderosa pine up to the red fir zone but require a good supply of ripe cones or other foods before they settle in any particular place. Unpredictable food supplies in the mountains make these nomadic birds disappear mysteriously from areas where once common and not return for several years or more. They forage in oaks, pines and cedars, but seem to prefer rather dense stands of white or red fir. Areas chosen for nesting have adequate food, a source of water and often a mineral spring or salt lick nearby. They construct loose nests and position them high in dense conifer foliage. Females incubate the eggs alone; most clutches are started in June, and young typically fledge by August. In fall and winter, Evening Grosbeaks roam the Sierra at least up to the mixed-conifer zone, and some years they descend into foothill oak and pine woodlands. Flock size tends to swell somewhat during the nonbreeding season.

It is uncertain how Evening Grosbeaks acquired their name. One theory is that an early ornithologist believed they lived in the deepest, darkest forests during the day, and only emerged at dusk to sing. They do inhabit dense woods, but also forage at forest clearings and open meadows where they utter loud, unmusical calls in broad daylight.

Where Found:
Yosemite: Yosemite Valley, Wawona, Mariposa Grove, Chinquapin, Badger Pass, Tuolumne Grove, Crane Flat, Gin Flat, White Wolf, Porcupine Flat.
Sequoia-Kings Canyon: Grant Grove, Lodgepole, Giant Forest, Crescent Meadow, Log Meadow, Mineral King, Ash Mountain.

WEAVER FINCHES *(Family Passeridae)*

House Sparrow *(Passer domesticus)* Plate 37

If seen for the first time in the picturesque countrysides of their native Europe, House Sparrows might seem handsome with their tailored patterns of black, brown and gray. In North America, however, they are often viewed with disdain. These boisterous birds were introduced from Europe to New York in the mid 1800's. Since then they have spread and increased enormously and now abound wherever humans or livestock dwell. These alien "sparrows," which in fact are not true sparrows but Weaver Finches, did not invade the Sierra for some years following their arrival in California. The first ones reached Yosemite Valley in 1920, presumably having followed the railroad or stock trains into the mountains. They are now very rare above the ponderosa pine zone but fairly common in the foothills where they have colonized towns, farms and livestock pens. They were even more common in California and elsewhere before the automobile replaced the horse, for the waste grain and manure around stables allowed them to flourish.

Introduction of the House Sparrow to North America was unfortunate both for humans and native birds. House Sparrows damage grain crops and usurp cavity nesting sites needed by Western Bluebirds and other birds as well as nests built by Cliff and Barn Swallows. Almost any crevice or cranny will do for a nest, including the eaves or decorative grillwork of buildings, as well as holes in trees. House Sparrows typically raise two or three broods a year. The promiscuous black-bibbed males actively court as many females as possible. Males have no musical songs to attract their mates; rather, they screech "cheep-cheep-cheep" in shrill, tedious tones.

Male House Sparrows are distinctive, but the females look something like immature Golden-crowned Sparrows. The House Sparrows have brown, unstreaked crowns and buffy eye lines.

Where Found:
Yosemite: Mostly west of the park, as at Big Oak Flat, Groveland, Buck Meadows, Hardin Flat, Mariposa and El Portal; very rare in Yosemite Valley.
Sequoia-Kings Canyon: Three Rivers, Ash Mountain.

APPENDIX I. Marginal, occasional and extremely rare bird species in the western Sierra Nevada. The following list is not comprehensive, but represents all species for which actual records of occurrence were located. Written documentation will be supplied by the authors on request. Address inquiries c/o Yosemite Natural History Association, Yosemite National Park, CA 95389. Additions to this list are welcomed.

Red-throated Loon
Arctic Loon
Common Loon [1]
Horned Grebe [1]
Western Grebe
Blue-footed Booby
American White Pelican [2]
Magnificent Frigatebird [3]
American Bittern [3]
Least Bittern [3]
Great Egret [1]
Snowy Egret [1]
Tundra Swan [1]
Snow Goose [1]
Green-winged Teal [1]
Northern Pintail [1]
Blue-winged Teal [3]
Cinnamon Teal*[1]
Northern Shoveler*[1]
Gadwall [1]
American Wigeon [1]
Canvasback [1]
Redhead [1]
Lesser Scaup [1]
Surf Scoter
Hooded Merganser [1]
Red-breasted Merganser
Mississippi Kite
Ferruginous Hawk
Rough-legged Hawk
Sage Grouse
Common Moorhen [1]
Sandhill Crane [2]
Black-necked Stilt
American Avocet
Greater Yellowlegs [1]

Lesser Yellowlegs [3]
Solitary Sandpiper
Willet [3]
Wandering Tattler [3]
Whimbrel [3]
Long-billed Curlew
Marbled Godwit [3]
Western Sandpiper [1]
Least Sandpiper [1]
Dunlin [3]
Long-billed Dowitcher [1]
Wilson's Phalarope
Red-necked Phalarope
Parasitic Jaeger [3]
Franklin's Gull [3]
Bonaparte's Gull [3]
Caspian Tern [3]
Forster's Tern [1]
Black Tern [3]
Yellow-billed Cuckoo*[3]
Lesser Nighthawk [3]
Costa's Hummingbird [3]
Allen's Hummingbird
Yellow-bellied Sapsucker
    (Red-naped subsp.)
Ladder-backed Woodpecker*[3]
Northern Flicker
    (Yellow-shafted subsp.)
Gray Flycatcher [4, 5]
Brown-crested Flycatcher [3]
Purple Martin*
Bank Swallow*
Pinyon Jay [4]
Black-billed Magpie
Cactus Wren*[3]
Sage Thrasher

Brown Thrasher [3]
Bohemian Waxwing
Northern Shrike
Virginia's Warbler
Magnolia Warbler
Blackburnian Warbler
Cerulean Warbler
Black-and-white Warbler
American Redstart
Ovenbird
Northern Waterthrush
Summer Tanager*[3]
Scarlet Tanager [3]
Rose-breasted Grosbeak
Indigo Bunting*[3]
Brewer's Sparrow [4]
Black-throated Sparrow*[3, 4]
White-throated Sparrow
Harris' Sparrow
Dark-eyed Junco
   (Slate-colored and
   Gray-headed subsp.)
Chestnut-collared Longspur
Yellow-headed Blackbird
Rusty Blackbird
Hooded Oriole
Scott's Oriole*[3]

Additional Species:

Brown Pelican
Black-crowned Night-Heron [3]
White-winged Scoter [3]
Blue-throated Hummingbird
Eastern Kingbird
Scissor-tailed Flycatcher
Northern Parula
Painted Redstart
Clay-colored Sparrow
Lark Bunting

*Nesting has been recorded in the western Sierra.
[1]May occur regularly in small numbers at low elevation aquatic habitats, with scattered records higher up.
[2]Flocks occasionally fly over the Sierra, but seldom land.
[3]Recorded in the South Fork Kern River Valley, but few if any records elsewhere in the western Sierra.
[4]May breed on the Kern Plateau and perhaps very locally elsewhere on the west slope.
[5]Regular spring migrant in the foothills.

APPENDIX II. Common and scientific names of plant species mentioned in the text.

Coniferous Trees
white fir *(Abies concolor)*
red fir *(A. magnifica)*
incense cedar *(Calocedrus decurrens)*
western juniper *(Juniperus occidentalis)*
whitebark pine *(Pinus albicaulis)*
foxtail pine *(P. balfouriana)*
lodgepole pine *(P. contorta var. murrayana)*
Jeffrey pine *(P. jeffreyi)*
sugar pine *(P. lambertiana)*
singleleaf pinyon *(P. monophylla)*
western white pine *(P. monticola)*
ponderosa pine *(P. ponderosa)*
gray pine[1] *(P. sabiniana)*
Douglas-fir *(Pseudotsuga menziesii)*
giant sequoia *(Sequoiadendron giganteum)*
mountain hemlock *(Tsuga mertensiana)*

Broadleaved Trees
bigleaf maple *(Acer macrophyllum)*
California buckeye *(Aesculus californica)*
white alder *(Alnus rhombifolia)*
California sycamore *(Platanus racemosa)*
Fremont cottonwood *(Populus fremontii)*
quaking aspen *(P. tremuloides)*
black cottonwood *(P. trichocarpa)*
canyon live oak *(Quercus chrysolepis)*
blue oak *(Q. douglasii)*
California black oak *(Q. kelloggii)*
interior live oak *(Q. wislizenii)*
California-laurel *(Umbellularia californica)*

Woody Shrubs
chamise *(Adenostoma fasciculatum)*
mountain alder *(Alnus tenuifolia)*
greenleaf manzanita *(Arctostaphylos patula)*
whiteleaf manzanita *(A. viscida)*
Great Basin sagebrush *(Artemisia tridentata)*

[1]*Often called digger pine; see footnote on p. 19*

golden chinquapin *(Castanopsis chrysophylla)*
bush chinquapin *(C. sempervirens)*
snowbrush *(Ceanothus cordulatus)*
buckbrush *(C. cuneatus)*
redbud *(Cercis occidentalis)*
curl-leaf mountain mahogany *(Cercocarpus ledifolius)*
kit-kit-dizze *(Chamaebatia foliolosa)*
common rabbitbrush *(Chrysothamnus viscidiflorus)*
dogwood *(Cornus spp.)*
toyon *(Heteromeles arbutifolia)*
desert bitterbrush *(Purshia glandulosa)*
huckleberry oak *(Quercus vaccinifolia)*
shrub live oak *(Q. spp.)*
California coffeeberry *(Rhamnus californica)*
currant *(Ribes spp.)*
gooseberry *(R. spp.)*
willow *(Salix spp.)*
poison oak *(Toxicodendron diversilobum)*
California wild grape *(Vitis californica)*

Nonwoody Plants
wild onions *(Allium spp.)*
sedges *(Carex spp.)*
paintbrush *(Castilleja spp.)*
shooting stars *(Dodecatheon spp.)*
rushes *(Juncus spp.)*
penstemon *(Penstemon spp.)*
bracken fern *(Pteridium aquilinum)*
tule *(Scirpus spp.)*
cattail *(Typha spp.)*

Annotated Bibliography

Listed below are some of the most useful references on life histories, distribution, habitats and identification of Sierran birds.

American Ornithologists' Union. 1983. Check-list of North American Birds, 6th edition. Allen Press, Lawrence, Kansas. 877 pp.

The official reference for taxonomy, nomenclature, and general distribution.

Bakker, E. S. 1972. An Island Called California. University of California Press, Berkeley. 357 pp.

A wonderfully readable, ecological introduction to California's biological communities; sophisticated, with detailed examples, but not too technical.

Bent, A. C. Life Histories of North American...(birds).

A monumental and invaluable work covering every subspecies in a series of volumes first published between 1919 and 1968. Reprints now available from Dover Publications, Inc., New York.

Cogswell, H. L. 1977. Water Birds of California. University of California Press, Berkeley. 399 pp.

Particularly useful for identification, California distribution, and seasonal status, with much life history information.

Dawson, W. L. 1923. The Birds of California. South Moulton Co., San Francisco. 4 vols., 2121 pp.

A monumental classic by a great American ornithologist, with color plates, photos, technical information and expansive, colorful accounts of each species.

Farrand, J., Jr., ed. 1983. The Audubon Society Master Guide to Birding. Alfred A. Knopf, New York. 3 vols., 1243 pp.

Too bulky for a field guide, but probably the most complete reference on identification, packed with excellent photos and color plates.

Gaines, D. 1977. Birds of the Yosemite Sierra: a distributional survey. California Syllabus, Oakland. 153 pp.

A useful distributional reference for the Yosemite Sierra, covering the west slope above the foothills and the east slope down to Mono Lake and vicinity.

Grinnell, J., J. Dixon, and J. M. Linsdale. 1930. Vertebrate Natural History of a Section of Northern California Through the Lassen Peak Region. Univ. Calif. Publ. Zool. No. 35. 594 pp.

A useful study on an area just north of the Sierra.

Grinnell, J., and A. H. Miller. 1944. The Distribution of the Birds of California. Pacific Coast Avifauna No. 27. 608 pp.

Still the definitive work on the subject, by two of the greatest California ornithologists, although the status of many species has changed. Excellent descriptions of habitat needs and seasonal status of each species.

Grinnell, J., and T. I. Storer. 1924. Animal Life in the Yosemite. University of California Press, Berkeley. 752 pp.

A classic reference, and the informative first-hand accounts of each species make enjoyable reading.

Harrison, C. 1978. A Field Guide to the Nests, Eggs and Nestlings of North American Birds. Collins, Cleveland. 416 pp.

Packed with useful information, much of it hard to find elsewhere.

Hoffman, R. 1927. Birds of the Pacific States. Houghton Mifflin Co., Boston. 353 pp.

An excellent early field guide that is particularly successful in depicting the personality and behavior of each species as well as the markings, songs and calls.

Manolis, T., and B. Webb. 1977. The Birds of Butte County, California. Altacal Audubon Soc., Chico. 40 pp.

An excellent distributional list with seasonal bar graphs.

Martin, A. C., H. S. Zim, and A. L. Nelson. 1951. American Wildlife and Plants, a Guide to Wildlife Food Habits. McGraw-Hill Book Co., New York. 500 pp.

Specific data on food habits of most birds, by season; a 1961 Dover edition is available.

McCaskie, G., P. DeBenedictis, R. Erickson and J. Morlan. 1979. Birds of Northern California: an annotated field list. Golden Gate Audubon Soc., Berkeley. 84 pp.

This authoritative list has seasonal bar graphs and distributional notes, as well as identification tips for problem groups. It is useful as an up-to-date supplement to Grinnell and Miller (1944).

National Geographic Society. 1983. Field Guide to the Birds of North America. National Geographic Society, Washington D.C. 464 pp.

The best, most complete single-volume field guide, with illustrations and descriptions of nearly every species and most important plumage variations.

Orr, R. T., and J. Moffitt. 1971. Birds of the Lake Tahoe Region. California Academy of Sciences, San Francisco. 150 pp.

A useful distributional reference on a region just east of the area covered by the present volume.

Peterson, R. T. 1961. A Field Guide to Western Birds. Houghton Mifflin Co., Boston. 366 pp.

One of the best general references for field identification.

Pough, R. H. 1949. Audubon Land Bird Guide. Doubleday and Co., Garden City, New York. 312 pp.

Pough, R. H. 1951. Audubon Water Bird Guide. Doubleday and Co., Garden City, New York. 352 pp.

Pough, R. H. 1957. Audubon Western Bird Guide. Doubleday and Co., Garden City, New York.

Out of print, but still an extremely useful set of field guides for identification and list history information. These volumes are filled with useful illustrations—especially the western guide.

Robbins, C. S., B. Bruun, H. S. Zim, and A. Singer. 1983. Birds of North America. Golden Press, New York. 360 pp.

One of the best general references for field identification.

Small, A. 1974. The Birds of California. Collier Books, New York. 310 pp.

Good chapters on California habitats as well as distributional information on each species.

Storer, T. I., and R. L. Usinger. 1963. Sierra Nevada Natural History. University of California Press, Berkeley. 374 pp.

This compact volume contains an astonishing amount of information on geography, geology, and biology of the range, including sketches and identification tips for most of the plants and animals likely to be encountered.

Sumner, L., and J. S. Dixon. 1953. Birds and Mammals of the Sierra Nevada, University of California Press, Berkeley. 484 pp.

Good life history information, with detailed distributional data from Sequoia and Kings Canyon National Parks.

Terres, J. K. 1980. The Audubon Society Encyclopedia of North American Birds. Alfred A. Knopf, New York. 1109 pp.

Concise, informative entries on each species, as well as a wide range of ornithological subjects.

Udvardy, M. D. F. 1977. The Audubon Society Field Guide to North American Birds. Alfred A. Knopf, New York. 855 pp.

This field guide has color photos of most western birds and nearly all Sierran species. The descriptions of calls and songs are particularly useful.

Verner, J., and A. S. Boss, tech. coord. 1980. California Wildlife and Their Habitats: Western Sierra Nevada. U.S. Dep. Agric., For. Serv. Gen. Tech. Rep. PSW-37. Berkeley, Calif. 439 pp.

Concise accounts of habitat needs and life histories of all amphibians, reptiles, birds and mammals found regularly in the region; plus a good list of references.

Whitney, S. 1979. A Sierra Club Naturalist's Guide to the Sierra Nevada. Sierra Club Books, San Francisco. 526 pp.

A well-written ecological approach, with comprehensive discussions of climate, geology and biological communities of the range, plus species accounts for many plants and animals.

Index to Common and Scientific Names

The first index below lists the common names of all species and subspecies of Sierran birds mentioned in the text. A second index provides the scientific names of species and subspecies discussed in the species accounts. Both the common and scientific names are those officially designated by the A.O.U. Check-list, Sixth Edition (1983). Older common names that were mentioned in the text are also included. Plate numbers and pages of figures are listed in bold type; pages of species accounts are shown in italics; and other important references to a species are indicated in regular type.

Index to Common Names

223

225

Index to Scientific Names

Illustration Credits

Keith Hansen: Cover illustration. Plates No. 1, 4, 6, 10-20, 24-27, 30-32, 34-37, 39-41. Drawings on title page and in Figures No. 3-18.

John Petersen: Plates No. 2, 3, 5, 7, 9, 22, 23.

Tad Theimer: Plates No. 8, 21, 28, 29, 33, 38.

Malcolm Holser: Graphic artwork in Figure 2.

Figures 1 and 2 were modified from Storer and Usinger (see Bibliography) with permission from University of California Press.

Photography by Ted Beedy, Steve Granholm, and John Harris (credits are shown by each photograph).